Degrees of Excellence

The Story of Queen's, Belfast, 1845 - 1995

Graduation, July 1994

1845 – 1995
QUEEN'S
150

Degrees of Excellence

THE STORY OF QUEEN'S, BELFAST
1845~1995
by Brian Walker *and* Alf McCreary

Consulting editor: R.H. Buchanan
Picture editor: Ivan Strahan

Published by
The Institute of Irish Studies

First published in 1994
by The Institute of Irish Studies,
The Queen's University of Belfast,
Belfast BT9 6AW

ISBN 085 389 535 X

Designed by Rodney Miller Associates, Belfast
Printed in Northern Ireland by W. & G. Baird Ltd, Antrim

Contents

Stained glass window "dedicated to the memory of all Queen'smen and Queen'swomen" in the entrance hall of the Lanyon building.

Foreword

I have watched this book grow from its genesis to final publication to mark the 150th Anniversary of the foundation of Queen's, first as a college and from 1908 a university. A university is about people, and Brian Walker and Alf McCreary have captured fascinating glimpses of people, and of their contributions to Queen's. However, our authors' task has been difficult, for much has had to be left out. The outcome of their research, including their conversations with many people, has produced a vivid story of the past century and a half. It is dedicated to all those, mentioned and not, who have helped by their presence and contribution to make Queen's the great university it is - and a fitting base for its development towards the next century and beyond. What, then, will our descendants think of us?

My special thanks, on behalf of Queen's, now go to Professor Emeritus Ronald Buchanan, who acted as editor, and to his wife Gwen who corrected the manuscript. Particular thanks are due to Ivan Strahan, who undertook the photographic research and wrote a large number of the captions to the illustrations which are a major archive of the university's life and activity. Thanks are also due to Bryan McCabe of W. G. Baird Ltd, the printers, and to designer Rodney Miller and his colleagues, for the production of such an attractive book.

Many others have supported our authors in various ways, but above all it is Alf McCreary and Brian Walker who made all the choices and who deserve all the credit.

Sir Gordon Beveridge
President and Vice-Chancellor

1850's engraving of Queen's College, Belfast.

Part One

Early Days 1845–89

"IN or near the town of Belfast, in our province of Ulster, in Ireland," declared the charter of Queen's College, Belfast, dated 30 December 1845, "there shall and may be erected and established one perpetual college for students in arts, law, physic, and other useful learning, which college shall be called by the name of Queen's College, Belfast". This charter, a result of the Irish colleges act of July 1845, laid the formal foundation of an important new centre of higher education in Belfast. By late 1849 the main building for the college was complete and the first lectures commenced in November with an intake of 195 students. In the years which followed the founding of this new institution, remarkable changes have occurred. After various arrangements under subsequent educational acts, the college in 1908 became an independent university, to be known as "The Queen's University of Belfast." In 1908–9 the number of students stood at 456. By 1948-9, when the university marked the centenary of the arrival of the first students, numbers stood at 2,762. By 1995 the figure will be around 14,000 undergraduate and post-graduate students. Clearly then, this new centre of education in Belfast has faced well the challenge of its description in the original charter of 1845 as a "perpetual college".

Origins

The establishment of the new Queen's college in Belfast in 1845 was heavily influenced by both national and local developments. Up to this time Trinity College, Dublin, was the only university institution in Ireland, but it retained strong links with the Church of Ireland, and consequently it was not thought to be a suitable

1

venue for higher education by many, especially Catholics and Presbyterians. In order to placate denominational feeling on the matter and to meet demands from Ireland for social reform, the government under Sir Robert Peel introduced its Irish colleges bill in 1845. The bill, which became law in July 1845, allowed for the establishment of one or more university college in Ireland. This college or colleges would be built by a government subvention and then supported by annual parliamentary grant. This new institution was to be strictly non-sectarian. The legislation did not actually lay down where the new college or colleges would be sited but in the months that followed its passing, the locations chosen, after considerable debate and lobbying, were Galway, Cork and Belfast.

This fine portrait of the young Queen Victoria by Sir George Hayter hangs in the University's Senate Room.

In Ulster, and particularly in Belfast, there was already a strong tradition of higher education. In the eighteenth century, considerable numbers from the province had gone abroad for a university education. The Scottish universities had provided an education for many, mostly Presbyterians, and the Irish colleges on the continent had been an important source of learning for Catholics, especially before the founding of Maynooth College by an act of parliament in 1795. To meet the local demand, the Belfast Academical Institution ('Royal' was added in 1831) was established in 1810 and it provided education of a university type although it was not empowered to issue degrees. Among its departments, headed by professorial staff, was a flourishing Medical School. By the mid century, Belfast was a bustling port and industrial centre with a population of 75,308 in 1841 and 97,784 in 1851, compared with 20,000 in 1800. In his *Irish sketch book* (London, 1843) William Thackeray, who visited Belfast in 1842 described it "as neat, prosperous, and handsome a city as need be seen. It looked hearty, thriving and prosperous as if it had money in its pocket and roast beef for dinner." The strong educational background to the town, as well as its dynamic expansion, made Belfast an ideal centre for a new university college.

The first practical step for the establishment of the new Irish colleges was the selection of their Presidents and Vice-Presidents. Various names were put forward for the positions in Belfast and finally Dr Pooley Shuldham Henry was chosen as President and Dr Thomas Andrews was picked as Vice-President. Henry was a Presbyterian minister with experience as an educational commissioner, and "eminent for discretion, moderation and decorum"

Rev. Pooley Shuldham Henry was first President of Queen's College, Belfast. Born in 1801 in Randalstown, Co. Antrim, he attended the Belfast Academical Institution. He was minister of First Armagh Presbyterian Church, 1826–46, during which time he obtained his D.D. from Glasgow University (1841). He served as government agent for the regium donum, 1837–45. He acted as a commissioner for national education, 1838–81, and for charitable bequests, 1844–62. He played an important role in the establishment and early days of the Queen's College in Belfast. Professor J.C. Beckett has said of him: "he was not a man of academic distinction, but he was a good administrator, he had considerable experience of public affairs, and he inspired confidence both inside and outside the college." (J.C. Beckett, *A short history of Queen's College. Belfast and The Queen's University of Belfast* (Belfast, 1984), p.6.) He retired from his position as President in 1879 and died two years later.

Thomas Andrews was the first and only Vice-President of Queen's College, Belfast. Born in Belfast in 1813 he was educated at Belfast Academical Institution. He later attended universities in Glasgow, Paris and Dublin, as well as in Edinburgh, where he was awarded his M.D. in 1835. He was professor of Chemistry at R.B.A.I., 1835–45, and an attending physician at Belfast General Hospital, 1838–45. He served as Vice-President and professor of Chemistry at Queen's College, Belfast, 1849–79. During this time he continued as a consulting physician at the Belfast General Hospital. He died in 1885.

Andrews was a scholar of European reputation. His work on the liquefaction of gases was regarded as highly significant, and led eventually to such inventions as the domestic refrigerator. He was elected F.R.S. in 1849, became President of the British Association for the Advancement of Science in 1876, and was awarded honorary degrees at Edinburgh, Glasgow and Dubln. He declined a knighthood in 1880. *The scientific papers of the late Thomas Andrews*, edited by P.G. Tait and A.C. Brown, appeared in 1889.

in the words of the historians, Professors J.C. Beckett and T.W. Moody (*Queen's history*, i, p.34). He was chosen in preference to the strongly outspoken Rev. Henry Cooke. The two Presidents selected for Galway and Cork were Catholic so Henry's selection may have been influenced by the idea of creating a balance. Thomas Andrews was a distinguished chemist. The colleges were formally brought into existence on 30 December 1845, by charters of incorporation which drew up a structure of President, Vice President and not more than twelve professors.

Selection of academic staff for Belfast then followed, and in December 1849 another charter for Belfast allowed the number of professors to be increased to 20 and laid down statutes for the organisation of the college: this covered the powers of the governing council, establishment of faculties and duties and responsibilities of the staff and students. Finally, in 1850 letters patent established the Queen's University in Ireland as a federation of the three colleges of Belfast, Cork and Galway. The Queen's University, with offices in Dublin, acted as the regulating and examining body for the colleges which nominated members to the university Senate. This arrangement continued until the early 1880s when the Queen's University was replaced by a new body, the Royal University of Ireland.

A central aim in the establishment of the new university institution was to create a higher education system based on non-denominational principles. This soon proved, however, to be unacceptable to various sections of society. While the bulk of Presbyterians supported the new colleges, an important section believed that a higher education establishment with a strong religious element was needed for their community and eventually Magee College was inaugurated in Derry in 1865. Among the Catholic community there was even greater opposition to what were seen as "godless colleges". The Synod of Thurles in August 1850 decreed that no Catholic bishop should co-operate with the new colleges which should be shunned "as dangerous to the faith and morals of Catholic youth". The Catholic bishops believed that the higher educational needs of their people could only be satisfied with institutions under their direct control. In 1854 the Catholic University was founded in Dublin, with John Henry Newman as the first President. In spite of these drawbacks, the Queen's Colleges came into operation in late 1849.

Queen's College, Belfast, c. 1905

THE THREE QUEEN'S COLLEGES

Queen's College, Cork, 1890
(William Lawrence)

Queen's College, Galway, 1890
(William Lawrence)

Buildings

THE ORIGINAL DESIGN OF QUEEN'S COLLEGE, BELFAST, BY CHARLES LANYON

There is evidence that Lanyon changed his mind about the layout of the Central Tower on the University Building. His original sketch shows a building with the staircase turret at the front of the Tower as a feature. In the event it was built half-hidden at the back of the Tower. The original concept did not include a quadrangle or even the possibility of a quadrangle at a later date.

Portrait by an unknown artist of Charles Lanyon, who designed the original Queen's building when he was only 33 years of age.

During selection of the professorial staff, work was already in progress on the construction of the new college in Belfast. After considerable debate about location it was finally decided to build on a ten acre site beside the Botanic Gardens on the south side of the town. This area was still rural and largely undeveloped, but within easy reach of the town. The architect selected for the new building was Charles Lanyon, civil engineer, county surveyor for Antrim and the architect already of a number of important Belfast buildings. Early Victorian architects, such as Lanyon, chose building styles for their historical associations. Queen's College, Belfast, is a free translation of the Founder's Tower and other elements of Magdalen College at Oxford. The aim was to provide the new college with an architectural setting imbued with ancient learning and scholarly tradition. Lanyon's effective use of a Tudor-revival style has left us with an impressive building in a pleasant setting.

The original building included a great hall for public purposes and examinations, a library, a museum of natural history, laboratories, eight lecture rooms, a room for the professors, a students' cloakroom and residences for the President and Vice-President. A sum of £100,000 was allowed by the government for the building of all three colleges and the Belfast college was granted £34,357 to cover purchase of site, construction of building and furniture. To meet the budget Lanyon was obliged to curtail some of his ideas for extra detailing and elaboration. The original plans for the building contain amendments, drawn in red ink, removing various features for the sake of economy. The master stone mason on the building was Robert McCredie of Comber, whose family of six sons, all masons on the building, later went to New South Wales to become prominent builders, but which retained an unusual link with Queen's, Belfast. His granddaughter Marion married William St Clair Symmers of South Carolina who was appointed professor of Pathology at the Belfast college (1904–29): their son William Symmers was given an honorary D.Sc. at Queen's in 1990 for distinction as a pathologist and services to medical education.

The college was inspected in August 1849 by Queen Victoria and Prince Albert who were then in Belfast in the course of a state visit to Ireland. The President, Vice-President and professors met formally for the first time in the new building on 27 October and lectures for students began on 7 November 1849. The official inauguration of the college took place on 20 December 1849, in the presence of many local notables and representatives. In his *Tour of Ulster*, (London), p. 35, published five years later, J.B. Doyle paid a nice tribute to the new college:

> The situation of this building is well chosen. It is significantly removed from the bustle of the town, and not too far off for the convenience of the students resident in Belfast . . . The internal arrangements are commodious and elegant, and although to an eye accustomed to the venerable and time worn halls of Trinity or of Oxford and Cambridge, they have somewhat of a raw and unpoetical effect, yet it cannot be denied that they are well adapted to the great purposes for which they were designed.

Staff

When the college opened in 1849, the academic staff consisted of 20 professors (including Thomas Andrews) and the President. These were the only academic members of staff and there was no allowance for lecturers or demonstrators from the annual revenue of the college. Extra lecturers or demonstrator were paid either directly by fees from students or by the relevant professor out of his own salary. The professorial staff of 1849, as Professors J.C. Beckett and T.W. Moody have shown, reflected a wide range of talent, age and experience (*Queen's history*, i, pp.115-23). Four were in their twenties, six in their thirties, four in their forties and six in their fifties. Thirteen were Irish by birth: eight out of the twenty were from Ulster. Of the remaining staff, three were from Scotland, three from England and one from Germany.

Of the Irish born staff in 1849, six were graduates of Trinity College, Dublin, four had primary degrees from Scotland, one had a degree from Germany and two had no degree. Six of the eight Ulster born professors were former students or professors of the

THE ENIGMATIC CARVINGS

The original door in the north wing of the Lanyon building, which led to lecture rooms, the museum and the library, is flanked by two carved heads, whose significance has been lost in time. They may be fanciful representations of ancient scholars, or allegorical figures to inculcate in students a sense of awe at the level that knowledge had reached in 1845.

THE ANDREWS TREE

In a climate apparently more benevolent than today's, Professor Thomas Andrews had a habit of working while seated under a large laburnum tree outside the Chemistry Department in the quadrangle. It is said that much of his seminal work on the liquefaction of gases was written up in this idyllic situation in the second half of the nineteenth century. The tree became known as the Andrews tree and survived in its original form until the 1950s, when it succumbed to old age. A slip was grown from the original tree, but it was always a weak specimen and was finally removed in the 1980s.

Royal Belfast Academic Institution (R.B.A.I). As regards the denominational background of the Irish born professors we may note that members of the Church of Ireland were the largest single group, presbyterians were the next most numerous while catholics were the smallest group. This marked denominational disparity reflected contemporary inequalities in academic and higher education opportunities in Ireland, which also affected the recruitment of the staff in the other two Queen's Colleges, and served to highlight the need for the new educational arrangements.

Every professor, upon taking up his office, was obliged to sign a declaration stating his intention to carry out his duties faithfully. He also promised to "abstain from teaching or advancing any doctrine, or making any statement derogatory to the truths of revealed religion, or injurious or disrespectful to the religious convictions of any portion of my class or audience." In addition he had to undertake not to discuss "any subject of politics or polemics, tending to produce contention or excitement."

The President, Dr Pooley Shuldham Henry, had been minister of First Armagh Presbyterian Church and government agent for the regium donum. For three decades he provided able leadership for the college. Thomas Andrews, a former professor of Chemistry at the Royal Belfast Academical Institution, was Vice President and professor of Chemistry at the new college. He was a renowned scientist. As Professor J.C. Beckett has remarked: "Henry and Andrews, though very different in background, attainments and character, worked harmoniously together. Under their guidance the college advanced both in numbers and reputation..."
A short history of Queen's College, Belfast, and The Queen's University of Belfast (Belfast, 1984), p. 6.

The School of Civil Engineering was set up under John Godwin who was closely connected with the building of the new railways. He lectured in the college for two hours on two days a week, and on Saturdays held a drawing class in his office at the Ulster Railway headquarters: his salary from the Ulster Railway Company was £400 compared to the £150 he received as his professorial salary. Godwin resigned in 1857 and was succeeded by James Thomson, brother of the famous William Thomson, later Lord Kelvin, whose statue stands today in the Botanic Gardens in Belfast. Their father had been professor of Mathematics, first at the Belfast Academical Institution, 1815–32, and then at the University of Glasgow, 1832–49. In his day, James was well known, for his experimental prowess. After 16 years as professor of Engineering in Belfast he accepted the regius Chair of Civil Engineering at the University of Glasgow. Another Thomson on the staff who also became well known was Charles Wyville Thomson, professor of Natural History and Geology, 1860–70. He was appointed professor of Natural History at the University of Edinburgh in 1870 and achieved world-wide fame as scientific director of the 'Challenger' expedition which carried out a circumnavigational voyage from December 1872 to May 1876. The final scientific reports from the voyage form one of the classics of marine biology.

The Scotsman, Rev James McCosh, one of the best exponents of Scottish Common Sense Philosophy, became professor of Logic and Metaphysics in 1851. An important philosopher, some of McCosh's best work was written while he was in Belfast. He left Belfast in 1868 to become president of Princeton College. His work was important in forging a constructive religious response to Darwinism. The new professor of History and English Literature was George Lillie Craik who came to Belfast with a wide range of publications already to his credit, such as *Spenser and his poetry* (1845), but who published little in the subsequent seventeen years. His successor Charles Duke Yonge, in contrast, published extensively in the fields of History and Literature during his period in the Chair.

The Faculty of Medicine opened in a strong position at the new college, thanks to the medical traditions and personnel inherited from R.B.A.I. and the Belfast Medical Society. There were 5 professors in the faculty of whom the best known was probably Alexander Gordon, professor of Surgery at R.B.A.I., 1847–9, and at Queen's, Belfast, for 37 years, 1849–86. His writing on the investigation and treatment of fractures was seminal on the subject and 'Gordon's splint' for healing fractures had an international reputation. Of the second generation of medical professors the best known was James Cuming. A former pupil of St Patrick's College, Armagh, he was the first alumnus of Queen's, Belfast, to become a professor at the college. He graduated B.A. in 1854 and after extensive medical training in Ireland and abroad was appointed professor of Medicine in 1865, a position which he held until 1899. He became the leading member of the medical profession in Belfast and was internationally regarded for his research. Growing links with the expanding Belfast hospitals gave important extra teaching facilities to the Medical School.

THE McCOSH BUST

A bust of the Rev. James McCosh, who became Professor of Professor of Logic and Metaphysics in 1851, is housed in the Department of Philosophy. During the late 1950s and early 60s, when the bust gazed down from a high shelf in one of the philosophy lecture rooms, McCosh was adopted as a student mascot and treated with irreverent but benevolent abandon. It was not unusual to come into lectures to find McCosh wearing a sombrero and smoking a cigarillo. However, the point was reached when a group of students started to decorate the bust with paint, and Professor John Faris took pity on McCosh and removed him to the safety of his study.

9

The School of Mathematics built up a strong reputation in the nineteenth century, especially due to the work of John Purser, professor of Mathematics, 1863–1901. A student of his, R.M. Jones, later recalled his teaching skills:

> Purser, the mathematician, was the greatest and most enthusiastic teacher and lecturer one could ever imagine. He threw his whole physical as well as mental energy into his demonstrations, his students always following his movements – and he was always moving – as well as his ideas with admiration and delight.
>
> *The Northman*, centenary edition, 1945, p.19.

A considerable number of brilliant mathematicians emerged from his classes, many of whom later competed successfully at the Wrangler mathematical exams at Cambridge. His students included Sir Joseph Larmor, Lucasian professor of Mathematics at Cambridge, 1903–32, Sir John Henry McFarland, Chancellor of Melbourne University, 1918–35, and William McFadden Orr, professor of Mathematics, at the Royal College of Science for Ireland and at University College Dublin, 1927–33.

During Henry's presidency several Chairs were abolished or amalgamated. The Chair of Celtic Languages was held by John O'Donovan from 1849 until 1861 when he died. O'Donovan was a scholar of international renown for his work on the Irish language and Irish history. He had been one of the principal contributors to the Ordnance Survey Memoirs, a major survey of the antiquities, topography, economy and society of Ireland, written to accompany the first Irish Ordnance Survey maps. His course in Belfast, however, attracted no students and his main duty was to give 6 lectures per year at the college for the interested public. His scholarship was appreciated by his colleagues but the lack of response to his course meant that the chair was suppressed after his death. Another area which failed to attract students was Agriculture. The original holder of the Chair was the well known John Frederick Hodges, director of the Chemico-Agricultural Society of Ulster for many years, whose work on agricultural chemistry was widely recognised in Europe. Due to competition, however, from other more practically based agricultural schools, his lectures were not well attended and the department ceased to function in 1863. Since he was appointed before a retirement age was established, he remained in post and taught medical jurisprudence until his death in 1899, at the age of 76, having lectured at the college for 50 years.

AN ILLUSTRATED WEEKLY NEWSPAPER

NO. 536.—VOL. XXI.
Reg^d at General Post Office as a Newspaper]   SATURDAY, MARCH 6, 1880   WITH EXTRA SUPPLEMENT [PRICE SIXPENCE Or by Post Sixpence Halfpenny

TORCHLIGHT PROCESSION OF UNIVERSITY STUDENTS AT BELFAST, IN HONOUR OF MR. LARMOR, THE CAMBRIDGE SENIOR WRANGLER

The early staff contained the usual complement of unusual characters. The Chair of Modern Languages, which covered French and German, was held for 37 years by Albert Ludwig Meissner (1865–1902), who had a strong publication record and one of the heaviest teaching loads in the college, but who was frequently in dispute with the president and council over various issues: for example, Meissner had insisted upon access to the college at all times of the day and night and had fitted a special lock to a back gate, but this lock had been forced open by rowdy elements from the town, who invaded the grounds, and the president had ordered the door to be permanently closed, to Meissner's annoyance. This conflict led to Meissner appealing in 1878 to the Chief Secretary of State at Dublin Castle but his case was not upheld. A predecessor in his chair, Mathias Joseph Frings (1849–62), faced another problem with the authorities which a student of the time, J.B. Armour, noted to a friend in 1862:

> We have lost our French professor which is a sore grievance to us, as he was very much liked by all our students. But he was like all foreigners a little lax in his morals. His wife and he did not live

A TORCHLIGHT PROCESSION,

In 1880 the students of Queen's held a torchlight procession, illustrated here in The Graphic of 6 March 1880, a weekly magazine, in honour of Joseph Larmor, a Queen's graduate who became a Cambridge Senior Wrangler. He later became Lucasian professor of Mathematics at Cambridge, secretary of the Royal Society and M.P. for Cambridge University.

11

John Frederick Hodges,
Professor of Agriculture, 1849–99.

James Cuming,
Professor of Medicine, 1865–99.

George Lillie Craik,
Professor of History and English
Literature, 1849–66.

The Rev. Richard Oulton,
Registrar, 1852–77.

Alexander Dickey,
Bursar, 1849–72.

Sir Charles Wyville Thomson,
Professor of Mineralogy and
Geology, 1854–60,
Natural History and Geology,
1860–70.

Alexander Gordon,
Professor of Surgery, 1849–86.

Charles Duke Yonge,
Professor of History and English
Literature, 1866–91.

Rev George Hill,
Librarian, 1850–80.

together for some time past and as a substitute he kept a lady in the house with him whom he introduced to the professors as his niece, but in reality she was a concubine. She was very handsome and some medical student of Trinity College took a passion for her and was at church to get the words said but the vicar had heard that she had lived with our professor and was with child to him, so that he refused to marry her to the young fellow. This reached the senators' ears and they sent down word to the president to have the matter investigated. He knowing that the matter would not stand investigation, advised him to resign. So he took his advice and we are left without a man. For my part I would have like he had stayed on whatever his faults, as he was a remarkably good teacher and good linguist.

J.R.B. McMinn, *Against the tide: J.B. Armour, Irish presbyterian minister and home-ruler* (Belfast, 1985), pp 49-50.

College structures

How was the college run? The professors were organised into faculties of which there were four – Medicine, Law and the Arts which broke into a Literary division and a Science division. The faculties elected four Deans who with the President and Vice-President made up the Council which was responsible for the college administration and which met in the President's office, in the central tower above the front door, a room still occupied by the Vice-Chancellor. From 1863 onwards the professors elected six members to the Council. When a Chair fell vacant the post was advertised, and a ranked selection of candidates was then drawn up by the President and Vice President and sent to the office of Under-Secretary in Dublin for a final decision. Normally the President's recommendation was accepted by the government.

While control of internal affairs of the college lay with the Council, ultimate authority for deciding courses of study and examinations leading to degrees lay with the governing body of the colleges, the Queen's University in Ireland. With its offices in Dublin, this body was run by a Senate to which each college sent its president as a representative, alongside other leading educational figures, selected by government. From 1863 the Senate was expanded to include a professor from each college and also persons elected by the convocation of registered graduates of the university. Relations were good between the members of the three colleges. Final examinations were sat in Dublin and degrees were conferred in St Patrick's Hall in Dublin Castle.

Besides the professorial members, other staff played an important role in the administration of the Belfast college. The executive machinery of the college was run by the Registrar and Bursar, both of whom were part time officers. The Registrar acted as Secretary to the Council, handled the correspondence of the college under the direction of the President, dealt with admissions and looked after the college property. The first Registrar, W.J.C. Allen, held the post for only two years and his place was taken by Rev. Richard Oulton, who for the next twenty-five years efficiently conducted this office along with others of garrison chaplain and local inspector of Antrim County Gaol. The job of Bursar, filled by Alexander Dickey until 1872 and then by John Wylie, dealt with the finances of the college which in this period were fairly simple. The post of college Librarian was occupied for the first two years by James MacAdam and for the next thirty years by the distinguished historian Rev George Hill, whose work included *The Montgomery manuscripts, 1603–1706* (1869) and *An historical account of the MacDonnells of Antrim* (1873).

Students

What about the students and the courses they attended? The bulk of students gained admission through passing a matriculation examination after which they paid a college fee plus class fees to the professors whose lectures they were required to attend. Others could attend the college without a matriculation exam, pay a small fee to the college along with appropriate class fees, but could not compete for scholarships or prizes or take a degree. There was a number of scholarships available to those who had passed the matriculation exams and then successfully competed at special examinations. Throughout the Henry era the matriculation exams for all students contained a strong classics element of Latin and Greek. For Arts students the classics element remained important for their degree course.

Various features are worth noting about the students in the Henry period, as Professors J.C. Beckett and T.W. Moody have shown (*Queen's history*, ii, p.666). Numbers were low. The student body grew in total from 195 in 1849–50, to 257 in 1859–60, to 353 in 1869–70 and to a peak of 500 in 1878–9. Many in these early years entered college aged 15 – 16 years old but as time went on those in the youngest age group declined. This state of affairs was largely due to the lack of an adequate secondary school system to take pupils from the widespread national school primary system through to third level. Existing local secondary level schools were sometimes in arrangement with university institutions elsewhere to the disadvantage of the Belfast college: for example the Royal Schools in Cavan, Dungannon, Armagh and Enniskillen had links with Trinity College, Dublin, while St Malachy's, Belfast, established links with the Catholic University, Dublin.

In the early years a clear majority of the students were in the Faculty of Arts. The Medical School increased in importance, however, and by 1870–71 medical students were 51 per cent of the student body. By 1879–80 they had increased to a peak of 66 per cent of those at the college: thereafter, they remained constantly at over 50 per cent. An interesting feature of this major medical group is that many never actually completed their degrees through the Queen's University, preferring to take out a qualification from one of the main medical licensing bodies in centres such as Dublin or London, after a number of years as undergraduates in Belfast. The original student body was all male. A proposal to admit women to the college first came before the council in 1873 but was rejected. In 1876 Mary Edith Peechey obtained permission from the senate of the Queen's University to attend lectures at a Queen's college but the Belfast college refused to accept her.

As regards origins and denominational background of the student body we may note that the vast majority came from East Ulster and Presbyterians made up the largest single group. For example, in 1868–9, 69 per cent of students gave Belfast, Co. Antrim or Co. Down as their home residence, while 18 per cent gave Counties Londonderry, Tyrone or Armagh, 6 per cent recorded the remaining 4 Ulster counties and only 3 per cent came from the rest of Ireland. Over the whole period, 1849–1909, the percentage distribution of the different denominations was Presbyterians 64 per cent, members of the Church of Ireland 17 per cent, Methodists 6 per cent, Catholics 5 per cent and others 8 per cent. Catholic attendance was highest in the first two and last decades of this period.

The high percentage of Presbyterians and low percentage of Catholics is partly explained by the large number of Presbyterians and the small number of Catholics in East Ulster, from where the college drew most of its students. Because of the Presbyterian predominance in the area, Catholics may not have felt at home in a Belfast college, an argument put forward by the Catholic Primate in the 1840s as a factor against Belfast and in favour of Armagh as

Professor John Tyndall, an eminent geologist and engineer, was President of the British Association for the Advancement of Science when it met in Belfast for its conference in 1874. In his presidential address he delivered a paper with a strong materialist world view which stressed the importance of science and denied the value of religion. This address caused great controversy not just in Belfast where it remained a much debated topic during the British Association meeting and after but subsequently in religious and scientific circles throughout Europe. Many articles and pamphlets were published in response to Tyndall's challenge. Tyndall is seen here in a *Vanity Fair* cartoon of 6 Apr. 1872.

the centre for the new college. Economic factors also were important in limiting Catholic participation. Finally, of course, the denunciation of the Queen's Colleges as "godless" and the continued strong opposition of local bishops militated against significant Catholic involvement.

Facilities

In the early days of the college, facilities for students were fairly limited. There were no college residences and students away from home had to live in approved lodgings. In the college itself there was neither a dining hall nor a club-room for students. The original Irish colleges act and subsequent charter stressed that the college was to be non-denominational, but at the same time, emphasis was placed on strong spiritual care for the students through part-time university chaplains or deans of residence. The 1849 statutes for the Belfast college included a list of offences for which a student would be disciplined: top of the list was "habitual neglect of attendance for divine worship, at such church or chapel as shall be approved by his parents or guardians". All matriculated students were required to wear academic caps and gowns within college precincts; in 1876 this was amended so that academic costume had to be worn only at examinations. In February 1850 a group of students founded the "Queen's College Literary and Scientific Society" otherwise called the 'Literific', to serve as a society where papers could be read and debated before the student members. An athletic club was formed in 1871. Lack of suitable grounds, however, hampered sporting activities. Writing in 1930, James Brown Dougherty described the limited facilities at the Belfast college during his time there in the 1860s:

> When Queen's College, Belfast, was founded, but little provision was made for the students in the way of facilities for outdoor sports. There were no racquet courts, no cricket grounds, no football field. In the corner of the too-limited vacant space surrounding the college buildings there was a ball alley in which a primitive game of handball could be played, and on the narrow strip of ground surrounding the college, which is now covered with buildings, students could sometimes amuse themselves kicking a leather ball in a game which was but the germ of the highly-developed scientific sport of football as played today.
> W.S. Armour, *Armour of Ballymoney* (London, 1934), p.15.

SPORT IN THE 1880s

Sport played an important part in the life of Queen's in the late nineteenth century, judging by the prizes that were on offer at the Queen's Athletic Club Sports Day in 1882. While the Band of the 19th Regiment played music by Gassner, Verdi, Audran, Coote, Sullivan and Waldteufel, winners were presented with prizes that reflected the Victorian view of what the educated man needed in life – a brass Indian tray, a silver cream jug, a rose water dish, a pair of bronze candlesticks, a cigar case, a case of salts, a card tray and a horn snuff box. Competitors were dressed in such exotic colours as old gold and peacock, cream and cardinal, primrose and rose, with touches of cerise, silver, magenta, lavender and amber. The level of performance was also remarkably high, considering there was a total of only 567 students to choose from: for example the 120 yards was won in 14.2 seconds – a fast time even by today's standards. Note that the timekeeper is James Stelfox of the North of Ireland Cricket Club, great grandfather of Queen's graduate and Everest conqueror Dawson Stelfox.

Queen's Sports Day in 1889 turned out to be a sensational occasion. Billy Hume of the Cruisers Club won every cycle race which he entered by a long margin and there was considerable bad feeling when it was discovered that he was using a new device which many felt to be unfair. The new invention was the pneumatic tyre and its inventor was John Dunlop, a Belfast vet from Joy Street, where many Queen's students had lodgings at the time. The original purpose of the invention was to save sick animals from distress while being transported by bicycle trailer. The photograph shows John Dunlop on one of the first sets of pneumatic tyres in the Botanic Gardens behind the University.

After the construction of the main buildings in the 1840s, little additional building occurred in the succeeding decades, thanks to tight government monetary control. Facilities for the Medical School soon proved inadequate, but it was not until 1863–6 that new buildings were constructed at the rear of the college grounds (where the modern administration block is now placed) so that the whole Medical School could be housed in one suitable block. A new Library was begun in 1866 and completed in 1868 to the designs of the original architect, Charles Lanyon, and his partner William Henry Lynn. A small observatory, paid for by the private benefactors, was built in the college grounds in 1851–2 and a gymnasium was put up in 1873.

THE LIBRARY

Queen's Library, designed by the firm of Lanyon, Lynn & Lanyon and opened in 1868 is an imposing building of distinctly ecclesiastical lines, with a high imposing nave. It provided ample study space for staff and students until the early years of the 20th century, when expansion led to the building of an extension in 1912–14 in the same style. The illustration is taken from a supplement to The Graphic, 22 August 1874.

Alumni

The standing of the college grew as its graduates pursued careers at home and overseas. The medical profession in Ulster and the ministry for the Presbyterian Church in Ireland came to be dominated by former students of the college. In legal practice and public service in Ireland many graduates gained prominence. Others worked in the education field, at school and university level. By 1879 more than 25 had obtained Chairs in universities and colleges in Ireland and overseas. A considerable number went abroad either to Great Britain or to parts of the Empire. The Indian Civil Service recruited many graduates of Queen's, Belfast, as did the consular service. In the developing countries of Australia, New Zealand, Canada and South Africa, graduates served as doctors or lawyers or in other professions.

One of the most remarkable of those early graduates was Robert Hart (graduated 1853). After a time in the British consular service, he joined the customs service of the Imperial Chinese government. In 1863 he became Inspector-General of the Maritime Customs in China, a position which he held until 1908. As the chief fiscal administrator of the Chinese Empire, he helped to lay the groundwork for much of the modernisation of China in the late nineteenth and early twentieth centuries. He created the Chinese Post Office. His role in China has been well summed up in the conclusion to the recent edition of his early journals:

> Robert Hart as Inspector General not only supervised the Customs Inspectorate with uncommon skill and efficiency, but he also became at times a nearly indispensible adviser to the Chinese government. His advice at one time or another extended to virtually every major area of Chinese official problems, from fiscal affairs to railways and postal services, and to foreign relations and national defense. No single foreigner in nineteenth-century China had more sustained influence than Hart, and none enjoyed a greater measure of Chinese confidence.
>
> K.F. Bruner, T.K. Fairbank, R.J. Smith *Entering China's service: Robert Hart's journals, 1854–63* (London, 1986), p.325.

When Sir Robert Hart was due to return home in 1908 after 43 years distinguished service as Inspector-General of maritime customs for the Imperial Chinese Government, he was presented with this set of elaborate table silver, referred to as the 'Empress of China's silver', though the connection with the Empress remains obscure. After Sir Robert's death this silver was kept in the vaults of the Bank of England in London until 1971, when it was presented to Queen's by the Hart family.

Hart retained a strong interest in his old college. He responded generously to appeals in the 1890s and early 1900s for funds for the college and after his retirement he became a Pro-chancellor of the new Queen's University. There is a memorial tablet to him in the entrance hall of the Lanyon building.

Edwin Laurence Godkin entered the college as a scholar in 1849, was a founder member of the "Literific", but left in 1853 without taking a degree. In the words of the *Dictionary of American Biography*, he displayed "marked intellectual ability, along with a disinclination to apply himself steadily to the required work of the college". Godkin became a war correspondent in the Crimea, after when he went to America and for thirty-five years was editor of a weekly paper, the *Nation*, which became famous for its advocacy of good

causes. He received an honorary M.A. from Harvard and a D.C.L. from Oxford. Andrew Marshall Porter was called to the Irish bar in 1860 and became Irish Solicitor general, 1881–3, Irish Attorney General, 1883, and Master of the Rolls in Ireland, 1883–1906. In the entrance hall of the Lanyon building there are memorials to Porter and Godkin.

Many graduates excelled in the field of medicine. Sir William Mac Cormac (graduated 1855), was elected president of the Royal College of Surgeons on five successive occasions (1896–1900). The leading ophthalmologist in Ulster in the last decades of the nineteenth century was Joseph Nelson. He interrupted his studies at Queen's in 1860 to serve with Garibaldi's Red Shirts in Italy and after a time of training in Vienna returned to become a very prominent eye specialist, known popularly as 'Garibaldi' Nelson. Another unusual medical graduate was David Walker who obtained his M.D. in 1856 at the very early age of 19 and in April 1957 became a licentiate of the Royal College of Surgeons, Dublin. Later in 1857 he was appointed surgeon and naturalist aboard the ship, the Fox, on an expedition to the northern polar regions in search of Sir John Franklin, the lost explorer. The expedition found Franklin's remains and the crew achieved considerable fame. Walker went to America in 1865 to serve fifteen years as a doctor in the U.S. cavalry on the American Frontier.

Changes of 1879

The year 1879 saw the departure of both Henry and Andrews. Under their direction, Queen's College, Belfast, was well established. The student body numbered 500 and its graduates were to be found in many areas of responsibility in Ulster and in the rest of Ireland. However, there remained problems of funding and of the future of university education in Ireland. The Belfast college received a none too generous government grant and there were still major question marks over the subject of higher education in Ireland, in particular the question of the role of religion in education. Some Presbyterians continued to favour the Presbyterian run Magee College in Derry, but it is clear that the Queen's Colleges, especially Belfast, had gained broad support from the Presbyterian community. The Queen's Colleges had failed, however, to win significant Catholic involvement. For the Catholic bishops and laity, support for a Catholic university and colleges remained the preferred option.

Andrew Marshall Porter, born 1837, died 1919.

Born in 1836, William MacCormac was the elder son of Henry MacCormac, the well known professor of Medicine at R.B.A.I., 1837–49. He entered Queen's College, Belfast, in 1851, and obtained first an Arts M.A. and then a M.D. After studying in Berlin, Mac Cormac became surgeon and lecturer in surgery at St Thomas's hospital in London. He saw war service as a surgeon in France, Serbia and South Africa and became renowned for his work and publications on the subject of treating gun wounds. He was the first Irishman to become President of the Royal College of Surgeons in England, a position to which he was elected on five successive occasions, 1896–1900. He was knighted in 1881 and became a baronet in 1897. His portrait in oils, by Harris Brown, was presented to Queen's College, Belfast, in 1897 and now hangs in the Great Hall. He died in 1901.

A cartoon portrait from Vanity Fair, 1906.

The passing of the act for the Royal University of Ireland in 1879 was to create a wholly new scene. Under the new act the Queen's University of Ireland, with its three constituent colleges, was dissolved, although the old arrangements continued until 1882 for the Queen's Colleges. The new body, the Royal University of

This photograph may well be the earliest known photograph of Queen's students and staff. It is not possible to date the photograph precisely, nor to say with certainty what the occasion was, but the fashions point to a date in the late 1880s and the number of students, including eight women, would suggest a celebration of Graduation, 1886. The significance of the tassled staffs is not known.

Ireland, was a purely examining body. A series of professorial fellowships was established to provide extra funding, particularly for University College, Dublin (formerly the Catholic University), and to a lesser extent for each of the Queen's Colleges. The Queen's Colleges kept their endowments but they only numbered three among a wide number of colleges which could prepare students for exams at the Royal University. In Belfast institutions such as Victoria College and St Malachy's College also educated students for these exams. The Queen's Colleges were no longer able to decide their own courses for degrees. The Medical School, in particular, was affected by new examining procedures which involved lengthy residence in Dublin hospitals for all medical students. Whatever advantages this new system gave other educational establishments the arrangement was not beneficial to the Queen's Colleges, which now faced competition from these sources. As a consequence numbers at the Belfast college were to drop. After a peak of 567 in 1881–2, the student population had fallen to 422 by 1888–9.

The new President of Queen's College, Belfast, was the Rev. Josias Leslie Porter, a former moderator of the Presbyterian Church, who had worked for the intermediate education board and was well known for his administrative skills. The post of Vice-President was discontinued after the retirement of Andrews. In spite of Porter's ability, however, he was unable to deal satisfactorily with the two main problems facing the college. The first was the downgrading of the college under the new arrangements. Despite representation to various government ministers and official enquiries, Porter could not obtain an improvement in the new university arrangements as they affected the Queen's Colleges. The second difficulty was the need for new accommodation for the medical and science departments. Porter was unsuccessful in trying to persuade the government to provide extra funding for this purpose. Appeals to the Belfast public to provide money for extra building proved to be a failure. Social facilities for students were still very limited.

Admission of women students

In spite of these problems, the decade of Porter's presidency was not uneventful. The most significant event was undoubtedly the admission of women to lectures. In 1882 the Belfast Ladies' Institute approached the Council to allow women to attend the college. On 21 October 1882 the Council agreed that women should be admitted to arts classes and the first women attended during the session of 1882–3. Queen's College, Belfast, therefore became the first university college in Ireland to admit women. The next year women were admitted to science classes and in 1884 Alice Everett obtained first place in the first year scholarship examination and Florence Hamilton fourth place in the second year examination. (Florence Hamilton graduated in 1886 but died early in 1908; she is recalled with affection in the writings of her son, C.S. Lewis, the famous religious writer and author of children's stories.) Women were still not eligible for college scholarships and although Porter called for this to be changed, it was not until 1895 that the necessary legal changes were obtained.

Rev. Josias Leslie Porter, born at Burt, Co. Donegal, in 1823, was the second President of Queen's College, Belfast. He received his B.A. in 1842 from the University of Glasgow and served as a presbyterian minister in Newcastle-upon-Tyne, 1846–9, and a missionary in Syria, 1849–59, before becoming professor of Biblical Criticism at the Assembly's College, Belfast, 1869–78. He was moderator of the Presbyterian General Assembly in Ireland, 1875–6, and served as an assistant commisioner under the board of intermediate education in Ireland, 1878–9. He was appointed President of the Belfast college in 1879, a position which he held until his death in 1889. In spite of strong efforts he proved unable to increase support for the college, either from the government or the public.

President Porter died suddenly in March 1889. His decade of tenure had seen no significant improvement in the college's position, either as regards funding or broader community involvement. The new arrangements had not proved to be satisfactory and the number of students who attended the college had dropped: Porter had been unable to improve the facilities of the college. Still, the college was undoubtedly well established and continued to produce a good stream of able graduates. Porter's successor now faced a considerable challenge.

2

New Challenges 1889–1923

IN 1889 Thomas Hamilton became the third President of the college, following the unexpected death of President Porter. During Hamilton's lengthy period of office, not only did the number of students and the amount of building grow markedly but the college became a university in its own right, based firmly in the local community. At the time Hamilton was regarded as a compromise candidate and his career to this point was distinguished but not outstanding. In the event, however, Hamilton's time as head of the Belfast college and then as Vice-Chancellor of The Queen's University of Belfast, a period of over thirty years, proved to be most significant. Professor J.C. Beckett has written of him: "He is one of the greatest figures in the history of Queen's which probably owes more to him than to an other single person: by his persistence, his courage and his foresight he well earned the title of a second founder." (*A short history of Queen's College, Belfast, and The Queen's University of Belfast* (Belfast, 1984), p. 9). Other candidates with greater academic records were considered by the government but rejected in favour of Hamilton whose administrative skills were known and who was regarded as less controversial than the others. He soon proved to be extremely able in promoting the interests of the college, especially in areas of building requirements and the status of the institution.

THE STUDENTS' UNION BAZAAR, 1894

The Bazaar of May 1894, organized in order to raise funds for the building of a Students' Union, was one of the great social events of the year, largely because the college managed to persuade most of the aristocracy in the Province not only to be present, but to take part in running stalls. The temptation to rub shoulders with the like of Countess Annesley and Lady Dixon at the Bric-a-Brack Stall, or Viscountess Templeton and Lady Magheramorne at the Cornflower Stall was too great for the Belfast public, who turned up in large numbers. It is interesting to note that, as a result of the Fair, Queen's received a letter from the Board of Works, sharply criticizing it for using the college and grounds in this way without obtaining permission under the fire regulations! These snapshots of the Fair, most of which were found in an attic in University Square in 1993, provide a fascinating window on a bygone age.

The Students' Union Bazaar, 1894

Rev. Thomas Hamilton was the third President of Queen's College, Belfast, the first Vice-Chancellor of The Queen's University of Belfast, and the only person with a primary degree from the Belfast college or university who has ever held either of these positions. Born in Belfast in 1842, he attended R.B.A.I. and Queen's College, Belfast. He obtained his B.A. in 1863, his M.A. in 1864 and went to Assembly's College, Belfast, after which he became minister of York Street Presbyterian Church, Belfast, 1878–89. He served as an examiner for the board of intermediate education and was the author of a very popular history of Irish presbyterianism, *History of the presbyterian church in Ireland* (Edinburgh, 1886). His tenure of office at the Belfast college and university, began in 1889 and ended in 1923. He died in 1925.

Over a period of nearly 35 years, Hamilton played a vital role in persuading both the public and the government to give generous support to the expansion of the college and later the university. Student numbers grew from a total of 461 in 1889–90 to 1077 in 1923–4. He guided Queen's through the transition from university college to full university. The bronze tablet erected in his honour by friends and colleagues in the entrance hall of the Lanyon Building in 1907 states: "he has justly earned the gratitude of posterity and the enduring reputation of a second founder".

Improved facilities

An initial priority was to improve the condition of accommodation for the students. Writing of his time at the college in the 1880s, Robert Lloyd Praegar commented on the lack of student facilities:

> If you were adrift between lectures, the only place where you could even sit down was a wooden bench in a small severe room of the main [ie the entrance] hall where a silent man with a white beard, as uncommunicative as the professor of metaphysics, served plum buns and weak coffee at a reasonable charge.
>
> R.L. Praeger, *The way that I went* (Dublin, 1937), pp 7–8.

Previous appeals for support by Hamilton's predecessor had failed to win over either the government or the public. In early 1892 Hamilton initiated an appeal for the erection of a Students' Union building. In May 1894 a five day fund raising fair was held by students and supporters in the college grounds and in the Botanic Gardens. Afterwards, a *Book of the Fair* (Belfast) was published which described the numerous stalls, concerts and entertainments. It also pointed out the value of the proposed new building:

> Such an institution will undoubtedly contribute to the well-being and comfort of students in a thousand ways. It will prove an antidote, to a large extent, to the disadvantages of lodging houses. It will enable the students to dine comfortably together, if they so desire. In the evenings it will be a safeguard against the temptations of the city, and it will much conduce to the fostering of that common life and *ésprit de corps* which constitute such valuable elements in academic culture.

This event was followed in May 1896 by a large public meeting in the Great Hall of the college at which considerable sums of money were given. With the money raised, the foundation stone of the Union (now the Department of Music) was laid on 18 January 1896 and the building, to the design of Robert Cochrane, was formally opened a year later by the Lord Lieutenant, Lord Cadogan.

While this appeal to the general public proved successful so did Hamilton's approach to the government. Within a few years of taking office, he persuaded the authorities to provide funds for physiology and pathology laboratories which were also formally opened in 1897 alongside a new chemistry wing (opened in

1894), all on the site now occupied by the Social Sciences Building. Successful as he was in obtaining this financial support, unfortunately Hamilton was unable to take advantage of the sale in 1894 of Botanic Gardens, hitherto run as private gardens, which were purchased by the Belfast Corporation. With the extension in facilities at the college went the appointment of a number of new lectureships and professorships. The opening of the Royal Victoria Hospital in 1903 provided new teaching facilities for the Medical School at Queen's. By the early 1900s, however, Hamilton had found that once more the government was reluctant to grant support for further development and he now planned a full scale public appeal.

On 16 April 1901 Hamilton launched his new appeal at a well attended public meeting. A 'Fund for the Better Equipment of Queen's College' was established to seek financial support for additional facilities in the college. Backing for the fund was slow to materialise and by mid 1905 just £30,000 had been raised, of which a considerable amount was earmarked for special projects, such as £5,000 from Sir James Musgrave to endow a Chair of Pathology and £7,500 from Harland and Wolff for Physics and Engineering laboratories. A public meeting in June 1905 to encourage additional giving had minimal effect. The fund might well have been wound up at this stage, but in August 1905 an

(Top) The scene at the front of Queen's for the laying of the foundation stone of the Student's Union in 1896.

(Above) The stone-laying ceremony by Earl Cadogan, Lord Lieutenant of Ireland. In the background the Musgrave laboratories for physiology and pathology are under construction.

(Below) A formal photograph to mark the event. No copy of this photograph is known to exist.

unusual offer was received from the Scottish shipowner, Sir Donald Currie, who had attended school in Belfast. He promised to subscribe £20,000 on condition that another £20,000 could be raised by Christmas 1905. Since it had taken five years to raise £30,000, this posed an enormous challenge to the college and the organisers of the Better Equipment Fund.

In September President Hamilton published a letter of appeal in the Belfast press, outlining the offer from Sir Donald Currie. A remarkable response from the public, in particular graduates, now followed. In spite of this and the strong efforts of the organisers, the fund was £3,000 short of its target by the beginning of December. At this stage, Sir Otto Jaffé, a former Lord Mayor of Belfast and linen manufacturer, already a benefactor to the fund, stepped in and gave the final amount, after which Currie presented his £20,000. The fund provided an enormous boost to the college which was able to spend the money on urgent needs, without constant reference to government. New laboratories were established and the number of teaching staff, at both professorial and lecture level, was expanded. The contributions of Currie and Jaffé were commemorated in laboratories erected with this money and given their names.

Student life

Until 1900 there was no responsible body through which students could negotiate with the College authorities, although the Literary and Scientific Society had sometimes acted in this way. The Students' Representative Council was formed in 1900 with provision for 32 members. The photograph is of the first SRC which held office in 1900/01.

During the last decade of the nineteenth century and the early years of the twentieth century, the college experienced a very active period of student life. The new Union building provided good facilities. Several student magazines appeared in the 1890s. In 1900 the Students' Representative Council (S.R.C.) was formed. At this early stage there were ten college societies or clubs recognised by the S.R.C. The sports clubs were six in number and covered athletics, gymnastics, tennis, rugby, football, hockey and swimming. The other clubs were the Student's Union Society, (which ran the Union building), the Belfast Medical Students' Association (formed 1886), the Literary and Scientific Society (the 'Literific) and the Christian Union. Over the next two decades a number of other societies were formed, including the College Gaelic Society (Cumann Gaedhealach an Choláiste). The Officers Training Corps was established in 1908.

The turn of the century was marked by one of the most intensive periods of building in the history of Queen's. During the 14 years between 1894 and 1907, no less than seven new buildings were opened on the north-east corner of the main site, effectively almost doubling the size of the university. Chemistry was opened in 1894, closely followed by the Students' Union and the Musgrave Laboratories for physiology and pathology in 1897. The year 1907 saw the completion of the Currie Laboratories (Chemistry), the Jaffé Laboratories (Physiology), the Harland Laboratories (Engineering) and the Surgery Building. In addition, accommodation for Biology was ingeniously built over the north cloister of the Lanyon Building without disturbing its visual appeal. In fact, looking at the building today, few would realise that the whole building is not original.

The Chemistry Building (above) of 1894 and the Currie Laboratories of 1907, on the site now occupied by the Social Sciences Building.

The original Medical Building of 1863, extended in 1866 (below) and the Musgrave Laboratories of 1897.

The Students' Representative Council of 1909/10 shows the fashion of the time of wearing an academic hood with nonchalant abandon, even in a formal photograph.

Efforts were made in the 1890s to extend university teaching to a wider audience. The Belfast Society for the Extension of University Teaching was founded in 1889 and although it was not directly linked to Queen's, members of the college played a very important role in the society. Hamilton was president and other professors and graduates played a large part in the council and teaching of the society. Lectures were given on a wide range of subjects at a number of locations. This work laid the foundation for a programme of adult education which would be later taken up successfully by the new university after 1908.

The Literary and Scientific Society was the oldest of the student societies, though its origins are somewhat obscure. While there is no doubt that it was founded on 11 February 1850, it may well have developed from a private Literary Society which existed for the young men of Belfast long before the foundation of Queen's College. By the 1860s, in the opinion of the students, the Society's meetings were second in importance to the deliberations of the Westminster Parliament alone, and the annual elections of office-bearers equalled in excitement the palmiest days of the Irish elections before the Reform Bill was passed. The photograph shows the Society in 1906.

In 1882–3 women had been admitted to lectures in the Arts Faculty but it was not until the end of 1889, with the enrolment of women in the Medical Faculty, that they were able to attend all classes. They were still ineligible, however, to win college scholarships and prizes. In 1891 a petition from nine female and twenty-three male students was sent to the college Council to alter this situation. This won the support of Hamilton and the Council but the final say in this matter was governed by the original college charter and it was not until 1895 that this could be altered. In spite of these changes the number of women students at Queen's, Belfast, remained small. Victoria College, Belfast, which prepared women for the Royal University exams, continued to be the main source of university education for women in Ulster until after 1908. Between 1891 and 1900 only nineteen women graduated from Queen's College, Belfast, compared with ninety-five from Victoria College. By the year 1908–9, however, there were eighty-seven women students at Queen's out of a total of four hundred and fifty-six, and this was the highest figure achieved between 1882 and 1909.

Staff 1899

By 1899, fifty years after the first lectures were given at Queen's Belfast, striking changes had occurred in the make up of the professorial staff. The number of Irish born staff was now higher than in 1849 with a figure of fifteen out of a total of nineteen compared with thirteen out of twenty at the earlier date: this 1899 figure includes J.W. Byers who was born in Shanghai of Ulster missionary parents. Of the remaining staff in 1899, two were from England, one was from Germany and one was from Scotland. Of the fifteen Irish professors in 1899, twelve came from Ulster compared with eight out of a total of thirteen in 1849.

Civil Engineering has been a subject taught at Queen's since its foundation. This group of engineering students, photographed in 1905 in what is now the quad, includes the imposing figure of Professor Maurice Fitzgerald, a Trinity College Dublin graduate who came to Queen's with engineering experience gained in England and Russia. Note the photographic stowaways peering from the window and the state of the grass!

In 1849 there were six graduates of Trinity College, Dublin, and four graduates of Scottish universities and one German graduate among the Irish born staff, but in 1899 there were only three graduates of Trinity College, Dublin, one graduate of an English university and one graduate of a German university. Most significantly, there were now ten graduates of the Queen's University in Ireland or the Royal University of Ireland, of whom nine had studied in Belfast and one in Galway. Six of the twelve Ulster-born professors had been students at R.B.A.I. Among the Ulster professors a majority were Presbyterian: there was only one Ulster born Catholic professor, James Cuming, professor of medicine, the first graduate of the college to be appointed one of its professors. This small Catholic representation among the professorial staff was largely a reflection of the very low number of catholic graduates from the Belfast college in this period.

Anthony Ashley-Cooper, ninth Earl of Shaftesbury, First Chancellor of The Queen's University of Belfast, 1908–23.

The 1908 Irish Universities Act

During the first two decades of Hamilton's presidency, questions continued to be raised about the future of university education in Ireland. Finally in 1908 parliament passed the Irish Universities Act which abolished the Royal University and established new arrangements. The National University of Ireland was created as a federal body to embrace the old Queen's Colleges in Cork and Galway and University College, Dublin. The Belfast college became The Queen's University of Belfast. For Queen's, Belfast, the changes not only affected its title but its whole method of government, which for the first time became firmly rooted in its own academic body and the local community. Hitherto, the college had been under state control in appointments and general policy, and subject to outside examining bodies. Now it controlled its own appointments and policies and granted its own degrees, an autonomy which still exists.

Following the Irish Universities Act, the charter formally founding the Queen's University of Belfast was issued in 2nd December 1908. Under the charter supreme authority rested with the university Senate which drew its members from academic, civic and provincial interests. Bodies such as the Royal Victoria Hospital and the Belfast Corporation were represented. A group of commissioners was established to handle the establishment of the new arrangements. All members of the original Senate were nominated and it was not until 1914 that the first elections for the Senate took place. All existing appointments at the Belfast college were renewed in the new university. Thomas Hamilton was appointed Vice-Chancellor and the ninth Earl of Shaftesbury became the first Chancellor.

Along with these changes came an increase in annual income and capital expenditure from the government. New teaching posts were established. Separate Chairs were established in subjects formerly combined under one professor: for instance, the Chair of History and English Literature was replaced by Chairs of Modern History and English Literature. Lectureships were established in a number of areas, such as Biochemistry and Celtic Languages and Literature. A lectureship in Scholastic Philosophy was established amidst some controversy, but this new position, along with new university links with the Mater Hospital, was important in winning support of the Catholic bishops for the new university. The Faculty of Commerce (now Economic and Social Science) was created in 1910.

Building improvements included extensions to the Students' Union and the medical building, an addition to the Library and the construction of a new Physics block on the south side of the college, thus almost completing the south wing of the quadrangle. New attention was also paid to the question of purchasing playing fields. A fête of 1907 had raised substantial funds towards this purpose and Sir Donald Currie donated money to the sports' fund. From 1911 onwards the Better Equipment Fund laid aside money to increase the resources available for sports' land purchase. Finally, however, seventy-five acres was purchased at New Forge and the ground was opened in 1913.

This gymnastics photograph probably dates from around 1900. It was taken behind the old Medical Building (now demolished to make way for the Administration Building) in the area which is now a car park. The photographer had obviously failed to notice the small boy who had crept into the photograph.

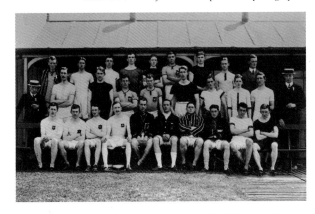

Student life post 1908

In the years immediately following the 1908 act the number of students at Queen's increased, although by 1914–15 it still stood at only five hundred and eight-four, of whom forty-seven per cent studied medicine. The number of Catholic students grew after 1908 so that by 1915–16 they numbered one hundred and forty-six out of a total of five hundred and sixty-seven full time students. The number of women students also increased because Queen's was now the only institution in Belfast allowed to provide university education. Magee College in Derry retained its univer-

(Above left) This photograph of the hockey team dates from 1904/5. The conditions for players may be judged from the changing rooms behind the team.

(Above) Queen's reputation in sport may be judged by the fact that the 1908 British Inter University Sports were held in Belfast. This 'Chariots of Fire' photograph shows four athletes from Queen's (wearing Queen's College crests) as well as those from Cork, Dublin, Liverpool, Leeds, London and Birmingham.

This photograph of the British Universities Students' Congress of 1908 includes the Lord Mayor of Belfast, Sir Robert Anderson (Centre front) and the President, Rev. Dr Hamilton.

sity role through a link with Trinity College, Dublin, but other institutions such as Victoria College and St Malachy's College were no longer able to offer university education, following the dissolution of the Royal University in 1908–9. By 1915–6 women students were one third of the student body.

Helen Waddell, later to achieve fame as a scholar and poet, came to Queen's in 1909 and in her correspondence and letters has left a picture of an inspiring intellectual environment, encouraged by George Gregory Smith, professor of English (1909–30), and a lively social centre. At the end of her second year she described her feelings about her exam efforts.

Thank goodness the class exams are over. In my last, we were told to compare Shakespeare and Ben Johnson, on which I could have written for a week. The day before, Gregory returned our essays. Well, as he once phrased it, I usually pursue the even tenor of my way along the A and I had given up all hope of a rise. He read out the seventeen names in alphabetical order – my miserable self coming last . . . Then, 'Miss Waddell'. Pause. 'An exceptional piece of work . . . an original treatment . . . in fact one of the best essays I have ever read . . . and I have judged it worthy of the highest mark to be given – A+'. He ended up 'By the way, if some of you have time, you might read it for yourselves, not merely for the matter – it has *literary merits*'. If they were not so nice, they would poison me, but I sat in the exam yesterday and wondered what it would feel like to drop from A+ to B-.

She set up a new society in the English department called the 'Tatlers Club', but the choice of president led to lively conflict with the 'Literific'.

Queen's was in a state of 'Sturm and Drang' all last week, and all over these unhappy Tatlers, or rather over the fool McCartney who, to our sorrow, we had elected President. There was an audience of about seventy. Gregory sat and beamed in his wonted chair, with the sheep on his right and goats on his left – namely, Mr Belfour and Mr McCartney. There was some speculation at first as to which was the goat, but events speedily cleared that up. For McCartney got up to deliver his Presidential address, and about half-way through began slanging the Literary and Scientific, the oldest society in Queen's and this in his most offhand Oxford manner. He meant it as a sort of burlesque, flinging down the gauntlet – or so he said afterwards. But as it happened, there wasn't a man there who didn't belong to the Lit. and Sci. and I sat and felt the atmosphere behind me getting electric – and I made agonized faces at McCartney which he was too short-sighted to see. And Gregory sat and buried his face in his hands and tried to look as if he were not laughing. It seems when he got McCartney out, he said very briefly – 'Well young man, you've done it now! Just you look out for the next *Q.C.B.*' Gregory knows his Queen's.

D.F.Corrigan, *Helen Waddell: a biography* (London, 1986), pp 81–3

In 1912 Eliza and Isabella Riddel provided £25,000 to establish a hall of residence for Protestant women students. Riddel Hall was designed in pleasant grounds at Stranmillis by W.H. Lynn and built 1913–15. It offered sixty-five places for women students. The building contains a fine bronze memorial plaque in the main corridor by Rosamund Praeger in memory of the Riddel sisters. A copy of the early house rules for Riddel Hall makes interesting reading. All students had to be back in the Hall by 7 p.m.:

Any student wishing to be out after 7 p.m. must, before leaving the Hall, enter her name in the Hall book, giving full particulars of her destination, and must sign it on her return. Students must in no case be out after 10.30 p.m. without special permission from the Warden, who may grant leave to be out until 11 p.m. for the purpose of attending theatres or concerts. Leave up to 11 p.m. may also be given by the Warden for dances but in this case the Warden must be furnished beforehand with the names of those composing the party, and with a written consent from the parents of the applicants.

Elmwood House with grounds in Elmwood Avenue was purchased by the university as a new residence for the Vice-Chancellor and, after Hamilton moved there in April 1913, his former quarters in the main university building were taken over and converted into class rooms, committee rooms and a common-room for women students.

During Hamilton's lengthy tenure in office, first as President and then as Vice-Chancellor, Queen's professorial staff was served by a wide range of able men. Perhaps the best known to the public of the professors was Sir William Whitla, professor of Materia Medica (1890-1919). Sir Ian Fraser has given a vivid description of Whitla:

Although Sir William Whitla had retired before I went up to Queen's he was still living in great style at Lennoxvale though very

SIR WILLIAM WHITLA

William Whitla entered Queen's as a medical student in 1870 and, following a period as house surgeon in the Belfast General Hospital, graduated MD with first-class honours in 1877. He was appointed Professor of Materia Medica in 1890, a post which he held for 29 years. He was knighted in 1902.

Sir William Whitla

Whitla's commemorative tablet on the Sir William Whitla Hall

This marble capital was brought back from Italy by Sir William and is now in the garden at Lennoxvale.

crippled with an arthritis of the hip. I remember him well at a grad-uation ceremony when he came dressed as a Deputy Lieutenant – brass buttons, coat, knee breeches, tricorn hat, and at the same time a Queen's hood around his neck. He was always very fond of regalia and decorations, a contrast to his wife who frequently dressed in her sober Salvation Army uniform – which she once wore to a garden party at Buckingham Palace. Sir William was a very interesting man. His daily readings were the Book of David and the stockmarket – this allowed him to keep his options open for both worlds. He produced several books. His *Dictionary of treat-ment* (published 1892) which was really a compilation with not much original work, was a best-seller. It went through twelve or more editions, including one in Chinese. It was a compulsory book for every sea-going captain in the Merchant Navy to have at his bed-side – of almost equal importance to the Bible.

Sir Ian Fraser "The personalities and problems of sixty years ago" in *The Ulster Medical Journal*, vol. 56, Supplement, Aug. 1987, p.521.

Whitla was an extremely benevolent individual. He part designed and paid for the Whitla Medical Institute, he endowed the Chair of Pharmacology at Queen's and in his will left his home at Lennoxvale to become the Vice-Chancellor's lodge and a sub-stantial sum of money which was to fund the building of the Whitla Hall. As Professor R.G. Shanks has commented:

"Unlike other distinguished graduates, his contribution to Northern Ireland has continued to develop through his generous legacies so that his name, although not the man, is probably more widely known now than at the time of his death.

R.G. Shanks 'The legacies of Sir William Whitla' in *The Ulster Medical Journal*, vol. 63, no. 1 p.52.

Johnston Symington was another distinguished medical professor during this period. He was appointed professor of Anatomy in 1893 and held the post until 1918 during which time he played a major role in the running of Queen's as Registrar. He was President of the Anatomical Society of Great Britain and Ireland from 1904–6 and achieved a national reputation for his work on Topographical Anatomy. Sir John William Byers, professor of Midwifery (1893–1920), combined a highly successful medical career with other interests, in particular Ulster dialect and folklore. His mother was the redoubtable Margaret Byers who founded Victoria College which, over a period of nearly forty years, educat-ed many women for the exams of the Royal University of Ireland.

John William Byers, Professor of Midwifery, 1893–1920.

In the Arts Faculty, one of the most distinguished scholars was Sir Samuel Dill, professor of Greek (1890–1923) and an expert on

Samuel Dill, Professor of Greek, 1890–1923.

Samuel James MacMullan graduated from Queen's College in 1861 and followed a distinguished career in education including: Principal of Cookstown Academy 1862–68; Assistant Librarian at Queen's College 1872–78; Assistant Registrar 1874–78; and Professor of History & English Literature 1892–1900. An unusual oil portrait of him hangs in the School of English in University Square.

Roman social history. Robert Lynd later recalled Dill's enthusiasm for Greek literature: 'while one was in his presence, Greek was no longer a dead language. One thought of him as a visitor from Pluto's world who had come with a message from the master.' In 1907 Robert Mitchell Henry was appointed to the Chair of Latin which he held until his retirement in 1938 along with the position of secretary of the academic council from 1908. Francis Maurice Powicke was appointed professor of Modern History in 1909, a position which he held for ten years. He established a high reputation for his work on the history of the middle ages and was professor of Modern History at Oxford, 1928–47.

Alumni

Queen's alumni continued to make significant contributions to various areas of life in both Ulster and further afield. In 1922–3, the last year of Hamilton's presidency, the Queen's calendar carried a list of all Queen's graduates from the first year of the college in 1849. The total number of names came to nearly six thousand, a figure which does not include the many students who studied at Queen's but took their degrees elsewhere. The single most important area of study was clearly medicine, and medical students made up around forty per cent of those listed in 1922–3. By this time medical graduates dominated the medical profession in Ulster but since this offered opportunities for only a limited number it is clear that the vast majority pursued their careers outside the province.

Many of these medical graduates achieved considerable prominence. Sir Edward Coey Bigger (M.D. 1883) was appointed medical chairman of the health ministry for Ireland in the early twentieth century, and was then professor at Trinity College, Dublin. Sir James W.B. Hodson (M.D. 1881), became senior surgeon at the Royal Infirmary Edinburgh, and was president of the Royal College of Surgeons, Edinburgh, 1914–17. Sir David Semple was founder and director of the Pasteur Institute, Kasauli, India, and later director of the Egyptian Health Department. Besides such men who achieved high office, others did invaluable work in countless public medical appointments, at home and abroad. In its obituaries, the Queen's *Annual Records* often carried mention of doctors who worked during this period. For example, in 1933 it records the death of Dr William Roulston:

Dr Roulston graduated in 1880 and worked in London during the epidemic of smallpox which occurred in that year. He had been in practice in Wakefield since 1881 till his retirement in 1925.

In 1935 it lists the death of James Whitefield Ritchie (M.B. 1899):

Dr Ritchie was one of the most popular practitioners in Belfast. He had practiced for thirty-four years in the Crumlin Road district, where he was a prominent figure in the social, political and public life of the people.

Samuel Dill, William Whitla and Thomas Hamilton were the best known members of Queen's staff who had attended the college as students. Sir Joseph Larmor was undoubtedly Queen's most

A rare snapshot of Professor J.A. Lindsay and Professor A.L. Meissner taken about the turn of the century. They are standing between the Engineering Building (now Information and Finance) and the Chemistry Building (now demolished and replaced by the Social Sciences Building) on the north side of the quadrangle. University Square is in the background.

Sir Joseph Larmor (on right) with Lord Balfour in 1921.

distinguished graduate at the national level in the academic world in this period. He graduated in 1874 and was senior wrangler (the top mathematical student) at Cambridge in 1880. After a time as professor of Natural Philosophy at Queen's Galway, he was appointed Lucasian professor of Mathematics at Cambridge, 1903–32. Knighted in 1909, he served as Secretary of the Royal Society, 1901–12, Vice-President, 1912–14, and was elected M.P. for Cambridge University, 1911–22. His works marked a number of significant developments in the fields of Mathematics and Physical Science for which he received honorary degrees from five universities. Benjamin Moore graduated from Queen's, Belfast, in 1890 and after pioneering the whole area of Biochemistry was appointed to the first Chair in this subject in Great Britain at Liverpool in 1902. He was later elected F.R.S.

BENCHMARKS

When the Cherryvale estate was purchased by the university in 1920 for playing fields, benches in the changing rooms were constructed from the reversed tops of old desks from lecture rooms in Queen's. When the old pavilion was demolished in the late 1970s, it was discovered that the desk tops were carved with the names of Queen's students from 1880 to 1913. Many of the carvers went on to pursue exemplary careers – thus has yesterday's vandalism become today's history.

Included in the 32 identified names are:–

Rev. Dr Robert Davey (B.A. 1900), father of Rev Dr Ray Davey, Presbyterian dean of residence at Queen's and founder of the Corrymeela Community;
Sir Robert Johnstone (B.A. 1893, MB 1896), professor of Gynaecology at Queen's 1920, President of the British Medical Association 1937;

Major General Samuel Kyle (M.B. 1906), with a distinguished career in two world wars in the Royal Army Medical Corps;
Surgeon Commander Robert McGiffen (MB 1905) with a distinguished career in the Naval Medical Service;
Robert Greer (B.A. 1899), Indian Civil Service
Rev. William O'Kane (B.A. 1892, LLB 1894), author of *With Poison and the Sword* (1910), *The King's Luck* (1912) and *Guppy Gyson* (1913);
Professor James Rea (B.A. 1885), first professor of Mathematics and Natural Philosophy, Church of Ireland Training College, Dublin.
Campbell Galway Robb (M.B. 1905), a gifted Rugby International and Chief Medical Officer, Egyptian State Railways;

The desk top also carries the exhortation 'Keep your hair on – use Sapplio'. It is believed that Sapplio was a well known proprietary product at the turn of the century.

and in 1920 he became professor of Biochemistry at Oxford, but died two years later.

Robert Lloyd Praegar, described recently as "probably the most important field botanist who has ever worked in Ireland", was a prolific writer of books and articles who graduated in 1885. Robert Wilson Lynd (graduated 1899) was a leading journalist for the *News Chronicle* and the *New Statesman* and the author of over thirty books. Samuel John Waddell, a brother of Helen Waddell, graduated with a degree in engineering in 1907. In 1904 he had helped to found the Ulster Literary Theatre. Under the name of Rutherford Mayne, he wrote various plays, such as "The turn of the road" and "The drone".

A number of Queen's alumni played a prominent part in politics, sometimes reflecting independence of thought and actions from their particular communities. James Brown Dougherty (graduated 1864) became a Presbyterian minister and professor of Logic at Magee College, Derry, but later held the post of Under Secretary for Ireland, 1908–14, and was Liberal M.P. for Derry city, 1914–18. James Brown Armour attended the Belfast college, 1860–2, completed his B.A. at the Cork college in 1864 and then took his M.A. in Belfast in 1866. He was ordained as a Presbyterian minister in Ballymoney and played a prominent role as a Home-Ruler in the early decades of the twentieth century. Denis Stanislaus Henry was a Catholic who studied law at Queen's in the early 1880s, became a barrister in 1885, served as Unionist M.P. for Londonderry South, 1916–21, and was appointed the first Lord Chief Justice of Northern Ireland, 1921–5. Sir Robert James McMordie was Unionist M.P. for East Belfast, 1911–14, and Thomas Sinclair was a leading Liberal Unionist.

Various Queen's graduates found employment with British colonial and diplomatic services as well as with foreign governments. John Newell Jordan obtained his B.A. in 1873 and joined the British consular service in the Far East. He served as consul general at Seoul, Korea, 1896–1906. In 1906 he was appointed British Minister to Peking, an important post which he held until 1920. He received a knighthood in 1904 and in 1921 he was given an honorary LL.D. by Queen's. Sir John McLeavey Brown (B.A. 1868) served as Chief Commissioner of the Korean Customs and Finance Adviser to the King of Korea (1889–1906). He received a British knighthood and Korea decorated him with the 1st class of the Order of Tai Kiek.

During this period a number of the first women students gained prominence. Edith Helen Major was a student at Queen's, Belfast, in the early 1880s and then attended Girton College, Cambridge, where she obtained honours in historical tripos. She became head mistress of Putney High School, 1900–10, and of King Edward's High School for Girls, Birmingham, 1910–25. She was appointed Mistress of Girton, 1925–31, and in 1932 was awarded an honorary LL.D. at Queen's. Anne Crawford Acheson graduated B.A. in 1904 and went to London to study at the Royal College of Art, Kensington. She became a sculptor and exhibited at the Royal Academy. She was the first woman to be elected a Fellow of the Royal Society of British Sculptors. During World War One she was involved in the invention of paper maché splints and in 1919 she was awarded the C.B.E.

Harriette Rose Neill, who graduated M.B. in 1894, was the first woman doctor to qualify at Queen's, Belfast. She later practised in Belfast before going to live and work at Bangor. Marion Braidfoot Andrews graduated with a M.B. in 1901, and received a M.D. in 1910 and a diploma in public health in 1914. She joined the staff of the Ulster Hospital for Women and Children. She took an active role in promoting public health in Belfast, and she contributed a report on maternity and child welfare in the city to the influential Carnegie report of 1917. She became assistant medical officer of health and school medical officer in 1921 in Worchester, a post which she held until 1936.

The summer of 1914 was one of the sunniest on record, at a time when Queen's had emerged from a period of uncertainty into full enjoyment of self-government with a renewed confidence in the future. The photograph by Hogg shows a carefree day of tennis on the front lawn in May, just three months before the outbreak of the First World War.

The First World War

The Great War of 1914–18 led to considerable changes to Queen's. It brought an increase in the number of students. In 1914–15 there were 584 students at the university but by 1918–19 the figure stood at 888, of whom sixty per cent were medical students. Large numbers of students received military training through the Officers' Training Corps and between the outbreak of war and the signing of the Armistice, over 700 of its members had received commissions. John Alexander Sinton (graduated 1908) was a doctor to the Indian expeditionary force, which saw service in Mesopotamia, and he was awarded a V.C. for bravery in 1916. His citation read:

> although shot through both arms and through the side, he refused to go to hospital, and remained, as long as daylight lasted, attending to his duties under very heavy fire. In three previous actions Capt. Sinton displayed the utmost bravery.

Part of the university grounds were given over for a military hospital for the Ulster Volunteer Force. Various members of staff volunteered for war service which created considerable problems in maintaining a viable teaching complement. The university also lost the services of Max Freund, professor of German, who was in Europe when war broke out. The Senate resolved to remove professor Freund from office as an enemy alien but after the war Freund successfully claimed against the university for arrears of salary. He later became professor of German at Rice University, Houston, Texas. In 1979, when Freund was 100 years old, Queen's senate made him a professor emeritus.

During the war many Queen's graduates lost their lives. The war memorial erected at the front of Queen's in 1923 carries the names of those two hundred and fifty-four Queen's alumni who died, including fifty-four doctors and medical students. A very moving account of the great personal loss of the war is given in the memoirs of Thomas M.Johnston, *Vintage of Memory* (Belfast, 1942). He records that in 1906 he served as secretary to the S.R.C. along with two good friends, Cecil R. Crymble, Auditor, and William Hamilton Davey, President. Crymble graduated B.A. in 1906 and B.Sc. in 1908, and achieved a D.Sc. in 1913, for which he was awarded special distinction and a gold medal. He was the first Queen'sman to fall in the war on 20th November 1914. Davey graduated B.A. 1902, M.A. 1903, and in his final law

Gregg Wilson (photographed in 1907), Professor of Natural History & Geology 1902–9 and Professor of Zoology 1909–31. In 1911 Professor Wilson, who had military experience with the Queen's Edinburgh Rifles and reached the rank of Major, took over the post of Commanding Officer of the Officers' Training Corps from Capt. H.H.B. Cunningham, who had established the Corps in 1908. Such was Gregg Wilson's impact that, for years after he left the post in 1920, cadets would be heard to refer themselves as 'Gregg Wilson's Army'. Professor Wilson subsequently served on the Military Instruction Committee until 1948.

Max Freund, Professor of Modern Languages 1903–09, Professor of German, 1909–14.

The Queen's Jesters, once referred to as 'the best Pierrot Troupe in Ireland', was most active between 1918 and 1923. It had close connections with the Officers' Training Corps which, in turn, drew heavily upon medical students in its recruitment. The Troupe probably grew out an OTC concert party, which had the benefit of the use of the Drill Hall for rehearsals and could draw on the services of the OTC band. It would seem that the Jesters also benefited from the fact that many of their number seemed to take an exceptionally long time to qualify, though a substantial number subsequently led distinguished careers. At the height of their fame the Jesters toured Ulster and could fill the Ulster Hall for their performances. The photograph is of the Jesters in 1923. In the centre, front, is Dickie Hunter when a medical student.

exams was bracketed first in all of Ireland along with the poet Tom Kettle, later Nationalist M.P. who died on the front in 1916. Davey was the last Queen'sman to die due to the war. A memorial in Carrickfergus Presbyterian church records how Major W.H. Davey of the Tyneside Irish Regiment "died from illness contacted on active service on 29 August, 1920".

In an interview in 1993, Mrs Florence Emeleus, who entered Queen's in 1918, recalled the end of the war and its memories:

> I remember Armistice Day. I was walking down near the bridge where the Lisburn Road joins Sandy Row. It was a foggy dismal November day. People were very excited. I remember the kind of rejoicings seemed to be very lonely because one knew so many people who had been killed. I'll never forget my first view of the *News Letter* on the day after the Battle of the Somme – pages and pages of people killed. Another thing I remember clearly is the Ulster Division marching through Belfast before they went away to the war. That added to the awful poignancy of the lists in the paper afterwards.

In October 1918, three weeks before the Armistice, the Queen's University Services Club was formed to encompass all university members who had served during the war. Membership of the club, which still exists, was extended to include Queen's members who served in later wars.

With the end of the war numbers continued to grow at Queen's. From 1915 attempts had been made to establish a department of social work, but they finally failed in the early 1920s due to lack of official demand for trained social workers. The dental school was founded in 1920. A new Faculty of Applied Science and Technology was established in 1921 through a special link with the Belfast Municipal Technical Institute. The new connections between Queen's and the local community now brought benefits in the form of many gifts and bequests for scholarships and the establishment of seven new posts. A Chair of Public Health was established in 1921. The Queen's Elms, a terrace of seven fine houses on University Road, directly opposite the university, were bought in 1920 for eventual conversion into student accommodation. Land was acquired in 1920 at Cherryvale for sports fields.

As regards the impact of political developments in Ireland on Queen's during the early twentieth century, it seems that events had little direct bearing on the university. When the third home rule bill was presented at Westminster by the Liberal government, successful efforts were made by Professor Douglas Savory and others to introduce an amendment underwhich Queen's was excluded from control of the proposed Irish parliament in Dublin and would have remained under Westminster. Concerns about a Dublin parliament were matched by concerns about a Belfast parliament and, following representations from Queen's Senate, section 64 was added to the Government of Ireland Act which ensured that the independence and income of the university were guaranteed by Westminster.

In early 1923 Hamilton resigned from the post of Vice-Chancellor at the age of eighty-one. In his last years he had become little more than a figurehead. Nonetheless, he had guided Queen's through a difficult period. During his time as President and then Vice-Chancellor, the number of students had doubled as had the amount of building on the university campus, and Queen's had emerged as a full university in its own right. Still restricted in social terms, nonetheless in terms of gender and denomination the university had a broader base in the comm-unity than ever before. The continuing growth in numbers now imposed new problems for the university but at least his successors were building on a strong foundation, a situation for which Hamilton was largely responsible.

The Hamilton Tower and gatelodge (above left) were erected at the front entrance to Queen's on 1907 in commemoration of the 3rd President. Although designed in a Tudor Gothic style in keeping with the Lanyon Building, the Tower came in for a great deal of contemporary criticism on aesthetic grounds. It was demolished in 1922 – one version of the story was that this was done to give lorries access to the main site; another was that the Tower was felt to obscure the new war memorial.

Parts of the Tower were preserved, built into the garden walls of Sir Willian Whitla's house at Lennoxvale (now the Vice-Chancellor's Lodge), (top and above).

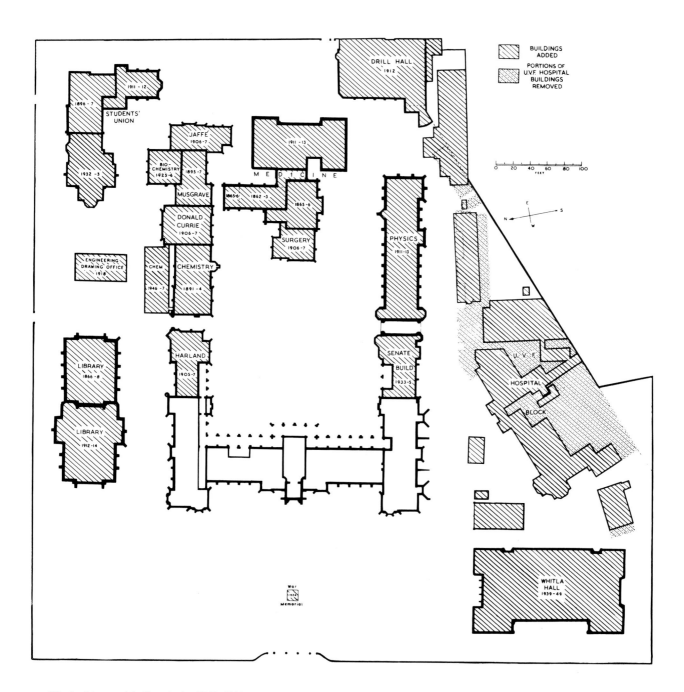

The development of the Queen's site, 1849–1949.

*This copy by James Atkins of **St Peter the Martyr** by Titian, presented to Queen's College by Charles Davis in 1847, hangs in the Great Hall of the University. It measures 15 feet by 8 feet. The original, which hung in the Church of SS Giovanni e Paulo in Venice, was destroyed by fire in 1867.*

Fingal's Cave, Staffa by Andrew Nicholl
(Lanyon Building)

Peat Stacks by Paul Henry
(Accommodation Office)

A Moorish Garden by Sir John Lavery
(Old Staff Common Room).

Connswater Bridge by John Luke
(Lanyon Building).

*Illuminated address to
Charles Stewart Parnell, from
the Belfast Parnell Leadership
Committee, 22 May 1891.
Illustrations by Patrick MacEnaney
and William Lynch.
(History Department)*

3

Changing times 1923–49

THE retirement of Thomas Hamilton in 1923 marked the end of the longest period of leadership by one individual in the history of Queen's. Hamilton had headed the college and then the university for 34 years. Three Vice-Chancellors now followed in the period of a mere 26 years. For the first time these appointments were the responsibility of the Senate of the university, rather than the government. R.W. Livingstone was Vice-Chancellor 1924–34, F.W. Ogilvie held the post 1934–8, and D.L. Keir served for the period 1939–49. Keir's resignation in 1949 coincided with the centenary celebrations of the founding of the original Queen's College, held over from 1945 because of the war. When these celebrations occurred in 1949, Queen's had been radically transformed, both in the size of campus and number of staff and students, from the college of the opening year of 1849. Many of these changes occurred in the period 1923–49.

Chancellor and Vice-Chancellors

The first Chancellor of Queen's, Lord Shaftesbury, also gave up his position in 1923 and he was succeeded by the 7th Marquess of Londonderry, Minister of Education for Northern Ireland. Lord Londonderry remained Chancellor from 1923 to 1949, covering the tenure of three Vice-Chancellors. Hamilton's successor as Vice-Chancellor, Richard Winn Livingstone, was a former Fellow of Corpus Christi College, Oxford, and a well known classical scholar. After his resignation in 1933, to become President of his original Oxford college, special tribute was paid to his efforts to bring greater community involvement in and financial support for the university.

RICHARD WINN LIVINGSTONE was Vice-Chancellor of Queen's University 1924–33. Born in Liverpool in 1880, he was educated at Winchester and New College, Oxford, obtaining his B.A. in 1904. He became a Fellow of Corpus Christi College, Oxford, 1905–24. He wrote extensively on Greek subjects and on the role of education: he placed heavy emphasis on the value of classical studies in modern education. After his time as Vice-Chancellor of Queen's, he became President of Corpus Christi College, 1933–50, and Vice-Chancellor of the University of Oxford, 1944–7. He was knighted in 1931.

In a speech at the 1959 celebrations for the golden jubilee of the founding of the university, Livingstone recalled Queen's of the 1920s: "what impressed me as a newcomer was the keen, vigorous life of the place. Its weakness was material, its strength on the human side . . .". He paid tribute to the staff: "The quality of the professoriate was partly due to the wise policy of the Senate which, in spite of shortness of funds, paid higher professoriate salaries than was usual elsewhere, and thus attracted good men." (*Belfast Newsletter*, 9 April 1959). He achieved considerable success at Queen's in increasing the funding and in bringing wider public involvement in the university: in particular he persuaded all the main county and borough councils to contribute to the revenue of the university and to participate in the Senate.

FREDERICK WOLFF OGILVIE'S period in office as Vice-Chancellor was the shortest in the history of Queen's. Appointed in 1934, he resigned four years later. Born in Valparaiso, Chile, in 1893, he was educated at Packwood Haugh, Clifton College and Balliol College, Oxford. His studies were interrupted by the Great War, during which he served in the 4th Bedfordshire Regiment, and he obtained his B.A. in 1919. He became a Fellow and Lecturer at Trinity College, Oxford, 1920–6, and then professor of Political Economy at the University of Edinburgh, 1928–34. He was Director General of the B.B.C. for 4 years after his resignation from Queen's in 1938. He was knighted in

1942. He became Master of Jesus College, Oxford, from 1944 to the year of his death, 1949.

DAVID LINDSAY KEIR served as Vice-Chancellor for a decade (1939–49). He was born in 1895 at Spennymoor, Co. Durham, and was educated at the University of Glasgow and New College, Oxford. He served in the King's Own Scottish Borderers during the Great War. He was Fellow of University College, 1921–39, acting as estates bursar, 1935–9. His area of academic interest was English constitutional history. During his time as Vice-Chancellor at Queen's he served as chairman of a number of government boards and other organisations, including the Ulster Young Farmers' Club. Knighted in 1946, he became Master of Balliol College, Oxford, in 1949, a post which he held until 1965. His death occurred in 1973

Keir faced the difficult task of leading Queen's during the difficulties and dangers caused by the Second World War. In the immediate post-war years he played an important part in putting forward Queen's case for additional funding and in laying much of the groundwork for the marked expansion of the university post-1949. When he resigned in 1949, tribute was paid in the *Annual Record* to his vision, his power and grasp of intellect, and his skill as a chairman.

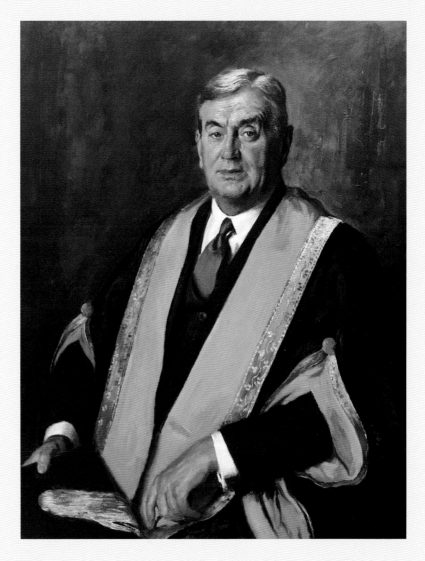

Professor Estyn Evans, 1950.

Estyn Evans came to Queen's in 1928, as the university's first lecturer in Geography. When he retired forty years later his Department was the largest in Ireland with an international reputation which reflected his own contribution to teaching research, and that of the staff and students whose work he had encouraged over the years.

To Queen's he bequeathed not only a flourishing Department of Geography but also the Department of Archaeology and Social Anthropology, both of which were founded under his influence and guidance. On his retirement from the Chair of Geography in 1968 he became the first Director of the University's Institute of Irish Studies, remaining as an Honorary Research Fellow until his death in 1989.

*The monumental **A preliminary survey of ancient monuments of Northern Ireland**, compiled with his colleagues Oliver Davies and H. C. Lawlor and published in 1948 provided the database for future study and research. Meantime he had also become aware of the traditional farming practices and crafts of the Irish countryside, and two of his books, **Irish Heritage** and **Irish Folk ways**, quickly became classics in that field. Works of synthesis followed later, notably his **Personality of Ireland**, first published in 1973, and with these came academic honours.*

In 1934 the Senate appointed Frederick Wolfe Ogilvie as Vice-Chancellor. He was a graduate of Oxford and the holder of the Chair of Political Economy in Edinburgh. His stay at Queen's was a short one which ended in 1938 when he was appointed Director General of the BBC. During this time, however, he was responsible for drawing up plans for expansion which saw fruition after his departure. In 1939 David Lindsay Keir, Fellow of University College, Oxford, was appointed Vice-Chancellor. The outbreak of war a few months after his taking up office caused special problems for the new Vice-Chancellor and restricted plans for expansion. Nonetheless, under Keir's leadership important developments did occur and with the end of the war significant steps for expansion were taken. Active in various local organisations such as the Northern Ireland Regional Hospital Board he played a key role in obtaining increased government funding for the university. He resigned in 1949 to become Master of Balliol College, Oxford.

Academic developments

Soon after Livingstone's arrival in 1924 important developments occurred in a number of academic areas. Renewed interest in provision of agriculture at Queen's had culminated in a decision of senate in 1923 to establish a Faculty of Agriculture. Discussion with the Department of Agriculture of Northern Ireland led to an agreement for joint appointments for new posts in this area, to be funded directly by government sources. In October 1924 appointments were made to two new Chairs and two new lectureships in agriculture. Discussion between Queen's and the government over the question of the training of teachers led to recognition of the newly established Stranmillis College.

Two fields of controversy during the early years of Livingstone's time as Vice-Chancellor were the questions of establishing a Theology Faculty and of creating an honours school in Scholastic Philosophy. Eventually in 1926 a Faculty of Theology was set up to create a link between Queen's and local theological colleges, in particular the Presbyterian college. In 1927, under the direction of Father Arthur Ryan, a new honours school in Scholastic Philosophy was established. An area in which Livingstone took a special interest was classical studies and both Greek and Latin were restored to an important place in the matriculation exams in 1931–2, a decade after they had been downgraded in 1922.

During the 1920s a number of new Chairs were established. A Chair of Biochemistry and a lectureship in Bacteriology were established in 1924 with a sum of £60,000 from the estate of J.C. White, a former lord mayor of Belfast. Changes in the legal system, in particular the establishment of a separate Inns of Court for Northern Ireland in 1926, led to the need for reorganisation of the law faculty and additional resources for legal education: extra appointments were made in the Law Faculty in 1926 and again in 1934. In 1928 the senate appointed H.J. Eason to the new position of lecturer and director of extra-mural studies, which put the earlier work of the university extension teaching movement on a formal footing. Eason had strong connections with the Workers' Education Association which were to be used to advantage to promote this extra-mural teaching widely in the community.

In the late 1920s and early 1930s lectureships were created in a number of areas, including Geography and Civil Engineering. Emyr Estyn Evans was appointed lecturer in Geography in 1928. He became the first professor of Geography in 1945 and proved to be a vital driving force in the fields of Archaeology and Social Anthropology as well as Geography. Changes occurred within departments such as History where in 1934 reallocation of teaching responsibilities led to the appointment of a specialist in Irish History. During the war there was a depletion of staff due to members joining the forces. Nonetheless, in response to the social upheaval caused by the war and the need for trained social workers, it was decided in July 1941 to establish a School of Social Studies and the following year a certificate in the subject was organised. Work in the school was carried out by existing members of staff until a full time lecturer in Social Studies was appointed in 1945. In 1948 arrangements were made with St Mary's Training College to allow students of the college to follow a combined course of university study and professional training.

The Quad in the 1930s. Note the Andrews Tree in the foreground.

QUEEN'S AT ITS MOST PICTURESQUE

Queen's in the late 1930s possessed a visual harmony rivalling the best of Oxford and Cambridge colleges. There was no residential accommodation within the college buildings, but the quad had achieved that air of learning and tranquility usually found only in idealized memories. The building of the Sir William Whitla Hall and the 1940s and the new Physics Building in the 1950s – whatever their individual architectural merits might be – marked the end of the coherence of the main site. Demolitions in the 1960s, which removed the fine old buildings on the north-east corner and

east side of the quad to make way for the Social Sciences Building and the Administration Building, together with the erection of the Library Tower, are now seen as acts of vandalism of our heritage, however necessary they might have been considered at the time. One can only be thankful that the proposal to build a multi-storey car park on the front lawn was successfully defeated. Fortunately, in an age now more sensitive to its environment, the rest of the old main-site buildings have been, and will be, sympathetically preserved.

Numbers of staff were restored in 1945 to the pre-war level but in addition the university received a considerable number of new posts as a result of additional funding due to the University Grants Committee. In 1945 and 1946 Chairs of Celtic, Geography, Mathematical Physics and Jurisprudence were established. Also in these two years, thirty-one lecturers, six part-time lecturers and ten assistants and demonstrators were added to the staff of the university. These changes meant that for the first time the professors were a minority of the academic staff. Analysis of the professorial staff in 1949 by Professor J.C. Beckett and T.W. Moody shows that important changes had occurred in their make up, compared to the situation half a century earlier (*Queen's history*, ii,p.634). Few of the professoriate were now locally born Queen's graduates (either protestant or catholic) and most were recruited from a wider network, except for the Medical Faculty with its close links to the Royal Victoria and Belfast City hospitals.

The number of professors had risen from nineteen in 1899 to thirty-five in 1949, but the number of Irish born professors had dropped from fifteen to eight. Of the eight professors in 1949 born in Ireland, those from Ulster numbered seven (compared with twelve in 1899) of whom five were in the medical faculty. In sharp contrast to 1899 only three professors in 1949 had studied at R.B.A.I. and there was just one with a Scottish degree and no one with a Trinity College Dublin degree. Besides the five locally born medical professors, who were graduates of Queen's, only one professor (M.J. Boyd of Latin) now had a Queen's primary degree: in 1899, 9 out of 19 professors had received their first degree through Queen's Belfast. Locals were even a minority of the Medical School, numbering five out of eleven professors, and were to be found almost entirely in the areas of clinical medicine which were attached to the main teaching hospitals.

Of the other non-Irish professors in 1949, there were seven from Scotland, eighteen from England and Wales, two from the Continent, and two from the British Commonwealth. The vast majority of lecturers in 1949 also were recruited from outside Northern Ireland. This whole trend, which seems to have begun early in the century, was found in other regional universities in the U.K. university system. No doubt it helped to increase the flow of new ideas and methods to Queen's and helped Queen's graduates find academic jobs elsewhere but it affected university involvement in the community and restricted local participation in the university.

Finance

Essential for such developments and expansion was an increase in financial support for the university. Soon after his appointment Livingstone began to seek additional funding. Thirty-five years later at the 1959 golden jubilee celebrations to mark the founding of the university, he described the challenge which faced him when he took up his new job in January 1924:

> In that year there were 1,169 students in buildings designed for 500, reinforced by a line of wooden huts in which geology, botany, dentistry and some other subjects were housed. These were survivals from a war hospital, which was substantially built on brick foundations, thanks to a prominent member of the senate, Dr A.B. Mitchell, who foresaw other uses for them after the war.
>
> Our annual income, about half that enjoyed by some contemporary British universities, was £62,000; from this it had to finance our scholarships, which in England were provided by the local authorities. There was a deficit of over £3,000 in 1923–4, which rose to £5,000 in the following year. The library was desperately overcrowded. The scientific departments were short of necessary equipment. Thus anatomy was without an epidiascope; it cost £150 and the annual departmental grant was £150. One could easily add to this list of deficiencies and needs.
> *Belfast Newsletter*, 9 Apr. 1959

Livingstone now turned not just to private donors and government sources but also to the public and to the local authorities, namely Belfast and Londonderry borough councils and the 6 county councils. In 1926 the first of a series of "Open Days" was held at the university. The purpose of this was to increase communications between Queen's and the general public. A booklet produced for the occasion highlighted the good facilities at the university. At the same time attention was drawn by Livingstone to the underfunding of Queen's compared to universities elsewhere. For example in 1924–5, as Livingstone pointed out, Queen's with 1,169 students had an income of £66,940 while Bristol with a student population of 775 received £113,496 and Leeds with 1,435 students had an income of £207,276. He appealed to local councils for support.

By 1929–30, when all councils finally agreed to help in some measure, the total of income from this source was about £5,000, a figure which compared with £26,000 in fees. Some councils made specific grants while others levied an extra sum on the rates in support of the university. The councils were now allowed to elect representatives on to Senate. Some success in attracting private donations was achieved but this money was often for specific purposes. Fees were raised in 1925–6 to increase the university income. During the 1920s the government gave only limited extra funding, in spite of appeals from the university.

By 1934, when Livingstone retired, the income for the university from all sources stood at £97,994, an increase of around 50% from 1924; but during this time the parliamentary grant had been raised by only £5,000 (in 1928), and the bulk of additional income came from local authority grants, private endowments and fees(due both to extra student numbers and an increase in their level). Nonetheless, good housekeeping along with the extra self raised income allowed the university to create a building fund in the 1930s. Then in 1938, thanks to a special appeal by Ogilvie, the main government grant was increased by £25,000 to £55,000.

In response to concern throughout the United Kingdom for improved university facilities after the war, the University Grants Committee visited Queen's in early 1945 and again in 1948. As a result of its reports, the Northern Ireland government increased very considerably its annual grant to the university and provided large sums for new buildings. The overall income of the university increased from £153,472 in 1944–5 to £316,516 in 1948–9, thanks largely to a growth in government grant from £62,500 to £190,000. Centenary celebrations after the war gave the opportunity to establish a Centenary Endowment Fund which by late 1949 had raised £292,000 for capital developments and ongoing revenue at the university.

New buildings

In spite of limitations of funding in the 1920s, new buildings were erected from early in Livingstone's tenure in office. Negotiations with the government over the establishment of an Agriculture Faculty included the provision of a new building, largely funded by government in Elmwood Avenue. Work on the building (now the Geosciences building) began in late 1925 and was fully in operation by 1928. The bequest from J.C. White in 1924 which led to the creation of two separate departments of Bio-chemistry and Bacteriology included finance for extensions to the northeast corner of the chemistry block. Early in Livingstone's time, steps were taken to make major improvements to the Library.

Late in the 1920s a decision was taken to build a new university Pathology Institute. A special arrangement was arrived at with the Royal Victoria Hospital for the erection of the Institute on a site at the hospital which allowed for even closer co-operation between the Medical Faculty and the "Royal". The building was opened in 1933. The same year also saw the opening by Stanley Baldwin of a major extension, including a new dining hall, to the Students' Union building. Funds for this addition came largely from the Pilgrim Trust. In the early 1930s work began on a block between the former President's house and the Physics department, so filling in the vacant space on the south side of the quadrangle. This new building provided space for a Senate room and accommodation for three Arts departments.

Building extension at Queen's suddenly received an important boost in 1933, thanks to a major bequest from Sir William Whitla, who died in December of that year. He left his house, Lennoxvale, to become the official residence of the Vice-Chancellor, and a sum of £35,000 to erect either an assembly hall or a student hostel. A decision was eventually made in 1935 to build the former. After considerable delay, the foundation stone was laid by the Chancellor, Lord Londonderry, in July 1939 and work continued, in spite of the war, until it was completed in 1942, except for internal fittings. The building was immediately requisitioned by the ministry of finance, and the assembly hall, called the Sir William Whitla Hall, came into full university use only in 1949, after its formal opening by Sir Henry Dale, former director of the Royal Institute for Medical Research. Other work, such as the proposed Geology building in Elmwood Avenue, was stopped by the war.

While the decision was made to build an assembly hall rather than a student hostel with the Whitla bequest, steps were taken at the same time to improve residential facilities for students. In the late 1920s money had been put aside from various sources to provide a hostel fund. This money was then used to convert four of the houses in the Queen's Elms, which had become vacant, into a hall of residence for 42 male students in study bedrooms. In October 1936 the formal opening ceremony of the new residence, called the Queen's Chambers, was performed by the Duke of Abercorn, Governor of Northern Ireland. Other residential accommodation was provided in the 1940s when Aquinas Hall on the Malone Road was opened as a hall of residence for Catholic women students under the care of the Dominican Sisters. The

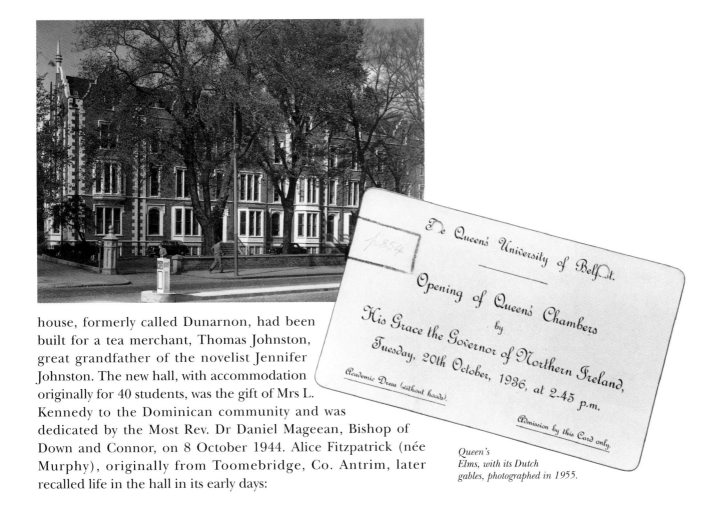

The Queen's University of Belfast.

Opening of Queen's Chambers
by
His Grace the Governor of Northern Ireland,
Tuesday, 20th October, 1936, at 2.45 p.m.

Academic Dress (without hoods).

Admission by this Card only.

Queen's Elms, with its Dutch gables, photographed in 1955.

house, formerly called Dunarnon, had been built for a tea merchant, Thomas Johnston, great grandfather of the novelist Jennifer Johnston. The new hall, with accommodation originally for 40 students, was the gift of Mrs L. Kennedy to the Dominican community and was dedicated by the Most Rev. Dr Daniel Mageean, Bishop of Down and Connor, on 8 October 1944. Alice Fitzpatrick (née Murphy), originally from Toomebridge, Co. Antrim, later recalled life in the hall in its early days:

> The régime was quite strict. Parents really knew their children were being supervised in those days. First years had to be in at 7.30 every night but you could get permission to go down and study in the library at Queen's but then again you had to be back when the library closed at nine. One night a week you had a late night when you had to be in by 10.30. The other students had to be in at 10.30 pm and one night a week at 11.30 pm. Twice a term the students were allowed to go to a late dance but any other late nights were allowed only after stringent conditions. A student could have gone to another function but it had to be known where they were staying and they needed their parents' permission. There wasn't the freedom that young people enjoy nowadays so we didn't feel badly done by although I wouldn't like to put anybody into that régime today. It was a social centre, as well as everything else in those days. I especially remember Mother Bertrand and Mother Augustine who looked after us well.
> (*Irish News* 6 December, 1993)

Sadly it closed in 1993.

When peace returned in 1945, and extra finance became available, a number of new buildings were constructed. Several houses in University Square were obtained for departmental purposes and so began a policy which would lead finally to the securing of the whole terrace by the 1970s. Chlorine House and grounds, situated between Malone and Stranmillis Roads, was bought to provide valuable space for later development. Work recommenced on the new Geology building in Elmwood Avenue and extra accommodation was provided at the Royal Victoria Hospital.

Students and student life

What about the students and student life during this quarter century? At Livingstone's arrival in early 1924 student numbers stood at 1,077. Ten years later when he resigned the figure had

The inter-war years were a time of increasing participation in sport by women. This photograph of the Ladies Hockey team dates from 1925–6.

increased to 1,484. Ogilvie's period in office saw little change and by 1939–40 students numbered 1,555. During Keir's term as Vice-Chancellor, however, numbers increased rapidly to 2,012 in 1944–5 and 2,762 by 1948–9. Students continued to be drawn from areas closest to the university. For example, in 1928–9, 95 per cent of students were from Northern Ireland, nearly 78 per cent were from Belfast or Counties Down and Antrim, 17 per cent were from the other Northern Ireland counties, 3 per cent were from the rest of Ireland, and only 2 per cent were from Great Britain or abroad. The 1940s, however, witnessed a rise in the number of outside students: by 1948–9 nearly 11 per cent of students were from Great Britain or abroad.

Throughout this whole period 1923–49 the Queen's student body in denominational terms was a mixed one, indeed more mixed than any other university in Ireland. At the same time Queen's was predominantly Protestant in the character of its student population. While the number of Catholics grew, their percentage of the total student body remained at only around 20 per cent. Various reasons limited Catholic attendance in this period, such as economic factors and the fact that many northern Catholics attended colleges of the National University of Ireland. In Fionnuala O'Connor's book *In search of a state: Catholics in Northern Ireland* (Belfast 1993), Cardinal Cahal Daly has recalled from his student days in the 1940s the good relations between students of different backgrounds and the lasting friendships that were formed: at the same time political and religious issues were usually carefully avoided.

Remembering his time at Queen's in the 1930s, Dr D.B. McNeill, who was an engineering student, has described the university as "a medical school with a university attached". There is considerable truth in this comment. In 1918–19 the number of medical students as a proportion of the student body had stood at nearly 62 per cent out of 888 students, but by 1923–4 the figure was 37 per cent out of 1,077 and by 1928–9 it was 30 per cent out of 1270. In the 1930s the percentage rose again with the result that by 1939–40 the medical students were 47 per cent of the student body. Their actual numbers continued to grow, but they fell as a proportion of the total student population so that by 1948–9 779 medical students were 28 per cent of the total population. The other major Faculty during most of this period was the Arts Faculty. From 1939 onwards, however, numbers in the Science and Civil Engineering Faculty were greater than those in the Arts Faculty.

Student life in the 1930s has been recalled vividly by Dr D.B. McNeill. The Students' Union, with various facilities such as a dining room and billiards room, provided the main social centre in the campus.

> The Union Building (now Department of Music) contained a café which was managed by the wife of William Fulton, the manager of the Students' Union. Here waitress service was provided for all customers who could obtain tea at 1p per cup and buns at $\frac{1}{2}$ p each; lunch was also available at 7$\frac{1}{2}$ p. The café also had a table reserved for the more sociable members of the academic staff such as Montrose (Law), Meredith (Commerce) and Dicky Hunter (Anatomy). The McMordie Hall, which formed part of the Union premises, was the venue for the monthly meetings of the Students' Representative Council and was also used for the more important student meetings.

Like the majority of students, McNeill lived at home. Besides those at Riddell Hall or at home, "all other students lived in lodgings which cost between £1.25 and £1.50 per week, a sum which included all meals with dinner on Sundays". The new Queen's Chambers hostel opened in the late 1930s to provide accommodation for male students, but, he recalled "the charges for accommodation in the Chambers were considerably more than those for lodgings and the majority of its early residents came from comparatively affluent homes".

AN EXTRAORDINARY CAREER

In 1906 retired R.I.C detective Thomas Carroll was appointed to the post of laboratory attendant in the Chemistry Department at the age of 46. He became so familiar with the material that, when there was a shortage of teaching staff during the First World War, he found himself called upon to take classes in Chemistry along with his other duties.

Such was the success of his teaching, in spite of the fact that he had never had any systematic training in Chemistry, that he continued to take classes after the war almost up his retirement in 1942 at the age of 82.

On his retirement, Vice-Chancellor Lindsay Keir wrote to him expressing the university's sorrow, and Dr A.W. Stewart of the Department of Chemistry said, '. . . you are not likely to be forgotten by any of us. No one could have done more for the place than you have done for the best part of a generation.' He died in 1944.

His successor in the post was his son, also named Thomas.

Women students had their own facilities on the campus. During the 1920s a women students' hall was based in rooms at the south of the original Lanyon building. In 1929 the hall was transferred to two of the houses in the Queen's Elms. Women were 34 per cent of the student population in 1924 but a decade later the figure had fallen to 25 per cent. Women students produced a magazine of their own, *Hall-marked*, which ran for three annual numbers from 1926 to 1928. Mrs Patsy Richardson entered Queen's in 1933 to study Science, and sixty years later she recalled her years at the university with affection: "I enjoyed my lectures and classes and practicals and I loved my sport. I met other people from other Faculties which was great as was going on tour [with the hockey team] and meeting people from other universities". In 1993 Mrs Kathleen Henry, who graduated in Arts at Queen's in the early 1930s, remembered vividly the debates in the Union and the enthusiasm for Drama. She also recollected classes in Political Science with Joseph Lemberger who was well-known as a mysogonist.

> Oh, he was terrible! I remember one day he was asking some questions in class and he said "what does the word 'Catholic' mean?" Catholic is a very tricky sort of word to use in the North of Ireland and there was dead silence and nobody answered – so at last I piped up and I said it means "universal" and he said "I didn't ask you". But in spite of that he passed me third in the exam. I sent a letter asking for a reference from all the teachers and he sent me back one without a stamp on the envelope, and I had to pay the stamp.

After the war, a number of improvements affected the well being of students. A permanent health centre was established in 1947 and a full time medical officer was appointed in the following year. The major religious denominations extended the scope of their work in the university with the appointment of full time deans of residence. Changes due to the introduction of the British Welfare State affected student life; in particular, the introduction of free secondary schooling for 1947 and the later increase in the number and value of university scholarships dramatically improved the opportunities for many to attend the university, although the full effects of this would not be felt until the next decade.

Several student magazines were produced during this period. The *Q.C.B.* had collapsed in 1920 and was followed in 1922 by *Fravlio-Queen's* which ran until 1926. These were student magazines which commented on university affairs. In 1926, however, there appeared the first issue of a rather different magazine, the *Northman*, which carried articles on literature and politics. It ran until spring 1951 and included material by a wide range of writers who later achieved considerable prominence such as John Hewitt, Bertie Rodgers, Hugh Shearman and Michael McLaverty. The magazine *P.T.Q.*, which first appeared in 1928, raised money for various local charities.

Sports continued to be popular and in the 1930s a number of new clubs were formed. D.B. McNeill and three other students were responsible for reviving rowing at Queen's in the Autumn of 1931, although it would be another 19 years before the boat club moved to its own boat house at Stranmillis. The Queen's Gaelic Football and Hurling Club was founded in 1931–2. Queen's hurlers formed their own separate club in 1943. The university produced many prominent international rugby footballers. George Stephenson played for Queen's as a medical student and won 42 rugby international caps for Ireland between 1920 and 1930. This period also saw the formation of a number of graduates' clubs, including The Queen's University Association, The Queen's Women Graduates' Association and The Queen's University Guild. The first of these organisations published an *Annual Record* from the early 1930's.

D.B. McNeill, a powerful presence in rowing at Queen's for over 60 years, photographed in 1991.

The Second World War

The outbreak of war in 1939 brought special difficulties to Queen's. Over 40 members of staff were released or resigned to take up national service. Special six month courses were provided for cadets preparing for entry to the Royal Air Force and to the Royal Artillery and Royal Engineers. The broadcaster, Sir Robin Day, was one such individual who as a cadet received part of his training at Queen's. The Senior Training Corps, which took over from the Officer Training Corps, and a newly formed air squadron provided training for hundreds of students. The war brought physical changes to the university. The Queen's *Annual Record, 1941–2*, noted:

King George VI and Queen Elizabeth visited Queen's in 1937. They are seen here being welcomed at the front of Queen's by the Chancellor, the Marquess of Londonderry. Standing in anticipation on the right is Vice-Chancellor Frederick Ogilvie.

During the Second World War the quadrangle and part of the front lawn at Queen's were turned into vegetable plots for staff during the government's 'Dig for Victory' campaign. In a rare show of university democracy for the time, plots were offered to all grades of staff, and the work commenced with an enthusiasm which was much more than a mere token gesture of contributing to the war effort.

However, all efforts were defeated initially by the amount of 1848 builders' rubble below the surface, including a quantity of discarded lead piping large enough to be worth sending to the smelter, and later by a lack of indigenous worms to aerate the soil, these having been removed over the years by Queen's groundsmen dedicated to eradicating unsightly worm casts from the lawns. Another factor in the small yields obtained was that academics proved to be no more competent at looking after their crops than any other group of first-time gardeners.

Among those who had plots were Dickie Hunter, Francis Newark, professor of Jurisprudence, and Estyn Evans, lecturer in Geography. Dickie Hunter purchased a silver cup to be presented annually to the person producing the greatest weight of vegetables. It was won by Dickie himself every year. He had been responsible for allocating the plots and had given himself a plot twice as large as any of the others.

(Top) The Quad in vegetables.

(Above) Dickie Hunter in his vegetable plot.

"Among the less important changes brought about in the university by the war, though among the most obvious, is the turning into allotments of the lawns in the quadrangle and immediately in front of the new building" It was alleged that air wardens on night duty on the roof of the main Queen's building spent much of their time looking after their vegetables in the allotments.

The real horror of the war, however, was never far from people's minds. In 1941–2, the Queen's *Annual Record* noted:

Apart from the general war situation, the air raids on Belfast during the session did not leave the university unaffected. For the greater part of a week, few classes were held, partly because of transport difficulties, but primarily because of the manful part which students were playing in connection with the A.R.P. services of the city. In particular, a body of over 250, drawn from all classes, was prominently engaged in demolition work. Inevitably all this effort on the part of students, as well as destruction and damage to the homes of some of them, interfered with their studies. The university authorities accordingly took steps to assess as far as possible the amount of interference caused in each case and made all practicable allowances.

The encampment on the front lawn of Queen's was part of the Salute the Soldier week in May 1944. Note the vegetable plots in front of the Lanyon Building.

The *Annual Record* now carried obituaries of those killed on active service. These entries make sad reading. They include:

Flight-Lieutenant Granville Wilson, D.F.M., D.F.C., D.S.O., R.A.F., a student of civil engineering; reported missing 6th September, 1944, now known to have been killed and buried in Holland. He was an old boy of Methodist College. He had 60 operational flights to his credit and had for some time been marker to the Pathfinders when he met his death.

Alexander McIntosh, Lieutenant, Royal Irish Fusiliers, a student of dentistry; killed in the Middle East, aged 23 years. A noted rugby player and oarsman, he had played in one of the schools' inter-provincial matches and had rowed for the university.

Thomas Dunwoody Mayne, Flight-Sergeant, R.A.F., a medical student of the university; died October 1943. He was the only son of Mr and Mrs Thomas Mayne, Antrim Road, Belfast.

A total of 2,335 Queen's men and women served in British and allied forces during the war. Bronze tablets containing the 155 names of those who lost their lives were placed on the plinth of the existing war memorial on 8th November 1948. Over a third of those killed were nurses, doctors or medical students.

The War Memorial records those Queen'smen and Queen'swomen who gave their lives in two World Wars.

THE COMMANDERS

In the spirit of celebration following the end of the Second World War, Queen's conferred honorary degrees in October 1945 on four of those instrumental in the liberation of Europe.

General Eisenhower, Supreme Commander of Allied Forces in Europe, Field-Marshal Montgomery, Commander of the British Forces, Field-Marshall Brooke (later Lord Alanbrooke, third Chancellor of Queen's) and Field-Marshall Alexander were presented for their degrees at ceremonies in the Assembly Buildings in Great Victoria Street.

An enterprising dental student, Bruce Hill, had the foresight to get his 1945 Graduation Ticket signed by the important people of the day.

Staff

As regards the academic staff, R.M. Henry was undoubtedly the leading figure during this period. He maintained the strong classics tradition in the university, after the retirement of Sir Samuel Dill in 1923. However, his chief role was as Secretary to the Academic Council from 1908 to his retirement in 1938. In his autobiography, *Out of my class* (Belfast, 1985), p.139, John Boyd, a student at Queen's in the 1930s, recalls Henry as "a stocky dapper figure with cloak and monocle. Henry had the reputation of being republican in politics and a martinet in class". A contemporary of Henry, Gilbert Waterhouse, later described graphically Henry's presence: "in the lecture-room he was majesterial, profound and illuminating: in the Council Chamber he was prudent in speech and eloquent in silence" (*Belfast Newsletter*, 9 April 1959) Besides his position as professor of Latin and key administrator, Henry had many interests outside the university. He helped to set up a distress committee during the industrial depression of the late 1920s and 1930s, he was involved with the National Council for Civil Liberties and he actively promoted adult education and Irish history. After retiring from Queen's in 1938 at the age of 65, he accepted a chair at the University of St Andrews for another 9 years before taking up an honorary Chair of Classical Literature at Trinity College, Dublin, until his death in 1950. His fine collection of Irish books was left to Queen's to become the core for the major Irish holdings in the library.

James Eadie Todd was professor of Modern History 1919–45. He published little significant work but under his direction the department of History achieved considerable eminence, due to the students who emerged from it. One of his students, J.C. Beckett, later holder of the first Chair in Irish history at Queen's, has recalled Todd and the department of the 1930s:

> He was a Scotsman. He was a very good teacher. It's surprising what was done in those days. The whole department was run by three people. There was himself, a lecturer in medieval history and an assistant lecturer who held office for three years. The honours school was small. In my final year there were just three.

In the words of another former student, T.W. Moody, professor of History at Trinity College, Dublin, 1939-77, Todd was "brimful of historical learning" and he "professed history as a high and holy calling". H.A. Cronne, later professor of History at Birmingham University, 1946-70 recorded how Todd took endless trouble with

SNAPPED BY SHEMUS---No. 72

PROF. R. M. HENRY,
Member of Fiscal Commission

Robert Mitchell Henry, who graduated from Queen's College in 1893 and was Professor of Latin 1907–38. This cartoon is from the Freeman's Journal.

T. W. Moody, 1950.

Theodore William Moody graduated with a B.A. from Queen's in 1930. After two years in London at the Institute of Historical Research, he returned to Belfast to become an assistant to Professor Todd and in 1935 he became a lecturer with special responsibility for Irish history. In 1939 he was appointed to the Erasmus Smith chair of modern history at Trinity College, Dublin. For nearly forty years until his retirement in 1977 he ran the history department at Trinity and, by his energy and scholarship, he established the department as a major centre of research. He died in 1984.

His first book, The Londonderry plantation, 1609–41: the city of London and the plantation in Ulster *(Belfast) appeared in 1939. This was followed by a succession of important books, including the two volumed* Queen's, Belfast, 1845–1949: the history of a university *(London, 1959) which he wrote with J. C. Beckett. In retirement he completed his masterial study of Michael Davitt,* Davitt and Irish revolution 1846–82 *(Oxford, 1981)*

Besides these important books, Theo Moody made other invaluable contributions to the development of Irish historiography. A prime mover in the foundation of Irish Historical Studies *he remained one of the two editors for over forty years. He established a monograph series in Irish history and was one of the originators of the Thomas Davis lectures on Raidió Éireann. He was the chief architect of the multi-volumed* New history of Ireland.

his pupils "collectively and individually, exhorting and encouraging them . . . safeguarding their interests and furthering their careers". Other students included J.L. McCracken, later professor of History at Magee College, Derry and D.B. Quinn, later professor of History at Liverpool University. A number of his students, in particular Moody, played a key role in establishing the Ulster Society for Irish Historical Studies which, with the Irish Society for Historical Studies, ran the highly influential *Irish Historical Studies.* Todd's efforts, in Cronne's words, were "to contribute greatly to the renaissance of Irish historical studies".

The departments of Physics and Mathematics also had notable staff and produced remarkable students during these years. A new lectureship in Mathematical Physics was created in 1933 and the first person to hold the post was Harrie Stewart Wilson Massey who stayed at Queen's for four years before he accepted a chair at University College, London, and continued on a career which would make him one of the world's leaders in atomic physics. He was succeeded by Peter Paul Ewald who was promoted to a chair in Mathematical Physics at Queen's in 1945 and who built up a strong reputation in this field. The Mathematics Chair was held by two distinguished academics, John Greenlees Semple, 1930–6, and William Hunter McCrea, 1936–44. William Blair Morton, one of the earlier generation of brilliant Queen's mathematicians of whom Joseph Larmor was the best known, was professor of Physics, 1897–1933, and he was succeeded by Karl George Emeleus.

During this period there emerged what Sir William McCrea later called "a set of students of commanding ability". The most eminent of these was Massey's student David Robert Bates who was appointed professor of Applied Mathematics at Queen's in 1951, was elected F.R.S. in 1955 and was knighted in 1978 for his contribution to planetary and space science. He worked daily in the department of Applied Mathematics and Theoretical Physics until his death in 1994 at the age of 77. Other graduates included James Hamilton, later professor of Physics, University College, London, and A.W. Macbeath, later professor of Mathematics and Statistics, University of Pittsburgh.

In 1909 the Chair of Natural History and Geology had been replaced with Chairs in Botany and Zoology and a lectureship in Geology. John Kaye Charlesworth was appointed to the first lectureship in Geology and in 1921 his position was elevated to a

Chair of Geology. Over the next 33 years he built up an international reputation in the field of Quaternary Geology. Charlesworth's *Geology of Ireland* has remained an important textbook. The chair of Botany was held by James Small (1920–54). In his memoirs, *An unquiet life: memoirs of a physician and cardiologist* (Antrim, 1989), J.F. Pantridge gives a description of Small:

> Small was a short, lowland Scot with a large head, and big feet frequently encased in bedroom slippers. He harboured a deep, long standing grudge against medical students because of an episode at the end of the First World War when ex-service undergraduates had thrown him into the pond in the Botanic Gardens. He lectured to both medical and science students and sometimes began his lecture: "Ladies and gentlemen and medical students".

Gregg Wilson, professor of Natural History and Geology (1902–9), became professor of Zoology (1909–31). His successor was the Australian Theodore Thompson Flynn, whose scholarly reputation was overshadowed by the growing reputation of his actor son, Errol. After his death in 1968, the Queen's *Annual Record, 1969* noted his role during the war.

> At the outbreak of war in 1939, Professor Flynn joined the Civil Defence organisation and became chief casualty officer of the Belfast district – for which service he was subsequently awarded the M.B.E. In those days it was not uncommon for him to deliver first-year lectures – a brand of teaching at which he excelled – still clad in full ARP uniform after a sleepless night touring the casualty posts throughout the city.

> Flynn was a man of considerable presence and enormous charm. With a tolerant, and at times rather wistful dignity, he supported the often exacting role of father to one of the cinema's great romantic figures, the late Errol Flynn. As Errol smote the ungodly in epic after epic, it was easy to discern from where sprang his undeniable appeal.

Medical studies at Queen's continued to prosper. In a confidential report to the Rockefellar Foundation in New York in September 1927, Dr A. Gregg wrote: "The Medical Faculty in Belfast is the best of its kind in Ireland. The Faculty is intelligent and progressive; considerable progress in building and in general conduct has been made, even in the past two years." (Rockefellar Foundation Archives. Tarrytown, New York)

By the mid 1940s, the Queen's Medical School was the largest in Ireland and the fourth largest in the United Kingdom, after

DR JOHN STEWART BELL

Dr John Stewart Bell, who graduated from Queen's with a B.Sc. in Experimental Physics and a B.Sc. in Mathematical Physics in the successive years 1948 and 1949 was one of the most outstanding scientists to have come from Queen's. Born on 28 July 1928, he was educated at Ulsterville and Fane Street Public Schools before completing his secondary education at the Technical High School, an integral part of the then Belfast Technical College.

At the age of 16 he began work as a laboratory assistant in the Physics Department at Queen's, under the kindly supervision of Professor K.G. Emeleus and Dr R.H. Sloan. At 17 he was able to obtain some financial support and to pursue his degree studies. He later said that he had very warm memories of the physics department of that time. He left Belfast in 1949 and worked for the Atomic Energy Research Establishment at Malvern and Harwell. In 1960 he moved to CERN (The European Nuclear Research Centre) in Geneva and worked there for some 30 years until his death in October 1990. In 1988 he was awarded an Honorary Doctor of Science by Queen's for distinction as a theoretical physicist, at which ceremony he was described as "an outstanding ambassador for Northern Ireland and this university".

London, Edinburgh and Glasgow. Probably the most prominent of the medical staff in the inter-war period was Andrew Fullerton, professor of Surgery, 1923–33. He had been a consultant surgeon in France during the Great War and he brought to his job not only the new skills which had been developed during the war but also contact with many of the leading surgeons from France, America and Great Britain. Sir Ian Fraser has described in *The Belfast Medical School and its surgeons* (Belfast 1981), how, in the 1920's, thanks to Fullerton, eminent surgeons and medical authorities, such as the Mayo brothers, came to Belfast to discuss and demonstrate their techniques. Fullerton was a distinguished, innovative surgeon in his own right who pioneered urological surgery in Belfast. President of the Association of Surgeons in 1931, he was the first Ulsterman to be president of the Royal College of Surgeons in Ireland, 1926–8.

Queen's Medical School during this time also had two very able medical brothers, Thomas Hugh Milroy, professor of Physiology, 1902–35, and John Alexander Milroy, formerly a demonstrator in Physiology and a lecturer in Biochemistry, and the first professor of Biochemistry, 1925–34. T.H. Milroy's successor, Henry Barcroft (1935–48) was elected F.R.S. and received honorary membership of the Physiological Society. In contrast to these three who took little part in university politics or public life, William Dalziel Thomson, professor of Medicine, 1923–50, played an important role in the Faculty, the Senate and other university committees as well as outside bodies such as the Tuberculosis Authority. Eminent as a teacher and physician, Thomson became a Fellow of the Royal College of Physicians, was elected President of the Association of Physicians of Great Britain and Ireland, and was knighted.

One of the many medical traditions at Queen's is the ragging of new professors on a grand scale. The year 1935 provided a double bill, with two new appointees, Henry Barcroft and Douglas Harrison. Henry Barcroft, who held the Dunville Chair of Physiology until 1948 was later knighted. Douglas Harrison held the J.C. White Chair of Biochemistry until his retirement in 1967. He played a leading role on a number of influential university committees and was a member of the university Senate until 1986.

In 1920, on the death of the professor of Midwifery, Sir John Byers, it was decided to create two Chairs of Gynaeocology and Midwifery. Robert James Johnstone, appointed to the first of these Chairs in 1920, took a considerable interest in medical politics and served on many medical committees. He represented the university in the Northern Ireland parliament, 1927–38, and was knighted in 1938. Charles Gibson Lowry became professor of Midwifery in 1920 and, when Johnstone retired in 1937, the two areas of responsibility were combined again under Lowry's care. Lowry was one of the leading figures behind the improvement of maternity care in Northern Ireland in the 1920s and 1930s and played a key role in the building of the Royal Maternity Hospital. In the tribute paid to him when he received an honorary degree from Queen's in 1949, it was stated how "his own enthusiasm and determination, and the enthusiasm with which he inspired others, have completely transformed maternity work in the Province."

During this time a small number of women joined Queen's academic staff. The first major appointment in fact, had occurred in 1916 when Maude Violet Clarke, who graduated in 1910, took over the Chair of History on a temporary basis. Her friend Helen Waddell wrote to an acquaintance on 21 June 1916:

> This is a dead secret, for the appointment has not been quite ratified yet – but unless the anti-feminism of Queen's is too strong, Maude, *my* Maude, is to have the Chair of History for a year – or until the end of the war. Professor Powicke, her old chief, is doing war work in the Economics Department in London, and he wants her to fill his place. There's just a chance that the Academic Council will cut up rough about it, but I don't think so.
> D.F. Corrigan, *Helen Waddell: a biography* (London, 1986) p 134.

She did take over the job with no objections but was obliged to give it up when Powicke returned in 1919. Dr Margaret Purce had a one year lectureship in Anatomy 1918–19, during a vacancy in the Chair of Anatomy. During the 1920s a number of women were teaching assistants and demonstrators.

The first permanent female appointment, however, came only in 1931 when Mary Johnstone Lynn, a Queen's graduate of 1912, was made a lecturer in Botany. Margaret McLean Pelan became a lecturer in Medieval French in 1938 and was appointed to a Chair in 1966. In the 1940s six other women were appointed to lectureships. They included Kathleen Atkinson (Ancient History, 1948), who sixteen years later became the first woman in Queen's to receive a Chair, and Elizabeth Florence McKeown, who was appointed to a lectureship in Morbid Anatomy in 1947 and was promoted to professor in 1967, succeeding John Henry Biggart in the Chair of Pathology.

One of the most colourful characters among the staff was Douglas Lloyd Savory, professor of French, 1909–40. In a lecture in 1983, Professor Henri Godin recalled his first day in Belfast with Savory when he

Professors T.W. Moody and J.C. Beckett, in their history of Queen's, say that it is possible that in the 1930s Greek literature exercised its widest and most important influence on the life of the university, not through formal teaching, but through the work of the Dramatic Society. Under the vigorous direction of H.O. Meredith, Professor of Economics, the society produced a series of Greek plays in translation, beginning with Sophocles's Electra in 1930. The photograph shows a performance in 1933, probably of Aeschylus's Seven Against Thieves, by the society's Unemployed Workers' Group.

arrived as a senior assistant in the French department in 1936:

> That first morning, I had breakfast and a few minutes before 10, a uniformed *chauffeuse* came to the door and invited me to join the professor in his limousine – an Austin 20. He sat in the back, his knees covered with a leopard skin rug which he pulled back to let me in and enjoy the comforts of the ride and thus we drove to Queen's in grand style.

After introducing him to various staff members, Savory then prepared for his morning class.

> He took off his bowler hat, replaced it with a mortar-board and put on his gown over a beautiful and, I thought, complete riding gear. I couldn't help gazing at him in wonder. He noticed this and said, in French: "You are looking at me with a critical eye." I said: "Certainly not, Professor; I am lost in admiration!" "Ah!," he said, "you are very polite like a Frenchman but you know very well what is missing." Once again I protested and he went on: "You noticed at once that I wasn't wearing my spurs. It is so very difficult to go downstairs with spurs on."

> He then went into the French lecture theatre with his lecture on Racine and as always gave a powerful performance. At 12, he would signal to Nellie in his car in University Square and go to Fortbreda to ride his horse over the Castlereagh Hills.

Savory resigned his Chair in 1940 to become the M.P. for Queen's at Westminster and when the seat was abolished in 1950, he was elected, at the age of 72, the M.P. for South Antrim, a position which he held until 1955.

Among the administrative staff of this period the most notable, and most eccentric, was undoubtedly R.H. (Dickie) Hunter. He qualified M.B. at Queen's in 1920 at the age of 38, after spending years in Paris in the theatre and art world and after service during World War I as a stretcher bearer in the French Red Cross. He became a lecturer in Anatomy at Queen's in 1924, but in 1937 he was appointed Secretary of the university, a post which he held until 1948. What was most unusual about Hunter was his active role in the Christmas circus in Belfast. Sir Ian Fraser has recollected how he served as both ringmaster, complete with 'pink coat, top hat and whip', and a director:

> one of his duties was to collect talent for the next year's performance. He took no money for his appointment but he did go on extensive European trips during the summer vacation – expenses paid – to look for suitable performers – perhaps a juggler from

Dickie Hunter's portrait by James Gunn, which hangs in the Great Hall. The unusual mode of dress for a formal portrait is the result of Gunn deciding that what was revealed beneath the hat, scarf and gloves would have detracted from the painting!.

Austria, a tightrope walker from Austria, or a loose rope walker from Scandinavia. Anyone can be a tightrope walker but to be a loose-rope walker one has to be exceptionally skilled. (*Queen's Newsletter* vol. 6, 3 June 1990).

His distinctive portrait by James Gunn in the Great Hall is often the subject of comment and curiosity.

Alumni

The alumni of the university continued to play an important role in the life of the community, both home and abroad. Among women graduates the most notable was undoubtedly Helen Waddell. Born in Tokyo, the daughter of Ulster presbyterian missionaries, she obtained her B.A. in English from Queen's in 1911, followed by an M.A. in the next year. In 1923 she was elected to a Fellowship at Lady Margaret Hall, Oxford. Her work on medieval Latin literature led to highly acclaimed and very popular books such as *The wandering scholars* (1927), *Peter Abelard* (1933) and *The desert fathers* (1936). After her death in 1965, an obituary in the London *Times* stated: "Among those who have opened our eyes to the dawning of romanticism and the humanism of the early Middle Ages, Helen Waddell stood out for the grace of her learning, her love of fine literature and her poet's gift of translation".

Helen Waddell, 1889-1965, photographed in 1923.

Maude Violet Clarke was a contemporary and good friend of Helen Waddell. She received her B.A. in History in 1910 and served as acting professor of History 1916–19, during Professor Powicke's absence on war work. She was appointed a History Tutor at Somerville College, Oxford, held a university lectureship in Medieval History from 1930 and was made Vice-Principal of Somerville in 1933. She wrote a number of important papers and books on medieval history. A promising career was cut short by her death in 1935 at the age of 43. Mary Johnstone Lynn graduated in Botany in 1912 and took an M.Sc. the following year. She served as a VAD during the first world war. She was appointed a lecturer in Botany at Queen's in 1931 and in 1937 she was awarded a D.Sc. for her work on the ecology of the tidal zone of Northern Ireland. She retired in 1953 and lived to 1994 when she died at the age of 103.

Mary Lynn's graduation photograph, 1912, and (inset) aged 100 in 1991 with a former pupil, Queen's Pro-Chancellor Clare Macmahon.

In the medical world a number of women gained prominence. Beatrice Helena Lynn (née Barbour) graduated M.B. in 1923 and

Ellinor Maude Buchanan in her graduation photograph, 1908. In his 1909 testimonial for her, Professor Samuel Dill wrote: "in my experience as a teacher, I have had seldom, if ever, a pupil whose progress was so rapid and so sure. Miss Buchanan is gifted with a strong, receptive and singularly accurate mind."

was elected F.R.C.S. in 1928. For 32 years until her retirement in 1964 she was eye surgeon at the Ulster Hospital for Children and Women. She was also consultant ophthalmologist to the Northern Ireland Hospitals. Eileen Hickey received her M.B. in 1921 and was elected Fellow of the Royal College of Physicians in Ireland in 1937. She became a senior physician at the Mater Hospital. In addition she served as one of the Queen's M.P.s at the Northern Ireland parliament, 1949–58. Among those who became teachers were Sister Jessie Cheyre Teresa Nolan (B.A. 1911) whose whole career, including six years as headmistress, was spent on the staff of St Dominic's School, Belfast, and Ellinor Maude Buchanan (B.A. 1908 with first place in Classics in the R.U.I.) who taught classics at Lisburn Intermediate School (later Wallace High School) for many years.

In an obituary in the London *Times* in 1948 Helen Waddell, in her unique style, described the life of another Queen's graduate, Edith Martin (née Sinclair):

> Edith Sinclair Martin died on September 23 in her seventy-ninth year, one of the remarkable women of her generation. Born into Victorian ease and convention, she died Minister Emeritus of a remote congregation in Perth, pioneer of a movement as yet hardly recognized. For half her life she was wife to a distinguished lawyer in Belfast, the mother of children, an admirable political hostess, gay, arbitrary, and charming to most of the eminent who visited the city or the university. In 1915 her only son was killed at Festubert: four years later she lost her husband also. *Hic incipit vita nova.* In a life that had lost its meaning she turned to the discipline of learning, entered Queen's University in her late forties as an undergraduate, and took her Master's degree in science. Still unsatisfied, she turned to theology: studied Hebrew with an aged Rabbi, took the degree of B.D., served as assistant in various churches, but was denied ordination till finally received by the Continuing Free Church of Scotland and ordained minister of Balbeggie. There she preached, a dignified ageing Portia, with no feminine art, but with a massive sincerity and scholarship. Old age sapped her vitality but not her courage; in the last year of her life she was planning a thesis for her doctorate – the theology of John Cameron, rival to Calvin of Geneva; and she had held her fourth grandson in her arms.

Among the male alumni, the medical graduates continued to figure very prominently. Ivan Whiteside Magill graduated in the Faculty of Medicine in 1913. In spite of the fact that his M.D. thesis was referred in 1920 he went on to a brilliant career as an anaesthetist in England. Professor John Dundee has commented,

"Magill could well be called the father of modern anaesthesia, having made notable contributions on the control of patient airway and ventilation". By the 1940s he was Consultant Anaesthetist to the Ministry of Health in England and to the Admiralty. Queen's awarded him an honorary D.Sc. in 1945. James Deeny obtained his M.B. in 1928 and, after a second attempt, his M.D. in 1931. In 1944, aged 38, he was appointed Chief Medical Adviser to the Department of Health in Dublin. He played a key role in promoting public health in Ireland and tackling diseases such as tuberculosis. He later worked for the World Health Organisation. For his contribution to public health Queen's made him an honorary doctor of Science in 1983.

Further afield in India were three Queen's medical graduates of great distinction, Sir Robert McCarrison, Sir John Megaw and John Alexander Sinton. Described by James Deeny as "the father of nutrition", McCarrison studied at Queen's in the last years of the nineteenth century, obtained an M.B. from the Royal University of Ireland in 1900 and joined the Indian Medical Service the following year. The author of 9 books and 159 articles, his research covered a number of areas, such as endemic goitre, but his fame rested on the work done in the 1920s and 1930s on nutrition at the Pasteur Institute at Coonoor in South India. Megaw also attended Queen's at the end of the nineteenth century and obtained his M.B. in 1899. He joined the Indian Medical Service in 1900 and rose to become Director General of the service 1930–33, as well as president of the Medical Council of India. Along with Leonard Rogers he conducted valuable

The origins of the Queen's University Club London lie around the turn of the Century, when an 'Association of Old Belfastmen' was formed and held an annual dinner. By the 1920s it had acquired its title incorporating the name of Queen's and its annual dinner, as shown by this photograph from May 1929, had become a very large gathering. The London Club still exists as the Queen's University Association, London, with a membership (in 1994) of around 200. The Annual Dinner attracts some 100 people.

A FAMILY AT QUEEN'S

In Northern Ireland there are many families for whom coming to Queen's is a tradition covering the generations. One such is the Calwell family, whose contribution to the medical life of the Province has been prolific and lasting.

(Above) 'H.G.' Calwell as President of the Students' Representative Council in 1926. His future wife, Margaret Earls is on the left of the photograph. (Right) William Calwell's graduation photograph in 1897.

The earliest recorded Calwell at Queen's was Robert Calwell, who graduated in Engineering in 1874 and acted as city surveyor for Belfast Corporation and for Belfast Central Railway. His brother William graduated in Medicine in 1883 and became a consulting physician at the Ulster Hospital for Sick Children and a Senator at Queen's. Another William graduated in Medicine in 1897 and joined the Naval Medical Service of the Shipping Federation; his brother Gault graduated in Medicine in 1907 and their sister Sarah Elizabeth graduated in 1912, also in Medicine.

Perhaps the best known of the family was Hugh Gault Calwell, known as 'H.G.', the son of the second William Calwell mentioned above. As a student he became President of the Students' Representative Council in 1926 and was involved in the student rag of Winston Churchill on his visit to Belfast in the same year. Following graduation in Medicine in 1931 he married Margaret Earls, who was President of the Women Students' Hall and immediately left for Africa, where he worked with the Colonial Medical Service in Tanganyika.

On returning to Northern Ireland, he became responsible for the successful introduction of the Mass Radiography Service and later became Archivist at the Royal Victoria Hospital.

The tradition continues today with a number of Calwells working in the medical field.

The ragging of Winston Churchill on University Road. 'H.G.' Calwell is on the right of the photograph. On the left is James Price, who became a well known Belfast gynaecologist. Apparently Churchill was taken to the City Hall to inspect a guard of 'Ulster Volunteers', which included the 'Rising Sons of Belial' under the charge of another student, George B. Hanna. A large copy of the photograph hangs on a wall in Blenheim Palace.

research into cholera. J.A. Sinton, V.C., carried out vital work for a period of 15 years, 1921–36, into malaria and kala-azar, for which he was elected a Fellow of the Royal Society in 1946. Dr John Weaver and Sir Peter Froggatt have commented on him:

> By any standards, Sinton was remarkable: physically, morally and intellectually courageous he had many of the characteristics of the martinet but he was in fact a disciplined intellectual, warm-hearted if exacting, a rigorous scientist and a glutton for work. He wrote over 200 scientific papers – bound chronologically in 12 volumes in the Thomson Room, QUB Medical Library – and ranks with the great names of malariology, an interest which inspired his first paper on the subject in 1921, while the last which he wrote, received in August 1955 just seven months before his death, was on the same topic.
>
> J.A. Weaver and Peter Froggatt, "The wild geese" in *The Ulster Medical Journal*, vol. 56, Aug. 1987, supplement, p. 538.

Other Queen's medical graduates achieved very high rank in the medical services of the forces. William Porter MacArthur who graduated in 1903 from the Royal University of Ireland, after studying at Queen's, joined the Royal Army Medical Corps in 1909 and became a leading expert in tropical diseases. He served as Director General of the Army Medical Service, 1938–41. Sir William Tyrrell enrolled at Queen's in 1903 but only graduated in 1913 after a remarkable sporting career during which he won international caps at swimming, waterpolo and rugby. He served with the Royal Army Medical Corps at the outbreak of the war and was awarded the D.S.O., the M.C. and the Belgian Croix de Guerre for bravery. He joined the medical section of the newly formed R.A.F. at the end of the war and by the late 1930's he had been appointed Air Vice-Marshall.

In the academic and teaching world, Sir Joseph Larmor continued to be a leader in the area of mathematics and physics until his retirement from Cambridge in 1932. Other prominent Queen's academics included Robert Foster Kennedy who attended Queen's in the early 1900s, graduated in 1906 with an M.B., and became professor of Neurology at Cornell University, a position which he held from 1918 until 1930. James Dixon Boyd obtained his M.B. in 1930 and eight years later he was appointed to the chair of Anatomy at the London Hospital Medical School. In 1951 he became professor of Anatomy at Cambridge, a post which he occupied for 17 years. Sir John Henry MacFarland, another of the brilliant mathematicians to study at Queen's in the 1870s, went on to serve as Vice-Chancellor of the University of

SIR IAN FRASER, 1980

Born in 1901, Sir Ian Fraser has recently been described as Ireland's most famous living surgeon. He attended Queen's in the years immediately after the First World War and obtained his M.B. in 1923, which was followed by an M.D. in 1932. He has received many other qualifications and honours. He was elected Fellow of the Royal College of Surgeons in Ireland, 1926, Fellow of the College of Surgeons, 1927, Fellow of the Royal College of Surgeons in Edinburgh, 1938, and Fellow of the American College of Surgeons, 1945. After working as a surgeon at the Royal Victoria Hospital and the Children's Hospital in Belfast in the 1920's and 1930's, he served overseas during the Second World War. He was awarded a D.S.O. for courageous work under fire during the allied invasion of Salerno, and he was appointed officer in charge of field trials into the use of penicillin, which later played an important part in improving health conditions in the last period of the war.

After the war he returned to work in Belfast and was appointed senior surgeon at the Royal Victoria Hospital and the Children's Hospital, 1955–66. Since retiring from these positions, he has continued to play a very active role in the world of medicine and public affairs. He has received many awards and honorary degrees. He was knighted in 1963.

Melbourne, 1910–18, and then Chancellor, 1918–35. Frederick George Donnan (B.A., 1892) was a leading scientist who held the chair of Physical Chemistry at University College, London, from 1913 to 1937. The *Dictionary of National Biography* noted of him: "A tremendous worker, he kept odd hours: to retire at 1 am was early for him and 2, 3, or even 4 am, were not infrequent".

Many Queen's graduates played an important role in the school teaching profession. One of the best known was Robert Millar Jones who, after a distinguished undergraduate career, which included winning the Peel Prize "for the best answering in ancient classics of all the students from the three Queen's Colleges of Belfast, Cork and Galway", obtained his B.A. in 1882 and entered teaching. From 1898 to 1925 he was Principal of the Royal Belfast Academical Institution. In an obituary in the Queen's *Annual Record, 1934–5*, the writer Robert Lynd paid tribute to "R.M.", as he was known: "He never preached, but he was the sense of duty incarnate, and the best of his pupils (of whom, I regret to say, I was not one), probably owed as much to him for the example of his single-minded character, as for his thorough grounding in the classical languages". Besides such well known names as R.M. Jones, Queen's graduates fulfilled an essential role in countless teaching posts.

Queen's alumni occupied influential positions in the ecclesiastical world, as the lists of appointments in the yearly lists of the *Annual Record* of the Queen's University Association clearly show. The biggest contribution of graduates was to the Presbyterian ministry, where many served as moderators of the Presbyterian church in Ireland. By this period there was also a considerable number of Catholic clergy with a Queen's background. One example was William Conway who graduated from Queen's in 1932 with a B.A. in English Literature, and held various ecclesiastical positions before becoming Archbishop of Armagh in 1963 and cardinal two years later. A number of Queen's graduates served as missionaries, especially in India and China: they included medical missionaries such as Emily Crooks (1899) M.B. In the legal profession, a growing number of judges now had a Queen's background. Charles Leo Sheil (1918) LL.B. and John Clarke MacDermott (1921) LL.B. were two Queen's graduates to achieve high legal office in these decades. MacDermott was later a prochancellor of the university.

In the literary field, both graduates and members of staff made valuable contributions. John Hewitt graduated with a B.A. in

SIR ALEXANDER FLEMING

Sir Alexander Fleming, who discovered penicillin in 1928, visited Queen's in 1944 to give the Robert Campbell Oration to the Ulster Medical Society. When in Belfast he stayed with Professor W.D. Thompson in his house at 25 University Square, which subsequently became the Faculty of Medicine Office and is now houses the University Health Service.

During his visit, Sir Alexander also gave a lecture in the Great Hall to the Belfast Medical Students' Association. A request for £15 to hire a public address system for the occasion (on account of Sir Alexander's weak voice) was turned down by the Secretary of the University, Dickie Hunter.

Such was Fleming's reputation at the time that, when it was discovered that he had inadvertently left his lecture slides at Queen's, the Larne train, the Stranraer ferry and the London express were all held up while the slides were retrieved.

The following year (1945) Fleming received the Nobel Prize for Medicine together with Lord Florey and Sir Ernest Chain.

Sir Alexander Fleming (centre) with (left to right) medical students S.R.C. Ritchie, J.D.E. Leith, and A.L. Wells, all of whom graduated MB 1945, and Professor Henry Barcroft (later knighted), Dunville Professor of Physiology at Queen's 1935–47.

Queen's in 1945 was on the threshold of change as universities prepared for the post-war world. Major expansion was soon to take place, but the life at Queen's in that year was still filled with images of the pre-war world as these photographs of 1945 show.

A seminar in English literature

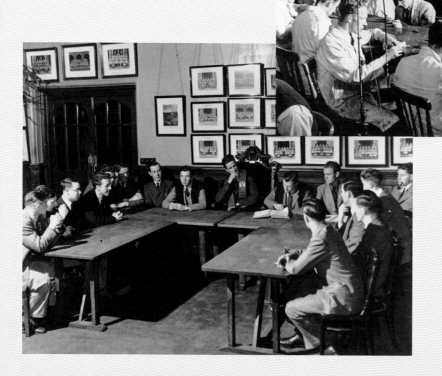

(Above) A dental class in the old wooden huts behind the Medical Building at the back of the Quad.

(Left) A meeting of the Students' Representative Council in 1945 in the McMordie Hall of the old Students' Union Building.

1930, after when he served on the staff of the Belfast Museum and Art Gallery, 1930–57. He wrote several volumes of poetry in the 1940s, including *Conacre* (1943) and *Compass* (1944). William Robert Rodgers obtained his B.A. in 1931 and in 1935 became minister of Loughgall presbyterian church, 1935–46. His first collection of poetry, *Awake and other poems* was published in 1941. Michael McLaverty graduated with a B.Sc. in 1933 and an M.Sc. in 1933. His first novel *Call my brother back* appeared in 1939, followed by *Lost fields* in 1941; his collection of short stories, *The white mare and other stories* appeared in 1943. Hugh Shearman (B.A. 1938), wrote various historical and political works and was the author of a novel set in Queen's, entitled *A bomb and a girl* (1944). Alfred Walter Stewart, professor of chemistry (1919–44), wrote many detective stories under the pseudonym of J.J.Connington. John Innes Mackintosh Stewart, lecturer in English literature, (1945–8) used the pseudonym Michael Innes for his detective stories.

A political career was pursued by some Queen's graduates in this period, although it is perhaps surprising that not more were involved. Graduates of Queen's elected an M.P. to the U.K. parliament at Westminister: no contest, however, occurred for the Queen's seat after the contested 1918 general election. Sir William Whitla held the university seat, 1918–23, and was succeeded first by Thomas Sinclair (the former professor of surgery), 1923–40, and then by Douglas Savory (the former professor of French), 1940–50, when the seat was abolished. Only a small number of other Westminister M.P.s had a Queen's connection. One of these was the redoubtable John Morrow Simms, a Presbyterian minister, who had been principal chaplain to the British forces in France in the First World War, was elected moderator of the Presbyterian church in Ireland, 1919–20, and then served as M.P. for Down North (later Down), 1921–31. All these M.P.s were Unionist. Another Westminister M.P. with a Queen's degree was James Little, independent Unionist for Down, 1939–50.

Queen's graduates also returned 4 M.P.s to the Northern Ireland Parliament at Stormont. In contrast to the Westminster university seat, these elections were usually heavily contested. At the first two general elections, all 4 M.P.s were Unionist but an independent held one of the seats from 1929 to 1945, when two independents were successful. In 1949 Samuel Thompson Irwin and William Lyle were elected as Unionists, while Eileen Mary Hickey and Lilian Irene Mercer Calvert (two out of four women M.P.s at Stormont) were elected as independents. In the general election of 1949, the other 6 M.P.s with Queen's degrees included Frank Hanna (Labour, Belfast Central), Dinah McNabb (Unionist, N. Armagh), James McSparran (Anti-partitionist, Mourne) and W.B. Topping (Unionist, Larne).

Official centenary celebrations to mark the establishment of Queen's College, Belfast, from which the university had grown, were held on 25th–30th September 1949, and not in 1945 because of difficulties arising from the end of the war. Beginning with denominational religious services, a series of receptions, dinners, exhibitions, lectures and conferring of honorary degrees was held. In many of the speeches, acknowledgement was made of the great changes which had occurred in the previous century. From an initial intake of slightly less than 200 students in 1849 the total now stood at over two and half thousand, while the size of the campus had grown very substantially from the single Lanyon building of the 1840s. For those present at these celebrations, changes over the next half century could only be guessed at, but in fact the two major factors in the even greater rate of future expansion were already in place. The growth in funding, thanks to the Universities Grants Committee, and a rise in numbers of students, due to the 1947 Education Act, would help to bring unforeseen opportunities for development and expansion.

A morning consultation – Secretary Dickie Hunter with Vice-Chancellor Lindsay Keir, 1945.

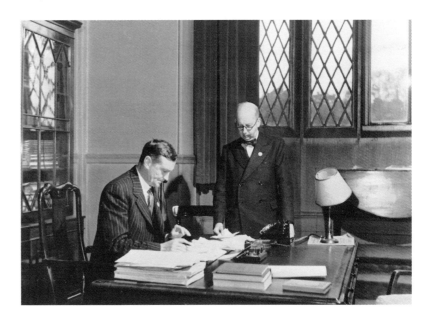

THE LIBRARY

The Queen's College of Belfast gave early recognition to the importance of a library, because just two weeks after the college opened the Council made a preliminary allocation of money for books among the various departments. (Parliament had given the College the princely sum of £4,000 for the purchase of books, specimens, apparatus and instruments. This was not augmented by an annual grant until 1854). Professors were invited to draw up lists of the books they considered essential and then the Council, showing great business sense, drew up a single list which they put out to tender. An early precursor of the co-operation between libraries was seen in the agreement with the Linen Hall Library to avoid duplication of expensive items. The first two Librarians of the College were clergymen: the Reverend James MacAdam, who stayed only one year before deciding that he could not afford the time the post demanded, and the Reverend George Hill, who was Librarian for thirty years and in many ways was the founder of the Library. He had been a Unitarian clergyman for fourteen years, but had become unfit for pastoral work through the loss of his voice.

The original Library building

Although often unhappy with his lot he was an excellent librarian. Under his watchful eye the collection grew to some 30,000 volumes, well organised and catalogued and, from 1869, housed in its own building. These clergymen were succeeded by incumbents who held simultaneously the post of Librarian and Professor and it was not until 1930 that the first Professional librarian was appointed.

The provision of accommodation for the Library has occupied the College and then the University throughout its history. The Old Library building, as built in

The old reading room, which was in use until the late 1960s

1866 and extended in 1914, is one of the most distinctive and loved buildings on the University campus. When readers were sitting under the high roof, in front of the huge fire which blazed in an open grate beneath the great west window, it must have seemed to them to be the very ideal of a library reading-room. (Alas the practice of lighting a fire disappeared during the Second World War and the fireplace has now disappeared.) To make full use of the building a huge metal book-stack was added, and in 1952 the great reading-room was divided by a floor at the level of the galleries. The affection for the Old Library makes it all the more surprising that the University planned to demolish it in the 1960's to allow the building of the second stage of a new Main Library, of which the first stage was the tower building designed to hold the Library's collections. Happily, wiser counsels prevailed and in the early 1980's the Old Library was completely refurbished.

While from the beginning there had always been just the one Library, where students of law, medicine, engineering and the arts worked together, post-war expansion caused a revision of this policy. The establishment of the Institute of Clinical Science at the Royal Victoria Hospital included a Medical Library, built as a memorial to members of the Medical School killed in the Second World War. The later aspiration has been to greatly enhance such provision. Also in the 1950's a new facility was opened in the David Keir Science Library and this continued to serve science and engineering users until the current Science Library opened in Chlorine Gardens in 1969. During the following decade, the Agriculture and Food Science Library was developed at Newforge Lane. The evolution of the branch libraries had the great advantage of bringing the Library to its users but inevitably led to a duplication of stock and of effort.

Refurbishment work in progress in the early 80s.

The Queen's Library is unique in Northern Ireland for the collections it has assembled over the almost 150 years of its existence. While the Linen Hall Library is older it never attempted to acquire material in depth across the range of disciplines which the University Library was called upon to support. The collections have grown mainly through patient accumulation, based on co-operation between the academic staff and the librarians, but throughout the years important collections have been bought or received as gifts. In 1929 R. M. Henry presented over 1,000 volumes relating to Ireland to form the collection subsequently named after him. He augmented this from time to time with further gifts and in 1951, after his death, the university purchased the greater part of his remaining library, to be added to the Henry Collection. There are many special collections ranging from a historical collection of economic theory, including part of the library of Adam Smith, to the Savory Collection of Huguenot Material, from the Hamilton Harty Music Collection to the Ross-Rosenzweig Collection of material on Jewish theology and the Dead Sea Scrolls. There are two almost intact eighteenth century libraries, the Thomas Percy Library and the Antrim Presbytery Library, and among the papers of individuals in the manuscripts section are the Bunting Irish folk melody and the Somerville and Ross manuscripts.

It is partly due to the existence of these collections that the Queen's Library has a role which extends well beyond its service to the University community. Researchers and scholars, professional and non-professional, want access to its resources, and the Library does what it can to facilitate this without detracting from its primary purpose. Formal agreements exist with the Department of Health and Social Services and the Department of Agriculture to provide a library and information service to their staff Province-wide, and the University hosts the library computer systems of the Linenhall

The library carrels under the roof were reserved for the use of honours students.

Library and the North-Eastern Education and Library Board. While Queen's is not the 'Provincial Library', as such, it undoubtedly has a very special place within Northern Ireland.

Although the Library at Queen's has constantly evolved over the years, with landmarks along the way as new buildings became available, as the collection grew from almost nothing to over one million volumes, and as readers were allowed to visit the shelves for themselves, there is no doubt that the recent pace of change has been unprecedented. The Library must provide full access to a world of information in electronic form as well as continuing to develop a collection of print-on-paper, and it has opened the first phase of the electronic library. It must ensure that as a service it meets the needs of the university and the local community while living within the same limited funding as the university itself. It is almost impossible to predict what the Library will be like when Queen's Bicentenary comes around, but it is difficult to imagine that it will ever be anything other than a key central information resource for the teaching and research of the University.

*The result of the refurbishment –
a harmonious blend of old and
new.*

Part Two

"The Golden Years" 1949–59

In the long history of Queen's, the 1950's came to be regarded widely as "The Golden Years", partly because of the comparative austerity of later decades and partly because people, then as now, recognised in Dr Eric Ashby, the new Vice-Chancellor, a figure of immense and pivotal significance in the development of the university. As a later Vice-Chancellor, Sir Peter Froggatt, noted in a tribute in *The Independent* of October 28, 1992: "Eric Ashby became Vice-Chancellor of Queen's University . . . at an important stage in the development of both. At 45, Ashby's aptitudes and ambitions stretched far beyond the laboratory and lecture room: while Queen's was poised for expansion in its size and horizons after its relative quiescence and continued provincialism between the wars. It was to prove a fruitful partnership." Ashby, it must be said, was fortunate. He came to Queen's at a time when Northern Ireland was in a period of comparative peace, which, although it had its share of violence, now seems idyllic. It was also a period, again by modern standards, of generous funding and with little or no government interference, when a strong Vice-Chancellor could stamp his authority, character and personality on as disparate an institution as a university. This is precisely what Ashby did.

Northern Ireland, like Great Britain, had lived through a major war, and there was a hunger for education, stimulated by returning ex-servicemen and women. Significantly the new Labour government had placed emphasis on a policy of education for all. It was a time ripe for expansion, and Queen's would reap the benefits.

LORD ASHBY OF BRANDON

Eric Ashby was an outstanding figure at Queen's University, where he was Vice-Chancellor from 1950–9 and Chancellor from 1970–83, and at Cambridge University where he was Master of Clare College from 1959–75, a Life Fellow from 1975, and Vice-Chancellor from 1967–9.

Born in 1904, he was educated at the City of London School, the Imperial College of Science, London and the University of Chicago. A scientist by training, he was Reader in Botany at Bristol University from 1935–37, Professor of Botany at the University of Sydney 1938–46, Counsellor and Chargé d'Affaires with the Australian Legation in Moscow from 1945–46, and Harrison Professor of Botany and Director of Botanical Laboratories at the University of Manchester from 1946, before coming to Queen's. Throughout his career he held many important posts on academic, government and public bodies and he was the first Chairman of the Royal Commission on Environmental Pollution, from 1970–3. He was knighted in 1956 and became a life peer in 1973.

Reflecting on his time at Queen's, he said in 1990:

> I had no experience of being a Vice-Chancellor, but nobody has that experience until the job begins! I came simply from being a professor in Manchester, but during the War I had run a government department in Australia, and as a Minister in Russia I had learned how to organise negotiations with other people. For example, I had to take part in international negotiations about navigation on the Danube. All this gave me experience. I had to learn the hard way, and I made some mistakes.

He had been sent by the Australian government to Moscow as a visiting scientist, from 1944 to 1945, but during the last few months he was acting as a diplomat, following the illness and departure of an Australian Minister.

He once recalled an important piece of advice he had been given by the Vice-Chancellor of Manchester University.

Coming up to the end of the day when you've had a particularly difficult and troublesome Senate, you haven't left much time, you have to go down town to the annual dinner of the Cost Accountants' Society and reply to 'the Toast of the University' and you haven't got your speech quite finished. There are two paths out of the university and you see coming up one path the professor you dislike most and you know he dislikes you. You go on his path and you ask him how his wife is and you hear that she has been ill. That's what being a Vice-Chancellor is like!

He always had a keen ear for the anecdote. "One evening I spoke at a Young Farmers' Club in Kilrea. I gave my speech between the 'Londonderry Air' and the 'Toreador's Song'. Quite suddenly they served sausages at about 3.00 am. I realised that these farmers were all waiting until milking time. They weren't going home at all!"

He also had an impish sense of fun, especially when dealing with the eccentricities of visiting lecturers, many of whom stayed at Lennoxvale. "On most occasions this was an enjoyable part of a Vice-Chancellor's duties, and it had its amusing moments. One guest put his shoes outside his room to be cleaned. The Lennoxvale staff did not rise to a shoe-cleaning maid, so around 7.00 am, the Vice-Chancellor himself could have been seen, in his dressing-gown, furtively cleaning the visitor's shoes and ready to scramble away if he heard the guest moving around in the bedroom!"

Lady Ashby also made a significant contribution to the university as the Vice-Chancellor's wife. A contemporary noted: "She was a shy person but she worked very hard at the job. She took a great interest in people and their families, and made them feel that they were people and not ciphers."

Sir Peter Froggatt in his tribute in "*The Independent*" neatly summarised the Ashby he knew so well:

Within Queen's, Ashby's authority was absolute. He was a formidable debater, lucid thinker, inspiring and humorous speaker, and with great personal charm and wide culture. These were allied to an impressive stature (he was well over six feet) and imposing patrician looks. By instinct a benevolent authoritarian he adopted the *persona* of a participative democrat more suitable to the labyrinthine decision-making processes resulting from a university's constitutional diffusion of power. He carried virtually every measure he supported through a combination of personal esteem and a shrewd regard to the art of obtaining consensus backed by a mastery of procedure if needed . . . He was a skilful exponent of the 'planted' idea, content to wait patiently for it to resurface through the committee system as someone else's. His talents and imposing authority were carried into the wider national university arena holding, during his time at Queen's, many memberships of national committees, most of which, significantly, he went on to chair. With only one university in Northern Ireland at the time, Ashby embodied higher education in the Province and truly bestrode the local scene. His kindness and courtesy were legendary and he was easily available to all levels of staff. His only enemies were those moved by jealousy or envy.

Lord Ashby left Queen's to become Master of Clare College, the first such appointment in centuries for someone outside the College. However, he retained his links with Queen's as Chancellor. "Being Chancellor was such an honour. If I was asked on 'Desert Island Discs' the appointment in my life I would put first, I would say 'Chancellor of Queen's.' It was the feeling that I was back among people who had liked me so much that they invited me to return."

Her Majesty Queen Elizabeth II on her visit to Queen's in 1953, accompanied by the Duke of Edinburgh, with Lord Alanbrooke.

LORD ALANBROOKE

Field Marshal the Viscount Alanbrooke was the third Chancellor of Queen's, from 1949–63. An outstanding soldier who played a major role in the Dunkirk evacuation of 1940, he became Chief of the Imperial General Staff in 1941 and contributed most significantly to the Allied war effort. Gifted with a wide strategic vision and a huge capacity for work, he was one of the ablest holders of his military office. It was said that one of his supreme qualities was a calm temperament and unlimited patience in dealing with politicians. Such qualities are equally valuable in any big university, and Alanbrooke fulfilled his role as Chancellor at Queen's with almost military precision.

Ashby said of him:

> He was modest, very considerate, made no demands on his hosts, and talked with the enthusiasm of a young man about the things he liked, mainly bird photography. And there were splendid stories from his wartime experiences – his meeting with Stalin and Roosevelt, his sessions with Churchill at Chequers (when Churchill would put the Wizard of Oz on the gramophone in the small hours of the morning when everyone else was exhausted). He always asked me to draft his graduation speeches and he wanted them typed entirely in capital letters. The one service he asked of my wife was typical of the simple life-style he led. He asked her to make up a packet of egg sandwiches to take on his return journeys to London. This was to be his breakfast which he had before he left the Stranraer-London sleeper the next morning.

Alanbrooke also had a distinctive approach at Senate.

> He rarely took the chair at Senate meetings but when he did he would arrive from the Larne-Stranraer boat and sit down in Lennoxvale to be briefed on the agenda straight away. If decisions had to be made on controversial matters I would try to give him an impartial statement of both sides of the question. He would then say 'Which way do you want it to go?' On the first occasion I offered opinions about the matter. And when the Senate met and the item came up for discussion, the Chancellor said: 'The way to decide this is . . .' and that was an end of the matter; the meeting was over in half the usual time!

Finance

The immediate problem to be tackled was finance, because Queen's had been seriously underfunded. In 1949–50, for example, the University of Bristol, with 2,371 full-time students had an approximate income per student of £338.00. At Queen's, which had only 10 fewer students, the figure was £157.00. In the 1950's the government grant to British universities came from the Treasury through the University Grants Committee. The Committee members visited every university once in five years and recommended a recurrent grant for the quinquennium, together with grants for capital expenditure. Queen's, alone among UK universities, was not financed in this way. Its grant came from the education budget of the Northern Ireland government. There had been, therefore, little or no formal opportunity for the financing of Queen's to be assessed against that for other universities.

Sir David Keir, Ashby's predecessor, took the first step to overcome this disadvantage. The UGC could not be asked to give grants to Queen's, but it could be asked to visit Queen's once every five years and to recommend to the Northern Ireland government what its quinquennial grant would be, as if Queen's were a university in England, Scotland or Wales. The next visit was due in 1952, to make recommendations for the years 1953–8. The university had to make a detailed case for its bid for a large increase in recurrent grant, together with money for an unprecedented building programme. Ashby put that case, and it was clear, during the UGC visit, that the message had impressed the Committee. As one of them said, after talking with a group of professors and lecturers: "The hungry pack hunts best." The Northern Ireland government accepted the Committee's recommendations, announcing recurrent grants totalling £1.9 million over the quinquennium 1953–8, together with grants for capital expenditure to be settled on a yearly basis. Ashby told Senate in his 1952–3 *Annual Report*: "This news was received with the greatest satisfaction by members and friends of the university. Together with our other sources of income, these promised grants will enable us to turn our blueprints into staff and buildings and equipment: and if price levels do not rise, we should be able to complete , by 1958, all we planned in our memorandum to do." Ashby, near the end of his tenure at Queen's was able to re-assure Senate, in his eighth *Annual Report* that the government grant for the period 1958–63 (£3.8m) was "very close" to the university estimate. The government also gave approval in principle of £1.9 million on capital expenditure during the period, subject to agreement about the exact amounts to be spent each year. Despite the problem of inflation and a sharp increase in the number of students, Ashby was confident that "our plans are laid for the next five years."

In a way, Queen's had something of the best of both worlds. On the one hand, Queen's was now being measured against sister institutions over the water by the UGC. On the other hand, the actual source of cash was fifteen minutes away, at Stormont; and the Vice-Chancellor and other university officers could visit ministers, or invite ministers to visit Queen's, to put the case for some additional capital grant for buildings or for the acquisition of property. Sir Peter Froggatt noted: "There was no stifling national-planning paraphernalia: during his nine years as Vice-Chancellor, Ashby wrote two reports for the University Grants Committee: the modern Vice-Chancellor writes at least two per month. Ashby told me that Queen's only once needed extra money. He went to see the Northern Ireland Minister for Education, told him how much he needed, and got it."

The 1950s therefore, were fortunate years for Queen's. New buildings were going up; the annual income, though still low by British standards, was rising substantially; new appointments were being made; relations with the City were amicable; and Queen's seemed to be preserving its friendly coherence.

Academic staff

Another of Ashby's major priorities was to raise the quality of academic staff. That is not to decry the contribution and service of a number of distinguished men and women already in post, several of whom were notable characters. One such was Professor Alexander Macbeath, the sort of man, it was said, who would not hesitate to dress down a Vice-Chancellor who showed the slightest sign of dirigisme in dealing with the academic staff. Despite what some contemporaries described as his 'Pickwickian' appearance, he commanded respect. Macbeath, a Scotsman whose first language in his youth had been Gaelic, held the Chair of Logic and Metaphysics until his retirement in 1954. He had been a member of several important committees including Standing Committee of Senate and had the rare distinction of having been successively Dean of the Faculty of Arts, Dean of the Faculty of Law and Dean

96

of the Faculty of Commerce. The citation for his Honorary D.Lit. conferred by Queen's on 19 December 1957 noted also his "respectable expertise upon such unlikely topics as drystone-walling, animal husbandry, and the drying and curing of fish."

At the same ceremony, an honorary D.Sc. degree was conferred on Professor John Kaye Charlesworth, the first Professor of Geology at Queen's from 1921 until his retirement in 1954. A Senator, thrice Dean of the Faculty of Science, and a member of many important committees, he took a heavy share in the administration work of the university, including the arduous Chairmanship of the Buildings Committee during a critical period when the planning of so

many new buildings was undertaken. Despite such duties, his scholarly work was paramount, and a contemporary said that Charlesworth described the Ice Age as if he had been there and seen it all.

Hugh Owen Meredith, the Professor of Economics who came to Queen's in 1911 and presided over the Faculty for more than 30 years, was a legendary figure for other reasons. Tall, with a full black beard, and a quiet Cambridge voice, he was in the generation of aesthetes at King's, Cambridge, and well known in the Bloomsbury Group. He called on the Vice-Chancellor shortly after he arrived and opened the conversation by saying: "Perhaps I ought to tell you that, in my opinion, a Vice-Chancellor is a fifth wheel on the coach and a waste of public money. But since you're here, I hope we shall be friends." And friends, indeed, they

PROFESSOR SIR JOHN HENRY BIGGART

John Henry Biggart, Professor of Pathology for 34 years, Dean of Medicine for 27, a member of Senate and a Pro-Chancellor of the university, was a legendary figure. He was extremely able, totally dedicated to Medicine and to Queen's, and tough, but with a kind heart and a sense of humour. In his prime, he was a powerful influence on policy-making in the university at the highest levels. Generations of doctors have their own anecdotes of 'John Henry', who was known as 'Harry' to his family and close friends. Behind the often formidable exterior, he was a complex man who noted in his personal biography: "In all things have I sought peace, but never have I found it, save in a corner with a book."

A former student wrote of him: "He became the father-figure of Queen's medical and dental graduates; many of them continued to write to him from all over the world, often seeking his help and advice. He would say: 'Don't come to me when the trouble has broken around you. Come when the clouds are on the horizon'". Biggart's basic philosophy on medical education was best summarised by his editorial in the *Ulster Medical Journal*: "In our own (medical) school we have endeavoured to lead the student to the belief that in spite of all its apparent fragmentation of the advances which sometimes come here and sometimes there, there is but one medicine and one medical problem – the sick patient."

Dr John Weaver, a friend and colleague and later a Queen's Senator, summed up Biggart's contribution thus: "In the almost 150-year history of Queen's, no-one controlled the destiny of the Medical School for so long or so totally as Harry Biggart – and no-one controlled it to such purpose."[1]

[1] Presidential Address to the Ulster Medical Society, 1 November 1984.

became. When a Staff House – a club for staff members – was started in University Square, Meredith came to see Ashby to ask whether retired professors would be eligible for membership. "No club is complete" he said, "unless an elderly person is visible through the window, reading a newspaper. May I offer myself in that capacity?"

It was not only retired members of staff who kept a proprietary eye on Queen's. Any unusual change in the flower-bedding on the front lawns would bring two or three letters (inevitably to the Vice-Chancellor), commending or criticising the garden policy, from passers-by on the Malone Road. Even the Vice-Chancellor's apparel did not go un-noticed – the University Printer, a formidable lady named Marjory Boyd, called on Ashby in his office and after brief introductory formalities, sized him up and said: "You don't dress as well as your predecessor."

The progressive retirement of the "Old Guard" made way for newcomers, and Ashby's single biggest achievement was the legacy of the academic staff he left to Queen's. Characteristically, he paid tribute to the Board of Curators, in his *Annual Report* for the year 1952–53:

> Responsibility for attracting and securing men of the right calibre rests with the Curators. It is fitting to pay tribute to their great service to the university during the past three years. They have filled 11 Chairs and dozens of lectureships, and this has entailed no less than 97 meetings and scores of interviews. It is no exaggeration to say that the prestige of the university depends more on the work of the Curators than on that of any other body. If they did not choose well, nothing could save the university from mediocrity.

Ashby, however, played a crucial personal role. The university granted him discretionary power to search out the really bright young scholars and scientists, and to invite them to meet the Curators at Queen's. His method was to visit three leaders in each field and to ask for the names of three potential candidates who, though not yet distinguished, were likely to be distinguished within the next ten years. Ashby found that in Science, the three referees sometimes came up with the same name, but in Arts subjects this rarely happened.

In an interview, nearly 40 years later, he reflected – with characteristic humour and frankness – on his methods of searching out the right people. He recalled:

Professor J. C. Beckett, 1990

James Camlin Beckett graduated with a B.A. from Queen's in 1934. After a period as a schoolteacher he became a lecturer in modern History at the university in 1945. He was appointed to a newly created chair of Irish History in 1958. He held this position until his retirement in 1975 when he was made emeritus professor. During his time in the History department at Queen's, he did much to encourage research in Irish History.

*Professor Beckett has maintained a distinguished publishing record. His first book **Protestant dissent in Ireland** (London) was published in 1948. Together with T. W. Moody he co-edited **Ulster since 1800: a political and economic survey** (London, 1954) and **Ulster since 1800, second series: a social survey** (London, 1957) and co-authored the two volumed **Queen's Belfast, 1845–1949: the history of a university** (London, 1959). His general survey, **The making of modern Ireland, 1603–1923** (London) was first published in 1966 and remains a key university textbook.*

*Recent books are **The Anglo-Irish tradition** London, 1976) and **The Cavalier Duke** (London, 1990). Professor Beckett retains a keen interest in Irish History and continues to play a lively and valuable role at seminars at the Institute of Irish Studies.*

We had appointed six new Professors in a two year period, and this was immensely encouraging. You can imagine the effect these people had on one another – they were all young, they found the place immensely exciting, and they all in fact became roaringly successful. Somebody said there was a man called Michael Roberts and if we got him we would have the best historian on Scandinavian affairs in this century, but some other university had offered him a Chair. I remember finding out at a Vice-Chancellor's Committee that he had indeed been offered a Chair. I came straight back and sent him a telegram. I think he was in South Africa and I appointed him entirely on my own with a certain amount of grumbling from some of the other Queen's professors. I thought, "If this chap fails I shall be in trouble." But, of course, he was very good. I think he was the only one for whom I really broke the rules! I came at a time when it was ready for change and the money was available. I think what I did achieve was appointing a staff who really put Queen's on the world map in a way it hadn't been before. Some one called Queen's "Britain's nursery for good professors!" That summed up the position admirably.

There is ample evidence that the Board of Curators was indeed

PETER RICE
– ENGINEER EXTRAORDINARY

Peter Rice, who graduated from Queen's with an honours degree in Civil Engineering in 1956, became one of the greatest structural engineers of his generation, and he was described as "perhaps the James Joyce of structural engineering". He died on 25 October 1992, at the age of 57.

He worked on many world-famous buildings and structures including the Sydney Opera House, and the Centre Pompidou in Paris, and in Britain his best-known works include the Lloyds Building and the new terminal at Stansted Airport. His last finished design was the Pavilion of the Future at Expo '92 in Seville. He was made an Honorary Fellow of the Royal Institute of British Architects and an Honorary Member of the Royal Institute of Architects Ireland. His finest hour came when he was awarded the Royal Gold Medal for Architecture by the Royal Institute of British Architects in June 1992, shortly before his untimely death. A commemorative exhibition of his work was staged by the Civil Engineering Department at Queen's in 1993–94, and some items are being kept on permanent display.

expert in the selection of outstanding staff. In the period 1950 to 1960, and excluding promotions within Queen's or to any other university or college in Ireland, there were no less than 24 lecturers who moved elsewhere to Chairs or posts of equivalent or higher status in Great Britain or the Commonwealth; 9 professors who moved to Chairs in Great Britain; and 4 professors who became Vice-Chancellors; and some of the 24 and 9 above also subsequently became Vice-Chancellors.

Ashby, later on, made light of the extraordinary achievement of infusing the academic life of Queen's with such rich new blood. He said: "Having the right staff was the only thing that mattered. I think if anyone asked me now 'What is the job of a Vice-Chancellor,' I could answer straight away 'Appoint the right academic staff and administrative staff and you are home and dry. You needn't do anything else except go around and be nice to people!'"

Buildings

The enormous change in the physical fabric of the university was the third major achievement during Ashby's years, made necessary by the increase in the number of staff, and latterly students, and the creation of new Departments. As Professor J.C. Beckett noted:

> Between the late 1940's and the early 1980's there was hardly a year in which some new building was not either being planned or actually in course of erection. It was recognised from the beginning that only a fraction of the new accommodation now required could be provided on the original college site; and the policy of moving further afield, which had been somewhat reluctantly embarked upon in the 1920's, was now accepted as the natural line of development.
>
> *A short history of Queen's College, Belfast, and the Queen's Universtiy, Belfast*
> (Belfast, 1984), pp 16-17

The need for expansion had long been evident, and the first major initiative had been undertaken by Sir David Keir who acquired a site between the Stranmillis and Malone Roads – the largest the university had undertaken.

Since the establishment of the Faculty of Applied Science and Technology, in 1920, the Belfast College of Technology had provided most of the teaching facilities in the Faculty. By 1946 all of the teaching in the Faculty was carried out in the College, but by the early Fifties the university and Belfast Corporation had agreed that the education of Queen's engineering students should be concentrated on the Stranmillis – Malone site, as envisaged by Sir David Keir. Appropriately it was named the David Keir building, housing engineering, chemistry and the biological sciences, and was opened in May 1959 by the Duke of Edinburgh.

Several years previously, two important new buildings were opened – the first major permanent additions for teaching and research since 1939. On 30 April 1954, Sir Edward Bailey, formerly a Director of the Geological Survey, opened the new Geology Department in Elmwood Avenue, and on 7 May the same year, the new Institute of Clinical Science at the Royal Victoria Hospital was opened by the Governor of Northern Ireland Lord Wakehurst.

The Stranmillis Road aspect of the David Keir Building, 1990.

Despite such achievements throughout the Fifties, the university remained aware of the need to plan further for the future. However, the Vice-Chancellor pointed out to Senate (and anyone else who cared to listen) that the new buildings, including the Keir, were not for any future expansion of Queen's, but merely to accommodate the current student population and to relieve the overcrowding from which the university had suffered for two decades. He concluded: "The accommodation per student in 1914 was considerably greater than it has been ever since." The next year he noted, somewhat impishly in the face of the long haul to finish the Keir Building, that the academic staff had to resign itself to lecturing to background noises of hammers and concrete mixers, while the Building Committee resigned itself to lengthy agenda papers: "One thinks nostalgically of the medieval universities which owned so little property that they could, if provoked, pack their belongings and migrate to another city." By the end of the decade, an extension to the Physics Department – to the south of the quadrangle – had been conceived and largely

THE LISBURN ROAD SITE

Charles Lanyon's beautiful buildings for the Deaf and Blind Schools, standing on five acres of land on the Lisburn Road, were purchased by Queen's in 1954. It was intended that they should be converted into a Student Centre with refectories, private dining rooms, a theatre, a library and suites of study rooms, a debating chamber and club rooms. The grounds were to be earmarked for future student amenities, including a physical education centre, study bedrooms and a swimming pool.

Sadly it was not to be. In an age when our heritage was not given a high priority, the development was axed in favour of a less-costly solution and Lanyon's buildings (below) were demolished in the mid-sixties to make way for the Medical Biology Centre (right).

carried out (it was opened in 1962), alterations to the Library had taken place, and plans were being laid for major new buildings, some of which would be completed in the Sixties. In the mid-Fifties also, the university acquired the building and site of the Ulster Society for Promoting the Education of the Deaf and Dumb and Blind on the Lisburn Road to be used for a new Students' Union, but the best laid plans of university Vice-Chancellors and Senior Officers do not always work out as hoped.

The Fifties

The Fifties were the years when youth seemed to be in the ascendant. A new Queen was crowned; John F. Kennedy and Jacqueline Bouvier were married and went on to re-create the 'Camelot' years in American politics; Elvis Presley was already a millionaire by 1956 and influenced generations from 'Heartbreak Hotel' to 'Hound Dog'; and the film of Bill Haley and his Comets in 'Rock Around the Clock' created disturbances in cinemas around the country with police called to eject young people 'jiving' in the aisles. Sadly it was also the decade of the Suez debacle and the brutal repression of the Hungarian uprising, but notwithstanding such news about the dark side of humanity, there was a feeling of hope and of progress in the air. Against such a background, student societies at Queen's flourished. Among the long-established were the Literary and Scientific Society which nourished the oratorical powers of generations of lawyers and politicians, minor and major, and which celebrated its centenary in the 1949–50 session. Lesser known student societies attracted new members, while enthusiastic students formed new groups including a Radio Club, a Fencing Club, a Natural History Society and the '16' Club, showing 16 mm films which attracted a large membership – all of these, plus what Ashby noted, tongue in cheek, as the students' "indefatigable enthusiasm for dances."

There was also much enthusiasm for Students' Day, or 'Rag Day' when a motley collection of young men and women in fancy dress descended on the wary citizens of Belfast to raise money for charity. Mostly these safaris were well behaved, but in 1951 there was an unseemly scuffle between ragging students and a contingent of the B Special Constabulary who had been holding an inspection in the Drill Hall. The students' magazine *Pro Tanto Quid* was consistently criticised for its "scurrility"'and even the retired Professor Sir Douglas Savory told the Diocesan Synod of Down and Dromore in 1956 that *PTQ* was "a disgrace to the university." Some things never change.

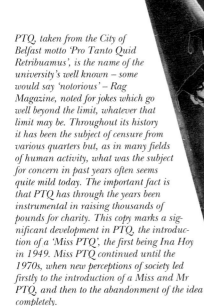

PTQ, taken from the City of Belfast motto 'Pro Tanto Quid Retribuamus', is the name of the university's well known – some would say 'notorious' – Rag Magazine, noted for jokes which go well beyond the limit, whatever that limit may be. Throughout its history it has been the subject of censure from various quarters but, as in many fields of human activity, what was the subject for concern in past years often seems quite mild today. The important fact is that PTQ has through the years been instrumental in raising thousands of pounds for charity. This copy marks a significant development in PTQ, the introduction of a 'Miss PTQ', the first being Ina Hoy in 1949. Miss PTQ continued until the 1970s, when new perceptions of society led firstly to the introduction of a Miss and Mr PTQ, and then to the abandonment of the idea completely.

Rag Day, with hundreds of students dressed in outlandish costumes to raise money for charity, reached its height in the 1950s. Each year the procession grew longer, with increasingly elaborate floats, lovingly built by students and their helpers during the Easter vacation in preparation for the big day in May. In the 1960s Rag Day was shifted to March. This gave little time and unfavourable weather for float-building and it was soon apparent that the spectacle of the procession was on the wane. These photographs by archaeology lecturer Basil Wilson capture the atmosphere of Rag Day at its height in 1958.

The Students' Representative Council continued to be a major influence in student affairs in the 1950s. For the session 1951–52, it elected its first woman president, Edith MacDermott (now Dr Edith Cunningham), daughter of the Pro-Chancellor Lord MacDermott.

The university was sufficiently small to enable the Vice-Chancellor to make personal contact with many students, and he was well known to the student body. Dr Edith Cunningham, whose father Lord MacDermott became a senior Pro-Chancellor, was President of the Students' Representative Council in the early Fifties and the first female to hold that post. She was later a Senator. Dr Cunningham remembers Ashby very clearly: "He was much keener on student participation in university affairs than his predecessor had been, so I saw quite a lot of him on a day-to-day basis. This was a great privilege for me, and I developed a tremendous admiration and respect for the man. He was always courteous, always fair, and always prepared to see the student point of view, but definitely no push-over. All requests had to be well thought through and clearly worded."

Academically there were problems about the quality of some of the student intake, and Ashby warned in his 1952–53 *Report* that Queen's could no longer smile indulgently at the student "now so rare as to be a curiosity who regards the university solely as a base for his sporting or social activities." The task of Queen's, he said, was to bring those freshmen who were educationally nearly one year behind their English cousins up to a degree standard on a par with an English university and to take no more time to do it than in England. There were 'controversial' issues, not the least of these being the wearing of undergraduate gowns. The problem was duly aired, and resolved in a most academic fashion, as the 1958 *Annual Record* of the Queen's University Association noted: "The perennial and much-debated problem of undergraduate gowns has for the present been resolved: two decisions have been taken, first that the official gown is to be a new one of St Patrick's blue, secondly, that students should not be required to wear it."

Student life in the Fifties was clearly enjoyable, a point made by Tom McAuley who graduated in Civil Engineering in 1953. He says: "It is difficult to look back objectively and avoid sentimentality, but the atmosphere at Queen's was everything one could wish for in a university, whether trembling before the gigantic intellect of a Professor Emeleus, or just mixing with motivated people. It was an ambition realised to go there, and it presented opportunities to be taken, if you were able. Above all it was such a pleasure."

A home from home – student accommodation in Riddel Hall in 1954.

Dr Moira McKelvey, who graduated in Medicine in 1958, agrees. "They were wonderful years. The university was small, many of us came from much the same background and there was a family atmosphere about the place. I would do it all over again." Dr McKelvey had other reasons for looking back with nostalgia, not least because her younger sister Thelma Hopkins, an outstanding athlete, had broken the world high jump record at Cherryvale on 5 May 1956.

Culture

Although the university had not yet reached the stage of conceiving, much less of sponsoring, a comprehensive. Arts Festival and cultural enrichment as witnessed later in the remarkable Belfast Festival at Queen's and the Queen's Film Theatre – both of which began to take firm shape in the Sixties – there was a great deal of artistic out-reach in the Fifties. Queen's, as it has done for many years, continued to acknowledge the role of the Arts in society and in education in the widest

sense, by conferring honorary degrees on a host of outstandingly creative men and women. They included the composers, Benjamin Britten and the Ulsterman Howard Ferguson, the poet Louis MacNeice, the local playwright Joseph Tomelty and the artist William Conor, whose portrait of Lord Londonderry, Chancellor of Queen's from 1923–49, hangs in the Great Hall of the university. The university in these years was also the 'home' of the distinguished English poet Philip Larkin who spent more than four years as a senior staff member of the Library.

Sport

Sport has always been an integral part of the life of Queen's, and in the late 1940's and 1950's the university had truly exceptional sports teams and individuals. The arguments will long continue as to which was the best rugby side – the teams of the 1920s, or the teams of the late 1940s and early 1950's. One of the most out-standing rugby players of all time was Jack Kyle, the Irish out-half who held the record of 46 caps. This was previously held by another Queen's player in the 1920's – G.V. Stephenson who

PHILIP LARKIN

Philip Larkin was appointed as Sub-Librarian at Queen's from 1 October 1950 and moved in March 1955 to take up a new job as Librarian at the University of Hull. He was, by all accounts, a most capable career Librarian who was sympathetic and skilled in handling staff and readers. Larkin the poet blossomed at Queen's, and he began to receive wider notice. This led to a collection called Various Poems, later The Less Deceived which gained him recognition as a major new talent in British poetry. A large proportion of the poems had been written during his time at Queen's.

Larkin left Belfast with mixed emotions. In a letter to Elizabeth Madill, a long-time member of the library staff, posted on 20 March 1955 he wrote: "I'd only been at Queen's for four and a half years but it was extraordinary how much at home I felt there and how much I disliked leaving . . . Queen's is a perfect little paradise of a library and I'm profoundly grateful for the demonstration of how harmoniously a library can run." Even five months later he was still missing Queen's. He wrote to Liz Madill: "I do have my low moments here, I'm afraid. I miss all the Queen's staff very much and also my few friends outside the Library - and most of all my flat".

Jack Kyle photographed in 1950.

played for Ireland on 42 occasions. Both these men became doctors. In Kyle's team there were 3 British Lions – Kyle himself, Noel Henderson, and Willie McKay – who toured Australia and New Zealand in 1950. Later, in 1955, Robin Thompson captained the British Lions in South Africa, and on that team was another Queensman Cecil Pedlow.

Off the field, Queensmen have always given something back to the game after retirement, and during the past 100 years they have been influential in Irish rugby. Sinclair Irwin and his father Sir Thomas Irwin both played for Ireland and both were President of the Irish Rugby Football Union. Jim Wheeler not only played for Ireland but was an international referee and later President of the Irish Rugby Football Union. In fact Queen's has supplied no fewer than 10 Presidents of the Union, while Sir Ewart Bell, a former honorary Treasurer of the university, was President of the Irish Rugby Football Union in 1986.

In the late 1950's Queen's Gaelic Football Club acheived considerable success. In 1957 the senior team won the South Antrim League for the second time in twenty three years and the seconds team won the reserve league. On the fifteenth of February 1959 the team won the Sigerson Cup for the first time in an exciting finals replay with U.C.D. The Queen's scorers were Kevin Halpenny, Seamus Mallon, Barney McNally, Leo O'Neill and Sean O'Neill (who later won three all-Ireland medals).

In the early 1950's there was a resurgence in cricket, with the first-eleven winning promotion to the senior league. The outstanding internationals were Bob Matier, Frank Fee and Jimmy McKelvey, who was a double international, having also been capped at rugby. Athletics were also very strong at Queen's in the late 1940's. The athletics club won several intervarsity matches and the outstanding athlete at the time was Prince Adedoyin, a Nigerian student who was studying medicine. He held the Irish high-jump, long-jump and hop, skip and jump titles, and he represented Great Britain in the 1948 Olympic Games, coming fourth in the hop, skip and jump.

Thelma Hopkins, a Queen's student in the Fifties, symbolised an outstanding decade in the history of Queen's sport. A great natural athlete, she was coached by Franz Stampfl, himself an Olympic competitor, and just missed a Bronze Medal for the high jump at the Helsinki Olympics in 1952. She won Gold Medals at the

Thelma Hopkins in practice at Cherryvale and leaving for the 1956 Olympic Games in Melbourne. She recalled the day of her world record: "Competitors from Manchester University were over when the conditions for competing were particularly good. Afterwards we organised a small dinner and we had a couple of bottles of wine - we never did tell the Bursar that we had bought booze with Club funds. I think we all went to the Student's Union dance later, it was mostly the centre of our social life in those days. That was my celebration for my world record!"

European, Commonwealth and British Games in 1954, and a Silver Medal for the high jump at the Melbourne Olympics in 1956. In all, she held some 30 Irish track and field titles, played more than 100 times for Ireland and Ulster at hockey, and was the first woman athlete to be elected to the Texas Sports Hall of Fame.

Her world record of 5 feet 8.5 inches at Cherryvale, on 5 May 1956, lasted only 5 months, but it was a major achievement. Her sister, Dr Moira McKelvey, herself no mean athlete who played hockey 22 times for Ireland, says: "Everyone thought that the record was fairly near because Thelma had been close to it for some time. At that age a world record seemed attainable, like most things when you are young. But, with hindsight, it was a remarkable achievement."

In the Men's Club there were 3 internationals – Jimmy Rodgers, sprinter; Artie Kerr, middle distance; and Victor Milligan, a civil engineer, whose prowess on the athletics track earned him the nickname 'Miler Milligan'. One of the highlights of his distinguished sporting career was the famous mile in the 1954 Commonwealth Games in Vancouver which was won by Roger Bannister with Australian John Landy second, and New Zealander Murray Halberg pipping Milligan into fourth place in a race of the truly great.

The 'buzz' of those sporting years is remembered by Tom McAuley, a contemporary and friend of Milligan who also captained the Men's Athletic Club in 1953.

Victor Milligan in 1953.

> Victor strained a hamstring in training for our match with Oxford, and I had to find someone to run second string in the mile at short notice. It seemed that Oxford had quite a promising miler called Bannister – yes, *the* Roger Bannister – and in the end I had to approach Willie McKay, who was down for the shot-putt and discus. I knew that Willie trained hard for the rugby season, and I really only wanted a second runner to gather the minor points. But I had reckoned without Willie's immense determination and fitness – he ran Roger Bannister to within a yard, coming second in 4 mins 21 secs! Imagine a back-row forward running that time on grass today . . . I doubt it very much.

Athletics apart, the rugby was breathtakingly exciting. Who could beat us? At one stage more than half the team were current internationals and the rest played for Ulster. The list of talent goes on and on.

107

Local community

Apart from their duties of teaching and research, Queen's academics played a leading role in the social and business life of the community, contributing – as they still do – to a wide variety of government-sponsored bodies and other public and private boards and institutions dedicated to the well-being of the entire community. The university's relationships with, and contribution to, that wider community were neatly summarised by Ashby in a radio broadcast on the then Northern Ireland "Home Service" on 12 January 1951. He said that Queen's touched the life of every Ulsterman. It was probable that a Queen's doctor presided over his birth. Likely as not, if he had an operation it was performed by a Queen's graduate, and another graduate fitted his false teeth. If his children were working for Senior Certificate, some of their teachers were sure to be Queen'smen or Queen'swomen. Many of the engineers who maintained the roads and railways were Queensmen. And if the Ulsterman was unfortunate enough to find himself in a Court of Law, there might well be a Queen's Graduate at the Bar, or on the Bench. (The same could equally be said of the Queen's of today.)

In May 1952 Queen's witnessed a most unusual ceremony, when the inauguration of the Commandery of Ards in the Venerable Order of St John of Jerusalem was held in the Sir William Whitla Hall. His Royal Highness the Duke of Gloucester, Grand Prior of the Order, presided and was received at Queen's by the Chancellor, Pro-Chancellor and Vice-Chancellor.

Queen's valued contribution to national and international scholarship was underlined by the visit of distinguished scholars to a large number of major conferences, including in September 1952 the visit of the British Association for the Advancement of Science, when some 4,000 members from the United Kingdom and the Commonwealth came to Queen's for 'a brilliant gathering'. This inspired, among much else, a handsome commemorative book *Belfast in its Regional Setting*, produced by the distinguished Queen's geographer Professor Estyn Evans. This glittering academic occasion characterised the optimistic and positive spirit of the Fifties, with Queen's becoming increasingly a significant player on the national stage. The *Irish News* extended a "cordial welcome" to the visit of the BA which it said, provided "an opportunity for the exchange and pooling of ideas with profit." A "youthful looking" Duke of Edinburgh, not unlike his son

SEAMUS HEANEY

Seamus Heaney, who graduated from Queen's with a first-class honours degree in English in 1961, is one of the finest poets of his generation. He has a world reputation and has been described as the best Irish poet since Yeats. Heaney was born on 13 April 1939 and brought up near Castledawson. He attended St Columb's College in Derry before coming to Queen's, and after graduation he taught at St Thomas' Secondary School in Belfast, and lectured at St Joseph's College of Education. He returned to Queen's as a lecturer from 1966–72, and then became a freelance writer. He has won numerous literary awards and travels widely to lecture and read poetry. He is also a noted teacher and holds the Boylston Professorship of Rhetoric and Oratory at Harvard University. He is a former Professor of Poetry at Oxford University.

Heaney's years as an undergraduate saw the beginning of a flowering of local writing and partly through the influence of Philip Hobsbaum, a Queen's lecturer in English, a number of talented newcomers burst on the scene including, among others, Michael Longley, Derek Mahon and James Simmons. Later, another group of notable younger poets included Frank Ormsby, Ciaran Carson, Tom Paulin, Paul Muldoon and Medbh McGuckian. Heaney, in the midst of a heavy teaching schedule at Harvard, reflected – in a letter – about his time at Queen's.

For the first two years I boarded on Park Road, opposite Ormeau Park, and walked to the University every day. I was studious and also a bit at sea. Hence my points of security were the library, which I loved for its woody warmth and faintly erotic ambience (all those young women adjacent and preoccupied – a bit of a change for somebody who had spent six years in a boys' boarding school); the Union Dining Hall, where a gang of Derry students tended to congregate; and the Catholic Chaplaincy on Fitzwilliam Street – not because of the devotional possibilities in the chapel, but because it was an alternative social centre. In time I moved out and got into the swim a bit more.

My own literary quickening happened shortly after I left the university, yet it certainly had to do with the nurture of the English Department, and not just in the area of modern poetry, where Lawrence Lerner was a lively promoter. Anglo-Saxon – with the jocund John Braidwood – was also important to me later, and memories of one to one tutorials under Matthew P MacDiarmid keep coming to the fore these days also.

My honorary degree in 1982 – perhaps to mark the coming of age of my 1961 B.A. – is a cherished link with Queen's and that occasion was conducted with fine grace by the then Vice-Chancellor Dr Peter Froggatt. The Great Hall, where I'd often eaten lunch as a student, was the setting for the pre-graduation dinner and it was a heartsome return to the old haunts, among the old faces. In recent years, my return visits to Queen's Festival to do poetry readings have also been most gratifying.

the Prince of Wales some 40 years later, attended the inaugural meeting in the Sir William Whitla Hall, and conveyed the good wishes of the Queen. Indeed, there were a number of Royal visits in the Fifties – the Duke of Edinburgh came to Queen's at least three times – and the undoubted highlight was the visit of the newly-crowned Queen on 2 July 1953, when according to the *Belfast Telegraph*: "The lawns never looked greener or the buildings brighter," and the "flags waved like corn in the fresh breeze".

These were heady days indeed and the mood of optimism and confidence was symbolised by the Jubilee celebrations of the granting of the Charter in 1908 to confer university status on Queen's. At the conclusion of his Vice-Chancellorship, Eric Ashby had the enormous satisfaction of knowing that he had left Queen's a much better place than he had found it but he was well aware of the problems facing his successor. He was fortunate in his times, not least in the service of senior administrative and other staff, including the redoubtable university Secretary George Cowie, a Scot with an appetite for work and an almost terrier-like determination to get things done. Ashby spoke highly of Cowie. He said: "I was inclined to act rather impulsively to get big decisions made quickly. Then there might have been complications that needed working out, and George Cowie would take care of this. He never minded coming to me and saying 'Vice-Chancellor, you've made a mess of it!' We knew each one another and we were fond of one another. It was an enormous success."

Ashby, like any human being, was not infallible and a contemporary says affectionately: "If he had a fault, it was his certainty almost always that he was right!" But as a consummate university politician and administrator he did an immense amount of good for Queen's, which will ever remain in his debt. Above all, he had the wisdom to realise that he had been indeed a man of his times and that a different set of skills would be needed today. He recalled: "I lived in an expansionist period and never had any financial worries. I would have had to run the university entirely differently now and I don't know whether I could have succeeded. I might not have done it very well." Near the end of his life he mentioned that he had spent his happiest years at Queen's. "This is partly because of the feeling of going into a university and coming out at the end and believing that I had been there when something was really happening. I'm not saying that I did it. But I was there while it happened."

5

Consolidation 1959–66

SHORTLY after his appointment as Vice-Chancellor of Queen's University, Dr Michael Grant – described by the *Belfast Telegraph* as a "Classicist with a modern outlook" – told an interviewer: "I am very deeply impressed by the extraordinary achievements of Sir Eric Ashby." Though very different to Ashby, who was described in the article as a Vice-Chancellor who "could pass as a business tycoon" whereas his successor "looks more nearly the academic of tradition", Dr Grant consolidated many of the measures set in motion by his predecessor. The massive expansion of Queen's continued, not only in buildings but also in student numbers. The academic momentum was maintained by the creation of new courses and the appointment of key staff, but this period also brought early warnings of a change in the government's approach to university funding, though not so severe as the "economic blizzard" described by Grant's successor, Dr Arthur Vick, in the mid-Seventies. By the time that the scholarly Dr Grant retired in 1966 to become a full-time writer in Italy, Queen's had made significant advances but the comparative tranquillity of the Fifties had gone.

Buildings

The physical transformation of the campus, which had characterised the Fifties, continued apace. On 6 April 1962, the Queen Mother, looking resplendent and robed as an Honorary Doctor of Laws (the degree which she received as Duchess of York at the university in 1924) opened the extension to the Physics Building and was quoted in the now extinct *Northern Whig* as saying that the aims of a university could not be fulfilled without adequate

DR MICHAEL GRANT

Michael Grant, a Classical Scholar, was Vice-Chancellor of Queen's University from 1959–66. He had been previously professor of Humanity (Latin Literature) at the University of Edinburgh from 1948 and was seconded to the Sudan where he was the first Vice-Chancellor of the University of Khartoum from 1956–58. Born in 1914, his father was an army officer who wrote much of the official history of the Boer War and he was also an art historian, recognised in his time as the greatest living authority on English landscape painting. Michael Grant was educated at Harrow and Trinity College, Cambridge, where he later became a Fellow. He joined the army during the Second World War and as he could speak Turkish he was seconded to Ankara where he set up the British Council. In Ankara, he met his future wife Anne Sophie Beskow, from Norrkoping, who was with the Swedish Legation during the war.

In his early thirties, Michael Grant was appointed to a Chair in Edinburgh, where he undertook the popularisation of aspects of Roman literature. He was also an expert on ancient coins. After resigning as Vice-Chancellor of Queen's, he lived in Italy and became a full-time writer, producing many books on ancient Greek and Roman history, and also publications with a religious theme, including a life of Jesus and of St Paul.

A contemporary at Queen's noted: "One didn't set out to 'follow' a man like Ashby, you set out to be 'different', but Michael really didn't do that. While Ashby and Vick were good academics, Grant was a distinguished international scholar in his own right. At Queen's he was keen to conduct his research, and this caused resentment from some Professors who had done little research and were being shown the way by the Vice-Chancellor!" Dr Grant was a charming and sensitive man, and he was well-liked at Queen's, though he was not generally regarded as a tough leader and administrator.

"Michael perhaps felt that Queen's was like an extension of an Oxbridge College where he could carry out his research without problems so long as he had an able team of administrators. He believed in job satisfaction and towards the end he did not seem to have this, and that may be one of the reasons why he left."

The Grants brought a number of excellent qualities to Queen's, and Mrs Grant had the skills of a professional diplomat. A senior colleague recalls:

> Michael was very concerned as to how the Establishment saw Queen's, and during his time the social ripples went wider and wider. That was very important for the university. The Grants also had a great lightness of touch socially, and transformed the fabric of the Vice-Chancellor's residence. They had a very fine collection of paintings at Lennoxvale. In administrative terms Ashby and Vick were built into the fabric of Queen's. Ashby led from the top down and Vick built from the bottom up. Grant had a number of fine qualities but his years at Queen's were essentially a period of transition.

buildings to house and staff the students. A number of important buildings were opened and new facilities were made available during Dr Grant's period. They included the massive new Ashby Institute for Electrical and Mechanical Engineering on the Stranmillis Road which complemented the David Keir Building and became a landmark in its own right. It was opened on 7 May 1965 by Sir Eric Ashby himself who made a characteristically impressive public speech about technology, science and the classics, and expressed private glee that the lavatory paper was embossed with the word "Ashby'"

The new Physics Building, on the site formerly occupied by the Ulster Volunteer Force Hospital, was opened in 1962, by Queen Elizabeth, the Queen Mother.

On 5 July 1966, the Queen, accompanied by the Duke of Edinburgh, opened extensive new playing fields at Malone (in pouring rain) and a splendid Social Sciences Building in the main quadrangle, on the site of the old chemistry, biochemistry and physiology building. A new Dental Hospital was opened during this period also, while a badly-needed new Students' Union, new Halls of Residence, a substantial extension to the Library and a new pre-Clinical block on the Lisburn Road were in various stages of completion. Such developments required a great deal of hard work, not least by senior staff, including the indefatigable George Cowie, the university's Secretary, and a great deal of detailed planning and heart-searching.

The purchase of land for the development of the Malone Playing Fields was a stroke of luck. For years the university had been trying to buy suitable premises to relieve serious overcrowding on the existing Cherryvale site, but in the late Fifties Malone Golf Club let it be known to Queen's that it was interested in selling its property to move to a new location nearby. Ashby, with a little internal prompting, was persuaded to seek the support of the Stormont Minister of Finance who in turn sought the advice of the University Grants Committee. The UGC sent across an assessor – the Bursar of Manchester, R.A. Rainford, himself no mean golfer – and the Queen's initiative was approved, provided the university would fund a proportion of the costs from its own resources. The Ministry was prepared to grant-aid the project to at least 85 per cent of the net cost, less the estimated proceeds of any sale of Cherryvale. The Queen's Senate approved of the proposal, and the agreement to purchase was completed in November 1960.

The major expansion of Queen's in the 50s and 60s included a massive development on the Stranmillis/ Malone site to cope with the growing numbers of Science and Engineering students. Work on the David Keir Building was commenced in the early 1950s and it opened in 1959. The original intention had been to clear away the houses at the fork of the roads, giving an unobstructed view of the building. With this in mind, it had been designed with an impressive main entrance at the apex, to give an appearance somewhat akin to an Egyptian temple. However the houses became too valuable to demolish, and the main entrance stands discarded and forgotten at the end of a back entry behind the houses. The Ashby Building was completed in 1965 and the university held a party for local residents to mark the end of 15 years continuous building on the site.

There was much controversy inside and outside the university, however, over the future of the Deaf and Dumb Institute, a building of special architectural merit which had been designed by Sir Charles Lanyon, and which had been purchased by Queen's in 1954. The original intention was to develop the site for a new Students' Centre, but this became less likely as time went on. Feasibility studies were carried out for the development of the site to include a Students' Union, a refectory, a physical education centre, a swimming pool, and also a theatre. It became clear, however, that there were inherent flaws in the fabric of the existing building, and that the cost of a conversion for the proposed facilities would be prohibitive. In 1960, some six years after the original purchase of the site, the Buildings Committee regretfully recommended to Senate that the building should be demolished. Professor A.D.M. Greenfield, Professor of Physiology, wrote to the Belfast Telegraph conceding that any new building on the site "must combine functional excellence with an appearance that will make it a worthy successor to the Lanyon Building." This drew a riposte from Henry Lynch Robinson who asked if it was fitting that Senate should do its best to see that the new generation of scientists and doctors "should be encouraged to turn out as a band of Philistines."

With Ashby at Cambridge, powerful voices in Queen's expressed increasing doubts about the suitability of the site for a Students' Centre, and Senate, with the approval of Academic Council, agreed in 1960 to cancel its previous resolution and the site became available for the development of what is now the Medical Biology Centre and the Whitla Medical Building. The problem of relocating the new Students' Centre was solved by pulling down the beautiful old Queen's Elms Halls of Residence opposite the front of the university and erecting the new building on that site – a development which no doubt had practical advantages in meeting the needs of a burgeoning student population but which, in the eyes of many, was a spectacular example of bad visual taste. On a happier note the university undertook to build an impressive Physical Education Centre on a site in Botanic Gardens. During Dr Grant's tenure of office, the university began to meet the growing need for Halls of Residence by building on a site in elegant, park-like surroundings just off the Malone Road. They were named Queen's Elms, after their lamented predecessors, and four of these five Halls were formally opened in 1968. The need for such Halls was clearly illustrated by Grant's first *Annual Report* to Senate in December 1960 when he noted that out of a total of 3,570 students only 221 lived in Halls of Residence, 151 in other hostels, 1,151 in lodgings and the rest at home.

The Ashby building on the Stranmillis Road, 1990.

Student numbers

Dr Grant was pre-occupied with student numbers right from the start. In his first report to Senate he noted that the total was "well over 3,000" and that Queen's needed to raise this to 4,500 "pretty quickly" to "fulfil the needs of Northern Ireland and of educational progress generally." A year later he stated: "None of us want to go above 4,700–4,800" but in his final report to Senate, seven years later, he expressed satisfaction that Queen's buildings

ART COSGROVE

Dr Art Cosgrove, who took up the post of President of University College Dublin on 1 January 1994, graduated from Queen's in 1961, with a First in Modern History. He was born and educated in Newry and came up to Queen's in 1957. "It was a place where Catholic and Protestant students were, perhaps for the first time, making friendships across the Divide. That was extremely important in the late Fifties and early Sixties. I was fortunate enough to experience great teaching in the History Department, under people like Michael Roberts, Lewis Warren, Jim Beckett, Alan Graham, and Jack Gray who encouraged me to be a Medievalist."

Above all, Queen's broadened his perspectives. "I met people from so many different backgrounds and this opened my eyes. I suppose that would have happened as I went through life anyway, but Queen's was a dramatic way of doing it. I've always felt that Queen's did very well by its students, and I think many other graduates would share that feeling, that they got a very good deal out of Queen's."

and equipment were "on the whole good enough to stimulate and challenge its 5,000 students". But that was by no means the end of expansion, as future statistics would show.

Higher education increasingly became a goal for a new generation of students who, for the first time, had access to university, and this pathway was eased by the decision of the Northern Ireland Government to implement the recommendation of the Anderson Committee that all students accepted by a university should receive a Local Education Authority grant – though it did not adopt the other recommendation that the "means test" on scholarships should be abolished. Faced with a population "bulge" in Great Britain (it was predicted that the number of eighteen-year-olds in 1965 would be 58.9 per cent higher than in 1959), the Government set up the Robbins Committee which reported in 1963 on the national pattern of higher education. The Stormont Government set up its own Lockwood Committee in November 1963 to determine Northern Ireland's particular needs. The Committee presented its report to the Minister in November 1964, and it was published in February 1965. It was to have far-reaching implications for higher education in Northern Ireland, and for Queen's in particular.

Initially, Queen's appeared distinctly cool in its reaction to the setting up of the Committee chaired by Sir John Lockwood, Master of Birkbeck College. Even the *Belfast Telegraph*, which under its distinguished editor J.E. Sayers was well-disposed to Queen's, noted that the university was a little slow off the mark on this issue. (Sayers, incidentally, was deservedly honoured in July 1964 with an honorary D.Lit. for his services to journalism.) Even prior to the publication of the *Lockwood Report* there had been intense speculation about a second university, with strong lobbies for a likely site at Armagh or Londonderry, though some people were prepared to consider the further expansion of Queen's to meet the need. Less than a year before the Lockwood Committee was established Dr Grant distanced himself from the issue. He stated at graduation on 18 December, 1962: "Queen's is not a Ministry of Higher Education, nor a part of the government obliged to decide what Institutions should be started elsewhere in the Province . . . it is not for us to decide whether our efforts need supplementation by another university or not."

There were influential elements within Queen's which believed initially that the university should have little to do with

Dr Wilson Johnston,
photographed in 1966.

UNIVERSITY HEALTH SERVICE

Dr Wilson Johnston was the first Director of the University Health Service, inaugurated in 1948. From its inception, the concept of full health screening was an integral part of the service, with a compulsory full routine medical examination for all first year students. Dr Johnston also introduced compulsory annual chest X-rays for all students. In those early days, broad spectrum antibiotics were still not available, and life-threatening infections were very much more prevalent. In 1950, some 52 of the 2,000 X-rays revealed evidence of tuberculosis, including many active cases. As the disease of TB was gradually conquered this screening process was slowly phased out, and eventually abandoned altogether in 1976. New serious diseases like Hepatitis B, and AIDS, waited in the wings. A particular innovation was the introduction of a specially designed record for each student. This system was maintained rigorously until 1992, and provides a remarkable database for every Queensman and woman during that

period. Dr Johnston also introduced a coding system for the different diagnoses made, and this too was maintained until 1993 – another superb research tool.

With a university population of 2,685 students in 1948, it was possible for Dr Johnston to carry out all his duties with the help of one nurse and one secretary. But ever-increasing numbers throughout the Fifties and Sixties led to a constant expansion of the work, with appropriate additions to the medical, nursing and secretarial staff. Dr F.E. ('Fuzzy') Anderson was the first Assistant Medical Officer, who was replaced by Dr David McLean in 1960. Dr McLean served the university with distinction, first as Deputy Senior Medical Officer, and latterly taking on the post of the Occupational Health Physician as well.

It was deemed essential to appoint a woman doctor to the staff, and between 1966 and 1970, the Service benefited from the successive help of Dr Megan Bull, Dr Katie McPhillips and Dr Eileen Robinson. Dr Johnston then arranged for the help of a psychiatrist on a sessional basis, to add another arrow to the quiver

Dr Robin Harland in 1970.

of talent in the department; the most significant professional to hold this post was Dr Arthur Kerr, from 1968 to 1987.

In the late Sixties the expansion was complete with the establishment of a branch surgery in Stranmillis College. The College had a medical officer, and the first holder of this post was Dr Robin Godfrey. He was succeeded by Dr George McCullough in 1972, and subsequently by Dr Denise Deasy in 1976.

Dr Wilson Johnston, a dapper, friendly man who was one of the characters at Queen's, retired in 1970, and was succeeded by Dr Robin Harland, a Queen's graduate. Robin had been a principal in a dispensing general practice in a pit village in County Durham since 1950, and regarded this experience as an apt apprenticeship for work in the University Health Service.

The period of rapid growth within Queen's was levelling out, but an annual student intake of 1,400 had vastly increased the work-load. But, far more significantly, there were several important social changes which occurred at this time. Dr Harland recalls:

'The Troubles' are well documented elsewhere, but their impact on the student body, on the staff, and on the fabric of Queen's cannot be over-stated. Coincidentally, what is now known as "The Permissive Society" arrived belatedly in Ireland. There was an upsurge in experimentation with all sorts of illegal drugs; homosexuality emerged from the shadows of illegality; and the non-judgmental availability of the Contraceptive Pill from the mid-sixties, and the legalisation of abortion on the mainland in 1967, changed sexual attitudes irrevocably. These changes demanded in-service training, and the weekly staff seminar, resourced by Dr Kerr, did much to meet these needs. Thus, the management of such psychological problems as examination stress, anorexia nervosa, obsessional neurosis, and the much rarer psychoses, was greatly improved.

With the exception of a new receptionist, the staff numbers remained static for over 25 years – a remarkable fact given that the annual first year student intake had gradually risen to 2,900. Dr Eileen Robinson decided to work half-time, and the concept of two half-time women medical officers was born. These duties were successfully shared by Dr Maureen Moore, and Dr Edith Cunningham. There have been no further changes in female medical staff since Dr Eileen Irwin and Dr Lesley Carnaghan joined the department in 1976. Dr Denise Deasy continued in her service to both Stranmillis College and Queen's since 1976.

Team-work is a characteristic of any modern group practice, and the nursing staff acquired a number of specialist skills from venupuncture, to the development of a skilled inoculation service, for home and abroad. One of the best examples of team work was the long standing co-operation between Dr Harland and the Senior Nursing Officer, Mrs Nan McBride, on the research into the problems of allergies in the student population. This culminated in the publication of a joint paper in 1993 confirming a remarkable 300 per cent increase of asthma in Queen's students between 1970 and 1990.

The medical staff, despite the pressures of work, still found time to publish relevant research in their discipline and in 1978 Dr Harland was awarded the Butterworth Gold Medal of the Royal College of General Practitioners for a paper on the management of hay fever. The University Health Service gained continual national recognition – Dr Johnston, Dr Harland and Dr McLean were all Presidents of the British Student Health Association, while Harland and McLean were both invited to deliver the prestigious Malleson Memorial Lecture.

In any university, the treatment of injuries through sport is important. Dr Harland and Dr McLean had wide experience in this area, and had acted as managers to the Queen's Rugby Club in its tour of Japan, Hong Kong and Malaysia in 1976. The provision of sports medicine was much appreciated by a wide range of sportsmen and women, and perhaps most acceptably by those involved in contact sports like Gaelic Football and Rugby. The expansion of knowledge in this area was continuous throughout the Seventies and Eighties, and the work culminated in the creation of the Isaac Agnew Sports Injury Clinic at Queen's in 1987. The Seventies and Eighties was a time of great expansion in numbers, despite financial stringencies. But even with the difficulties, the health of the student body as a whole remained good, although some members exhibited considerable signs of stress, as they were forced to adapt to the new severe economic climate. Dr Robin Harland retired in 1991, and was replaced by Dr Denis Todd. His background and experience in occupational health and administration, in addition to general practice, brought special management, organisational and human resource skills so valuable in harsh economic times.

Though the number of staff has scarcely altered since the early Seventies, the greater work-load reflected in a student intake which has itself vastly increased, has led to changes in the University Health Service. The long-established practice of routine medical examinations of all first-year students has been partially abandoned, as has the collection of research data, and staff consultations have had to be limited. Nevertheless, the caring service to the academic community has been maintained, despite the modern development of the National Health Service in terms of purchasers and providers, a concept so alien to the visionaries of the original NHS some 50 years ago.

Lockwood, but wiser counsels prevailed and the university – following detailed discussions at Academic Council and Senate – presented a submission to the Committee. The proposals in the report which raised most discussion, both in Parliament and in the Province at large, were for the establishment of a new university in the Coleraine area – much to the anger and disappointment of those who had championed the new city of Craigavon, Armagh and Londonderry – and for the discontinuance of Magee College as a university institution. The government accepted the first proposal but not the second, and it was finally agreed that Magee should develop as a constituent college of the new university.

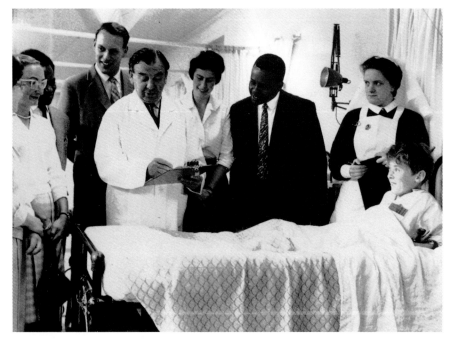

Medical education at Queen's is an integrated effort involving both the university and the teaching hospitals. A practical aspect of undergraduate tuition is the 'ward round', where students accompany a consultant and attempt diagnoses under the watchful gaze of the professor, their fellow students and, of course, the patient. This ward round in the early 1960s shows Sir Ian Fraser with a group of students. Looking over his right shoulder is third-year medical student Bob Stout, now Professor of Geriatric Medicine, Dean of the Faculty of Medicine and Provost of Health Sciences in the University.

Among the most important proposals affecting Queen's, apart from the establishment of a second university, was the emphasis on promoting technological development, the curtailing of the growth of certain Faculties, particularly Arts and the biological and environmental sciences in the Faculty of Science, and that the Faculty of Agriculture should be moved from Queen's to Coleraine.

Queen's deep misgivings on these and other issues were discussed with senior civil servants and the university was assured that, among other things, the government would find even the thought of having to interfere with the university's traditional independence as "repugnant", that the university still had flexibility for the distribution of its students between Faculties, that the further substantial development in the Faculty of Science should allow growth in all its disciplines, that there could be further diversification and growth in Arts subjects, and, most important, that the Faculty of Agriculture would remain at Queen's where it had been established in the early Twenties. The university, for its part, agreed that there would be special growth in Applied Science and Technology.

A special meeting of Senate on 6 July 1965 considered a letter from the Stormont Minister of Education, Mr W.K. Fitzsimmons, giving assurances along the lines outlined above. The Senate approved of a reply to the Minister noting its satisfaction with his assurances and expressing its willingness "to offer whatever help lies within our power" towards the successful founding and development of the fledgling Coleraine institution which came to be known popularly as the NUU.

Dr Brumwell Henderson, Managing Director of Ulster Television from 1959–84, whose 'Midnight Oil' series with Queen's academics in 1962 had pioneered adult education on television in the United Kingdom, was a member of the Lockwood Committee. He observes:

> It could be argued that Queen's did not play its cards well and that it did not welcome the prospect of new directions or offer new fields of study with sufficient vigour and appeal. On the other hand, to play from strength is often wise in these matters. The prevailing wind of the Sixties was for change, departure from tradition, for expansion and new horizons. But Queen's elected to 'stand on the record'. Accordingly the great expansion did not take place, and instead there was a steady growth along traditional lines. The Lockwood proposal that the Faculty of Agriculture should move to Coleraine was thwarted by a determined rearguard action by QUB and this dealt a severe blow to the environmental and biological emphasis which Lockwood had suggested as a distinguishing characteristic of the new institution. In this, Queen's was aided by the Department of Agriculture; and this action as well as the onset of 'The Troubles' caused the NUU considerable pain for many years.

Controversy

There was – as ever – controversy of different kinds in and around the campus, despite the carefully written, and sometimes sanitised, version of contemporary events in official university documents. For example the Vice-Chancellor in his *Annual Report* for 1963–4 stated blandly: "Sir Tyrone Guthrie succeeded the late Lord Alanbrooke as Chancellor of the University." But his words did not mention that, somewhat to the University's embarrassment, the Chancellorship, for the first time, was decided by an election.

There was controversy too on the academic front though the details were carefully tucked away in Academic Council reports. As ever, the *Annual Record* of the Queen's University Association –

a spirited publication – did not ignore the big story, in its report for 1962–3.

> It would be a quite inappropriate expression of judicial ignorance to pretend to know nothing of the dispute in the Faculty of Law, which during the year attracted the attention of the Press and distracted that of the students. By a narrow majority . . . Professor F.H. Newark was elected to succeed as Dean Professor J.L. Montrose, who had held office for 29 years. Montrose's ceasing to be Dean will mark for many the end of an epoch; they will find it difficult to think of the Faculty of Law without him at its head, fighting for what he believed to be right, for what he believed to be the interests of his students, who have always found in him both an understanding mentor and a doughty champion.

At the Academic Council meeting of 3 May, 1963 the Vice-Chancellor indicated that Montrose wanted an enquiry into "alleged academic improprieties in connection with the Faculty of Law". An enquiry was duly held and the university told the press that there had been no academic improprieties of substance. The investigating committee, however, had been disturbed by "evidence of recent disharmony and tension as well as a measure of confusion, in the Faculty." The Faculty's re-organisation and the election of Newark as Dean were confirmed. A year later, Professor Montrose announced his retirement and was granted a year's leave of absence before finally relinquishing his post in 1965. He died shortly afterwards, and a tribute in the *Annual Record* stated:

> Few men are adequately appraised or worthily recognised in their lifetimes and it may be that many years will pass before Montrose's great reputation will be consolidated. . . He was kind, agreeably mannered and deeply interested in the welfare and fortunes of his students and friends. If at times he appeared to be unbending and unwilling to compromise it was because he had, after analysis and deliberation, reached a reasoned conclusion to support the principle on which he acted.

Francis H. Newark himself was a major figure at Queen's. An Oxford graduate with a First in Jurisprudence and a First in Civil Law, he came to Queen's in 1937 and was appointed to the new Chair of Jurisprudence in 1946. From 1940 he was Secretary of the General Board of Studies until 1947, when he became the third Secretary to the Academic Council, a position he held for 17^1/$_2$ years, succeeding Professor Alan Sinclair, the Professor of Greek. He was also one of the Vice-Chancellor's key administrators, and his influence was important in providing continuity between Keir, Ashby and Grant. (It was during Grant's period

PROFESSOR J.J. PRITCHARD

Jack Pritchard was appointed Professor and Head of the Department of Anatomy at Queen's in 1952. An Australian, he was an able Professor and a noted wit, ranconteur and after-dinner speaker. His kindness was well known. The writer Bernard MacLaverty wrote a pen-portrait for the book Fullness of Life compiled by Jack's widow Muriel. He described how, typically, Jack Pritchard helped him find part-time employment when – like many a young man with a wife and family – he found it difficult to make ends meet when he embarked on a career as a student. The Pritchard Lecture, on a topic dealing with Multiple Sclerosis, is still delivered in his memory every other year at Queen's. The portrait was painted by Raymond Piper in 1969.

SIR TYRONE GUTHRIE

Sir Tyrone Guthrie, the internationally-acclaimed theatre Director, seemed an inspired choice as the fourth Chancellor of Queen's, succeeding Lord Alanbrooke who died in 1963. Guthrie was larger-than-life in every way, and his great presence and his habit of speaking his mind promised to be a refreshing experience in the traditionally conservative world of university politics. From the outset the search for a successor to Alanbrooke provided headlines. For the first time in the university's history the office of Chancellor was contested, and members of Convocation (the body representing all Graduates who have the right to appoint a Chancellor) cast 2,087 votes for Guthrie, 1,611 for the Duke of Abercorn (thought to be the Establishment candidate), with 521 votes declared invalid (mainly postal votes which were incorrectly addressed).

The new Chancellor was officially installed on 17 December 1963, and in the early days Sir Tyrone Guthrie followed the normal paths so carefully trodden by Chancellors, becoming – appropriately in his case – Patron of Festival, and confining himself to home-spun philosophy on graduation day. In 1964, however, Sir Tyrone electrified 400 guests at the City Hall during the 40th Anniversary Dinner of the Trinity College Dublin (Northern Ireland) Association by suggesting that the Irish Border was "hopelessly artificial, and desperately detrimental to the interests of our country." This led swiftly to a political uproar, with Sir Tyrone being predictably criticised by Unionist politicians and praised by Nationalists. The hapless Guthrie swiftly apologised to the Lord Mayor, and issued a statement to the Press claiming that he had been misrepresented.

The university, however, distanced itself and stated that the Chancellor's remarks were made "without the knowledge or authority of the university . . . and they run contrary to the established policy of the university which is to stand clear of party politics and controversies." Sir Tyrone also apologised in a statement to Senate at its December meeting.

Her Majesty Queen Elizabeth II touring Queen's with Sir Tyrone and Lady Guthrie in 1966.

Unpredictable as ever Sir Tyrone made headlines again when, at a Charter Day Dinner of the Queen's University Association, he decided not to speak – following a scintillating address by a previous speaker – and indicated that he would inevitably be tedious by comparison. Given that there had been several previous speeches and that the hour was indeed late, Sir Tyrone showed uncommon commonsense by speaking (or not speaking) his mind. However, he had learned the hard way that personal views and the duties of a Chancellor do not sit easily side by side. Sir Tyrone stepped down as Chancellor in 1970, due to ill-health, but some people still remember him as a welcome breath of fresh air in stuffy corridors of power.

that the university purchased a large green limousine for the Vice-Chancellor. Newark's response was to change his black saloon for a red MG soft top – with a consequential change from a trilby to a duncher!) He was a first-class teacher and administrator who expected, indeed required, very high standards. A colleague who knew him well said that it was an exhilarating experience to work in his office even though the common courtesies such as "Please, thank you, good morning or good night" rarely, if ever, passed his lips. His notoriously brusque and abrupt exterior was a cover for a form of shyness that was not based on a sense of inadequacy but rather a protection of the inner self he was reluctant to reveal. His staff loved him – in any form of trouble he was kindness itself, and very generous. His wit in debate and his repartee were renowned.

Newark, as Secretary to the Academic Council, played a leading role in disciplinary matters although the Students' Representative Council also had an important part to play, and in this respect Queen's was in the vanguard of United Kingdom universities. The matter of behaviour requiring disciplinary measures had changed since the Fifties. For example, in January 1955 the Academic Council asked the Committee of Discipline to report on its existing rules. The Committee reviewed Rule Six: "Students interfering with or disturbing the work of the university by snowballing, and snowballing persons outside the university precincts, will be severely punished." The Committee commented drily: "This curiously drafted rule appears to permit the snowballing of the Vice-Chancellor providing the work of the university is not thereby disturbed." There were, however, more serious matters in the Sixties.

In March 1963, the Committee of Discipline ruled that two law students had been guilty of conduct prejudicial to the interests of the university, and they were suspended for several months. In November 1964, the Committee suspended the entire Literific Society for several weeks "in view of the disorders and improprieties of conduct and obscene language" at a recent meeting at which a guest speaker had removed his shirt and trousers, for a brief period. And in March 1965 a final-year psychology student was expelled by the Committee for behaviour which was deemed to be "dishonourable and prejudicial to the interests of the university". The Committee also ruled that the student's name be removed from the books of the university.

Student Body

Despite such serious matters, life went on as normal for the vast majority of students. The Annual Rag effort continued to raise large sums of money for charity, while it also annoyed the general public through some of the more outrageous student pranks. In 1964 the citizens of Belfast were perturbed by the sight of six-foot high black letters 'PTQ' painted on the dome of the City Hall. Three students and another youth were bound over for a year by a local court as a result of this irresponsible but daring stunt. *PTQ* itself continued to attract a steady stream of complaints from enraged letterwriters, while on another topic entirely Senate received a large number of letters from Churches, Presbyteries and Temperance Societies objecting to its decision to allow a beer bar in the new Students' Union and at the Malone Sports Pavilion. Senate, as ever, had an enviable knack of noting such complaints but quietly carrying on with its business. The student newspaper *Gown* lived through one of its periodic crises when the senior editorial team resigned, and the Sports' Editor took over. He was required to raise money as an indemnity fund against possible future libels – no printer would touch *Gown* otherwise – and the students and staff responded generously to ensure the paper's future. However, it was a hard fact of life that some channels of communication did not survive and in 1965 the University Guild – a body set up to provide a point of contact between 'Town and Gown' – ended its 35 year existence, due to falling membership.

PUBLICATIONS

Queen's has long been a centre of lively publications, and one of the oldest is the independent student newspaper Gown. It was launched in 1955 by an American medical student Richard Herman, and throughout its history Gown, like many other student publications, has had a chequered career with the standards of journalism ranging from the almost-professional to the gutter-press. The newspaper has been the training ground for a number of its editors and main contributors who went on to noteworthy professional careers, but Gown's real claim to fame is that it has actually managed to survive for so long as an independent publication.

More recently the Students' Union launched its own newspaper Press Release, while over the years other student publications have emerged to dazzle briefly before sinking into oblivion. On the non-student side, the Annual Record (later the Annual Review) of the Queen's University Association has provided a reliable account of university life, while the official publications including the Vice-Chancellor's Report, the Queensletter, Update, the Vice-Chancellor's Letter to Graduates and other publications have been providing a comprehensive view of university activities.

*Bill Savage, SRC President 1960–1
and N.U.S. President 1964–6*

Student leaders distinguished themselves by achieving the highest national office. Bill Savage was elected President of the National Union of Students from 1964–66, the first time in the 42 year history of the NUS that an Ulsterman had held this position. He was succeeded by Geoff Martin, who had been President of Queen's SRC from 1962–63 and who served for 2 years as NUS President. In April 1965 a new constitution was adopted unanimously at Queen's by the Students' Representative Council, the Students' Union Society and the Women Students' Hall Society which from 1 October 1966 was to establish a unified Students' Union as student governing body and to make the most effective use of the new Students' Union on the site of the former Queen's Elms.

Entertainment

An exciting development in these years was the emergence of Festival. In March 1964, the SRC elected Michael Emmerson and his brother Anthony as co-directors of an expanded and more professional Festival 64, and as a result of its outstanding success it was decided to appoint Michael as Professional Director and Anthony as Student Director to plan an ambitious Festival 65. Mike Emmerson, an Englishman, was an exotic character, even as a student, and he was a familiar figure around the campus often wearing sandals and a floppy hat. He had flair, artistic brilliance and extraordinary persuasive powers, and he helped to lay the foundation of Festival which became one of the major artistic attractions in Northern Ireland, with a wide local and international appeal. Emmerson had limited opportunity to present large-scale musical extravaganzas but he staged events of the highest quality. The highlights included recitals by Sviatoslav Richter, Julius Katchen and Ravi Shankar, as well as a tribute to Séan Ó Riada, and the introduction of late-night recitals. One memorable performer was the Ulster-born flautist James Galway and it was no surprise when Emmerson, having resigned from Festival, became Galway's manager and helped him to carve out an outstanding international career.

*Geoff Martin, SRC President 1962-3
and N.U.S. President 1966-8.*

Another memorable development was the emergence of the Glee Club. One of the founders was Phil Coulter, a music student from Derry, who also developed a brilliant international career as a song-writer, music-arranger and entertainer. Even in the Sixties many people predicted a very bright future for Coulter who combined natural musical talent with entrepreneurial flair. To

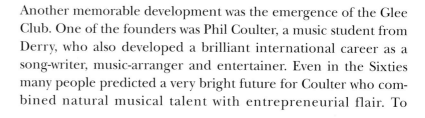

become a recognised Society, the Glee Club needed a constitution, so its stated aim was "To promote the lesser arts among the intelligentsia." A generation of graduates still has warm memories of the Glee Club meetings in the old Students' Union, with a hugely appreciative audience applauding Coulter, in a ridiculous "fez" and cloak, playing the piano, Stevie McKenna with his celebrated Cossack dance, the late Sean Armstrong (tragically murdered in the Troubles) reciting "The Shooting of Dan McGrew" by Robert Service, Willie Campbell, the "saw-player" and other "performers" of note. The Glee Club was so successful that it even arranged 'guest appearances' from international stars, playing in local theatres. They included Helen Shapiro, whose appearance surprised everyone, including the organisers and the friendly "bouncer" Ed the Ted, a young man who had a fearsome reputation because of his "Teddy Boy" garb, but who may well have been a gentle soul at heart. Coulter summed up the exhilaration of very many Queen's students of those days who appreciated actually being at a university, a privilege not given to their parents. "If we had to chose three or four years out of the last 30 we could not have chosen a better time to be at Queen's. There was a great sense of creativity and energy about the place, and Queen's gave me the opportunity to be what I wanted to be. It was as if some one had opened the toyshop and allowed us in."

For many they were comparatively carefree years, and this was typified by another phenomenon when students used to crowd into the McMordie Hall in the old Students' Union on a Friday afternoon to watch the cartoon character Yogi Bear on the communal television set – a good example as any of the maxim that "little pleases the innocent."

(Top) Phil Coulter first appeared on the university scene as a shy bass player in a jazz band at the Saturday night hops in the Drill Hall in the 1962, when all musicians looked like Edwardian waiters and singers looked like mannequins in Robinson & Cleaver's window.

(Above) After a sparkling career in the entertainment industry, Phil Coulter is seen here in 1992 trying to create harmony among politicians, the then Northern Ireland Education Secretary Dr Brian Mawhinney and Austin Currie TD, both Queen's graduates. This followed the filming of an Ulster Television programme "The class of '59".

DAVID HEWITT

David Hewitt (right), who graduated from Queen's in 1961 with a degree in Law, was one of the most brilliant rugby players of his generation. While still at school he played for the Ulster Senior team, and at the age of 19 he played for Ireland against Australia alongside Jack Kyle, Noel Henderson, Tony O'Reilly, Noel Murphy and others. He played for Ireland 18 times, and toured with the British Lions to New Zealand in 1959 and to South Africa in 1962. His outstanding ability was summed up by fellow Lion, Tony O'Reilly: "When David Hewitt was on his game he was an unstoppable force. He was not always consistent, but for sheer brilliance he must rank as one of the best centres of all time."

SEAN O'NEILL

Sean O'Neill (above), one of the greatest Gaelic Football players of his generation, graduated from Queen's with an honours Law degree in 1961. He was a member of the Queen's team which won the Sigerson Cup (the Inter-Varsity Championship) in 1959 for the first time in the Club's long history and also for the second time in 1964, thus becoming the first member of the Queen's Club to win two Sigerson medals.

O'Neill was also coach and manager of the Queen's team when it won the Sigerson Cup in 1982, the Club's Golden Jubilee Year and two years later when Queen's won the Ryan Cup (the Inter-Varsity League). He continued to serve the Club off the field and he has been a Vice-President since 1984. He was granted honorary life membership of the Students' Union in 1983 "for services to Gaelic sport at Queen's." He is currently Vice-Chairman of the Past Members' Union. Gaelic football writer Raymond Smith described him thus: "Sean O'Neill is the greatest full-forward I have seen . . . all the superlatives have been used to describe his unique talent and his genius . . . it was difficult indeed to pinpoint a flaw in his play."

Sport, as always, was extremely popular, with Queen's teams and individuals distinguishing themselves. For example, Dr Grant noted in his report for 1960–1, that the Boxing Club had made a "dramatic" re-appearance when three titles were won at the Irish Universities Championships. The Women's Athletic Club made a "no less dramatic" re-appearance when Joan Atkinson won the 100 yards and 220 yards titles at the Women's University Championships at Leicester. Both she and Thelma Hopkins were picked for the British team to compete at the World Student Games in Sofia. The Soccer and Swimming Clubs were also in excellent form and supplied almost the entire Irish universities teams in representative fixtures.

In Rugby, David Hewitt was the star of the Irish Rugby team in the Home Internationals while Ken Houston and Jimmy Dick went to South Africa with the Irish team. Incidentally, Jimmy and his brother Ian Dick created headlines by being capped for Ireland at the same time. In Gaelic Football, Queen's also had an outstanding player in Sean O'Neill who was a member of the victorious Down County team which first brought the All-Ireland Sam Maguire Cup to the North (See left). Another extremely talented Gaelic footballer at Queen's, later on, was Paddy Moriarty, who won two All-Star Awards when playing for Armagh county (including one when he was a Queen's student), and who went on to manage the county side.

Academic

While student societies and sport flourished, the main business of the university continued to be teaching and research. During Dr Grant's period a host of new academic appointments were made, and in his 1963–4 *Annual Report* he listed the names of no fewer than fourteen professors who had been appointed in the previous two years, including some whose names still retain a particular ring – Professors Charlton, Wells, Dundee, Pinkerton, Roddie, Carré, Owen, Jope, and the holder of a new Chair in Ancient

128

History, Professor Kathleen Atkinson, who was the first woman professor appointed by Queen's. Professor James Scott, who held a Personal Chair in Dental Anatomy, delivered his inaugural lecture in the form of a 5,000 word epic poem, which was given wide media coverage. He said: "I have taken this unusual step because I believe it is right that members of a university should every now and then attempt to break away from stereo-typed patterns of behaviour."

During Dr Grant's period, the university undertook many academic initiatives, including the establishment of a new Chair of Management Studies, as well as many new courses – indeed at one stage Dr Grant noted that there were no fewer than 29 different Honours Schools in the Arts Faculty. It also established in 1963 the Council of Queen's University and Schools, to further the already good relationships with local schools. The Institute of Irish Studies was founded in 1965 as the first institute of its kind in either Ireland or Britain. Its aim is to encourage interest and co-ordinate research in all those fields of study which have a particular Irish interest. It seeks to achieve these objectives through awards for advanced research and a programme of publications, public lectures and seminars.

Staff changes included the retirement of Professor A.H. Naylor, a significant influence in Civil Engineering in the university who was credited by Lord Ashby with providing the germ of the idea which later became the Keir Building, and Professor Karl George Emeleus, one of Queen's longest-serving and most highly-regarded professors. Emeleus came to Queen's in 1927, and became professor of Experimental Physics, 1933–1966. He was, for 13 years, Dean of the Faculty of Applied Science and Technology (at a time when the Faculty was split between Queen's and the Belfast College of Technology) and he acted as scientific adviser to various Government agencies, as well as becoming the first Chairman of the Northern Ireland Examinations Council. His main research interest was the study of the physical processes involved in the conduction of electricity through gases, an area in which he was an acknowledged world authority. "KG" as he was known to his col-

MIKE BULL

Mike Bull, who graduated with an Arts Degree in 1968 and later studied successfully for a Ph.D. in Philosophy, was an outstanding Queen's athlete and pole-vaulter. His many achievements include a Commonwealth Silver Medal in Jamaica in 1966, a Commonwealth Gold at Edinburgh in 1970, and Commonwealth Gold again in Christchurch, New Zealand in 1974, and membership of the British Olympic team in Mexico in 1968 (when he reached the final) and at the Munich Olympics in 1972. He continued to compete for Great Britain and Northern Ireland until 1978, taking part in a record 69 internationals and 13 AAA titles. He also won the World Masters Pole Vault title in Finland in 1991 thus fulfilling his "life-time ambition of becoming a World Champion." He recalls: "My memories of Queen's are dominated by the twin influences of sport and philosophy. My mentor, Professor Alan Milne, eventually became a friend. He was blind but loved to jog with me around the track. His humanitarianism and huge intellect were my inspiration."

Professor Karl Emeleus, professor of Experimental Physics, 1933–66.

leagues is best remembered as a teacher with the ability to present difficult topics in an interesting way, and his lectures, delivered with virtually no recourse to notes, were models of their kind. Even in retirement he continued to publish two or three papers a year – a record that would shame many younger academics. In recognition of his contribution to his subject for over 60 years, the university established the Emeleus Physics Prize in 1984.

Departure

Academics apart, there were other outstanding characters around the campus, including Lieut-Colonel S.A. Billington who was Steward of the Students' Union from 1952–64. Known as "the Major" he ruled over the billiards room with a rod of iron. Benign and belligerent by turns, he had a mastery of expressive language to put unruly undergraduates deservedly in their places, but beneath the crusty exterior there was a kindness which won the respect and affection of even those at the receiving end of a tirade.

When Dr Michael Grant announced his intention to leave at the end of the 1965–6 academic year, it marked the end of another distinct era in the history of Queen's. Shortly after he arrived, the government had fired the first financial warning shots across the bows of universities, and during the 1961–2 academic year the Committee of Vice-Chancellors and Principals was "profoundly disturbed by the government's announcement about the resources to be made available during the coming quinquennium, and, above all, by the fact that the advice of the UGC as to the grants required if the number of university places is to be increased to 150,000 by 1966–7, has not been accepted." This was a portent of much worse to come, and with hindsight, Dr Grant's comment in his *Annual Report* of 1960–61 provides a window into a different and much more genteel world: "I hope we do not have to think of a new era of cut-throat competition between universities, in which the Vice-Chancellors, after their monthly meetings, will no longer be able to lunch together on speaking terms." In his final *Report* Dr Grant noted: "Queen's . . . in my experience remains exceptional among universities because it is such a friendly and personal place." However, in face of the storm clouds gathering over universities in general, Dr Grant may well have embarked on a full-time writing career from his new Italian retreat with a sense of relief.

The Old Students' Union building, a core memory for generations of Queen's students, was taken over by the School of Music, which retained much of the old atmosphere.

6

Surviving the Troubles 1966–76

"THIRTY years ago, universities were arguably the most pampered institutions on earth. Governments showered them with money, convinced that they were engines of growth and agents of equality. . . ." stated *The Economist* in its 1994 New Year publication. It continued: "This mood has vanished. Universities are on the defensive everywhere, distrusted by governments, worried about losing income and influence . . . Nothing less than a populist backlash against academia appears to be under way."

Some 28 years before this article was published, Dr Arthur Vick became Vice-Chancellor of Queen's at a time when few people, if any, would have predicted the colossal changes in higher education in the next three decades or – equally significantly for Queen's – the immensity of the political and social upheaval in Northern Ireland due to 'The Troubles'. It was Arthur Vick's particular misfortune to encounter the beginning of savage government cut-backs which continue to create huge problems for his successors, while at the same time trying to maintain the university on an even keel during one of the most difficult and dangerous periods in the history of the Province. Nevertheless, Dr Vick displayed tenacity, tact and vision in leading Queen's through the continuing crisis, and the tributes to his leadership were thoroughly deserved.

SIR ARTHUR VICK

Sir Arthur Vick, in his final graduation speech as Vice-Chancellor on 6 July 1976, reflected on his top priority when coming to Queen's ten years earlier. It was "to endeavour to recruit the best staff available and then to give them the resources, conditions, atmosphere and encouragement to do their best work." He concluded "This, I am proud to say, we have in large measure succeeded in doing, in spite of the restrictions in resources suffered by all universities in these islands, and elsewhere in recent years, and our local context."

It was a fair assessment. Monsignor Arthur Ryan, a leading Roman Catholic and Queen's academic and Senator, at another graduation three days later, thanked Sir Arthur "for the quiet dignity and firm determination with which he has guided our university almost unscathed through most difficult years, and has succeeded in retaining the complete confidence and trust of every section of our community, apart from those whom no university has been able to reach – the irrational and the implacable."

Dr Vick, who was knighted in 1973, came to Queen's with an already distinguished record. A physicist, he graduated from the University of Birmingham, and during the Second World War he was Assistant Director of Scientific Research with the Ministry of Supply. After a period as a Physics Lecturer in the University of Manchester he became Professor of Physics and for a time Acting Principal at the University College of North Staffordshire, later Keele University. He later became Director of the Atomic Energy Research Establishment at Harwell, and was a member of the University Grants Committee for seven years, as well as serving on numerous advisory bodies and committees.

He brought to Queen's a wealth of experience gained in teaching, research and administration, and one of his strengths was his skill in committee work. He was also regarded to be one of the best administrators to have held the post of Vice-Chancellor. Despite his quiet approach, he had great determination and tenacity, and an eye for detail. Lady Vick was also a quiet person, and she was particularly fond of painting and gardening. A contemporary notes: "She was shy and retiring, but when she got to know you she was very friendly and hospitable."

Sir Arthur made a point of meeting students on their own territory. He was known to join the queue in the Great Hall, when time permitted, for lunch and then take the first vacant place at a table with students. "They were a little surprised at first, but they were very friendly. I learned a lot from them." He also kept closely in touch with staff. "If I wanted to see any Head of Department, I didn't ask him to come and see me. I went to see him because I could breathe the atmosphere of the Department and see what it was like."

He was not a man for an outward show, and his relatively scant references to the Troubles in his *Annual Report* to Senate may have been a reflection of his desire to stress that normal university business had to go on and that there was little point in labouring the Troubles which were obvious to all his contemporaries anyway. Some people believe that having adopted the right policies, he somewhat undersold the university's achievements in maintaining such a balance amid all the conflicting pressures, but he felt deeply about Queen's. As early as July 1970, following a difficult period of the Troubles as they affected Queen's, he told a graduation audience: "I am, of course, an Englishman, but I would like you to know that I am very proud of the staff of Queen's and cannot find words in which to express sufficiently fully my gratitude to colleagues, both academic and administrative, for all their hard and constructive work and for the help and advice they have given me through a difficult period . . . there is no other university in which I would prefer to work." On his departure the feeling was summed up by a senior officer who noted: "Sir Eric Ashby would have 'bled' with the people on the streets. Arthur Vick cared deeply, but he concluded that life in the university had to go on, even if the place was burning all around. If a Committee was scheduled to meet, that Committee would meet and get on with the business. He was very calm in a dry sort of way, considerate and practical. That was his training as a physicist, everything had to be tested all along the line. He left the university in surprisingly good shape, relative to the social chaos all around."

Finance

Although one of Dr Vick's early challenges was to present a case –
successfully – to the University Grants Committee regarding the
under-financing of Queen's compared to similar institutions in
England and the Irish Republic, the university was relatively satisfied with the proposed settlement for the new quinquenium
1973–8. Vick stated in his *Vice-Chancellor's Report* for 1972–3 that if
Queen's continued to receive adequate supplementation for
inflation, the block grant of some £38 m should be enough to
improve staff/student ratios, to undertake additional development and to provide for a target of 7,593 full-time students, very
close to the provisional figure of 7,500. He concluded: "This gives
us much encouragement . . . so we move into the new quinquennium in good spirits." The next year, however, brought a very different perspective, as in Vick's words "the economic blizzard
began to blow in the United Kingdom."

In 1974, the government announced substantial restrictions in
public expenditure. As a result, Queen's began the 1974–5 session with a projected deficit of over £300,000. At one stage it
looked as if it might rise to £450,000, but by imposing cuts, max-
imising income from interest from short-term loans, and other
measures, the deficit was reduced to £27,402, excluding catering
losses. Departmental and other academic grants were reduced by
10 per cent, nearly a third of the academic, administrative and
general posts were frozen, and there was deferment of some
maintenance and minor works, and economies in the use of fuel,
power and materials. Dr Vick concluded in his *Annual Report*,
however, that the university's development plans were in ruins.
"Money which had been set aside for future developments is having to be used for present needs . . . The quinquennial system is
effectively in abeyance." Sadly this depressing, though accurate,
summary set the tone for the next two decades when universities
had to survive as best they could in a harsh financial climate
where student numbers increased, staff salaries fell behind others
in traditionally comparable posts in the public sector, and governments expected more and more for less and less. The
"Golden Years" of the Fifties seemed far away indeed.

The view from the Lanyon building, largely unchanged for a century, was considerably altered in the 1960s with the demolition of the old Queen's Elms on University Road. Photographed in 1962, it is still greatly missed for its style and elegance. In its place arose the new Students' Union, a functional building which provided space for the rapidly rising number of students. It is ironic that the row of stately elm trees, the last link with the building famed for its Dutch gables, had to be felled in the 1970s as the result of Dutch Elm disease.

Achievements

Despite the financial gloom, there were many achievements to be celebrated by Queen's, not least the impressive headway made in the provision of new buildings. The programme included a £1m Students' Union on the former site of the Queen's Elms Residences to replace the old, much-loved but inadequate Students' Union at the rear of the Library; the official opening of the four tower-blocks of Queen's Elms Halls of Residence by Prime Minister Captain Terence O'Neill (work had already begun on the fifth Hall); the completion of the Medical Biology Centre, which received a Civic Trust Award, and a new Staff Common Room – a building of unremitting architectural blandness. The projects included a comprehensive and soon to be heavily used Physical Education Centre, a new building for the Departments of Applied Mathematics and Theoretical Physics and Computer Science, and, after some delay, for the Computer Centre, to house principally a powerful new computer, the 1906S – in addition to an extension building for the Department of Pure and Applied Physics on an adjoining site. In this period also there was an attractive conversion of the recently-acquired Elmwood Church into Elmwood Hall which was later leased, in 1989, to the Ulster Orchestra; the conversion of 12 student houses for 94 women and 87 men, and the completion of the first

Student President Ian Brick leading the academic procession to the new Students' Union for the opening ceremony in 1967 by Lord Murray of Newhaven. Recognizable in the line are Secretary George Cowie, Honorary Treasurer Sir William McKinney, and James Campbell (Head of the Institute of Education). Toward the rear are the Rt Hon. Terence O'Neill, the Prime Minister of Northern Ireland with Captain William Long, Cabinet Minister.

The new Queen's Elms Halls of Residence as viewed from Riddel Hall, photographed in 1982.

Queen's University apartments, a purpose-built block housing 36 male students. As well, the completion of Sinton Hall, the fifth of the Queen's Elms Halls, brought the total accommodation of the Malone Road site to over 800 places.

At the official opening of Queen's Elms are (L–R): Lord MacDermott (Pro-Chancellor), Dr Arthur Vick (Vice-Chancellor), the Rt Hon. Terence O'Neill (Prime Minister) and Dr John Benn (Pro-Chancellor). A few moments earlier the entire curtain rail had collapsed when the Prime Minister was attempting to unveil the plaque.

During the same decade the Geography Department moved into the former Agriculture building in Elmwood Avenue, the Whitla Medical Building on the Lisburn Road was opened, a new building for Botany and Zoology was being completed, and a new administration building was occupied from January 1975 "to mixed feelings of horror and delights in its unique "free flow planning"; later this was converted to more "private" accommodation. The Vice-Chancellor decided not to site his office in this building which remains as unattractive inside as its depressing exterior. Though all of these developments were welcome and necessary, there was some nostalgia about the demise of the old Students' Union, now the site of the School of Music. Apart from the "Diner", which served as a canteen during the day, as a community/concert hall on some evenings, and as a dance-hall on Wednesday and Saturday nights, the Students' Union was a largely male preserve with a billiards room and smoke room on the top floor, and baths in the basement. David Crawford, a former member of the Students' Representative Council and now a member of the Library staff at McGill University, Montreal, recalls:

Elmwood Hall, later to be the home of the Ulster Orchestra, 1994.

> The old Union was really from another era. Similarly to the area of Montreal in which I now live, the flats and rooms of many students in the Queen's district did not at one time have baths and the Union (or here the public baths) were really necessary. While it was fun to have a leisurely bath in the afternoon (with the ability to meet friends and shout from cubicle to cubicle), this was one of the amenities which was not moved over to the new Union. It had been agreed (or decreed) that when this building opened it would be run by SRC, and I was one of several students on its building committee. It was necessary to have a new Union but the new one never had the same clubby atmosphere of the old – though a bar was a welcome addition!

Generations of students remember affectionately some of the characters of the old Union, including "the Major" (already mentioned), Nellie the talkative waitress who took no backchat from unruly students, and "Whistlin' Rufus", a middle-aged "swinger" who used to haunt the twice-weekly dances in search of a young lady half his age.

The Hops themselves were an institution, with girls having to walk the gauntlet of wolf-whistles and stares in the McMordie Hall on their way through to the dance floor. In today's climate of political correctness such behaviour would be condemned as "ultra-sexist", but in the days of the old Union the girls merely took it in their stride, though a few habitually complained about the atmosphere of a "cattle-market". Whatever the advantages of the new Union, and there were many despite the unattractive exterior design, the old Union and particularly the Hops had a magic that lingers on for those who were privileged to be part of that experience.

Staff

While the university rightly devoted much time, effort and expense to providing the best possible facilities for its students and staff, the authorities never lost sight of Queen's central role which remained the gathering and dissemination of knowledge. In the quinquennium from 1968–73, a total of 91 new lectureships and a number of ancillary posts were established, as well as 13 new Chairs – ranging from Irish History and Social Anthropology to Ophthalmology and Cancer Studies, and Town and Country Planning. The university continued to attract such high-flyers as Professor Dan Bradley to the Chair of Pure and Applied Physics which he left in the early Seventies on his appointment to the Chair of Applied Optics at the Imperial College of Science and Technology, London, while Professor Phil Burke, another outstanding scientist, was appointed to the Chair of Mathematical Physics and continued to gain widespread recognition. Other staff who would make important contributions to Queen's, to the Province and to scholarship were appointed. They included Professor John Braidwood to a second Chair of English, Professor Bill Kirk who succeeded Estyn Evans in Geography, Professor Moiseiwitsch to a Personal Chair in Applied Mathematics, and Professor Peter Froggatt (who was to succeed Dr Vick as Vice-Chancellor) to a Personal Chair in Epidemiology.

It is important to stress that the Arts Faculty and other Faculties continued to make a significant contribution to scholarship, in a period when more emphasis was being placed on technology. It was fitting and timely, therefore, that Dr Vick – during his graduation address of 19 December 1973 – chose to congratulate Professor Lewis Warren, who had succeeded another distinguished historian Professor Michael Roberts as Head of the Department of Modern History, for the award of the Wolfson Prize for the best book on history published during the previous two years. This was Warren's *Henry II* which, like his earlier book on King John was internationally acclaimed. The academic legacy created by Ashby was still bearing fruit.

Chancellor Lord Ashby following Esquire Bedell Dr Richard Pink from the ceremony of his installation in the Sir William Whitla Hall in 1971. Behind Lord Ashby is the Vice-Chancellor, Dr Arthur Vick.

Happily, Eric Ashby was elected as Chancellor, succeeding Sir Tyrone Guthrie whom he praised as "a superb creative and imaginative Irishman." Ashby returned "in the disengaged spirit of a grandparent visiting a grandchild. I can just revel in enjoyment of the university and leave the Vice-Chancellor to do the worrying." As ever, his speeches were gems of philosophy and presentation, and as Chancellor he constantly challenged universities in general and Queen's in particular about the difference between knowledge and wisdom. In his first address as Chancellor, on 5 July 1971, he noted: "A university will teach us how to make a bomb or a church, how to increase food supplies or to diminish birth rates, how to write sermons or Communist pamphlets. But when we wish to know which of these choices to make, the university can give us only a technique for reflection, not the recipe for decision . . . So we have to find our own way into this other dimension of experience, the dimension requiring wisdom."

THE CHANGING FACE OF THE QUAD

The Quad underwent a dramatic change of appearance during the 60s and 70s, when the old Chemistry Laboratories and the Anatomy Building, photographed here in 1958, were demolished. The Social Sciences Building (centre, behind the trees) and the Administration Building (right) (photographed here in 1994) were erected in the Quad and opened in 1966 and 1975 respectively. Contributing to the new skyline is the Library Tower.

He told graduates: "Your degrees are not certificates in wisdom, but at least they should aid you to recognise wisdom when you see it . . . What this beautiful, ancient, troubled Province wants from the graduates of Queen's isn't only expertise. It is wisdom too." Two years later, on 3 July 1973, he returned to the same theme and noted, impishly, that:

> It is a commonplace that Fellows of the Royal Society are no better at making happy homes for their wives and children than plumbers are; and as for voting, it was a wise cynic in Cambridge who said that he would rather be governed by the first 100 persons whose names appear in the telephone directory than by the Faculties of the university. So although both personal and political decisions must take off from a firm runway of rational thought, accurate data and cool analysis, they must become airborne, as it were, on ideology, moral values and private or public conscience.

Throughout the decade, despite 'The Troubles' and other outside pressures, the scholarly output of the university continued unabated, with more than 1,000 publications each year ranging from a concerto for violin and orchestra to a Russian-English Dictionary, and from a paper on fish parasites of Ulster to one on noise from motorcycle engines. During this period also, much emphasis was placed on the university's technological outreach and particularly its interaction with industry, although it should be stressed that a Materials Testing Station associated with the Department of Civil Engineering had been operating successfully since 1945. Arthur Vick was keen on such links and after some 18 months of informal discussions with senior colleagues a University Industrial Liaison Committee was formed, and a Low Cost Automation Centre was opened on 16 October 1968. All these developments led to increasing co-operation with local industry and commerce, and culminated in the formation of QUBIS and QUBIS Ltd and the establishment of the Northern Ireland Technology Centre at Queen's, later on.

Ray McCullough, a technician in the Department of Mechanical Engineering, winning the 250cc class in the Ulster Grand Prix in 1976 with an engine designed by a research team from the department led by Dr (later Professor) Gordon Blair.

140

There were important academic developments in other areas of university life, including the establishment of a Faculty and Institute of Education and the development of an Institute of Professional Legal Studies. Incidentally, the initial groundwork for this latter and important development was laid in only one morning in a series of phone-calls between the Vice-Chancellor, the Permanent Secretary of the Department of Education and the Lord Chief Justice – a throw-back almost to the days of Ashby, and a reminder of the sheer intimacy of the Province and the good relationships between Queen's and the professions. Sir Arthur Vick repeatedly paid tribute to the quality and commitment of the staff at Queen's, but a great deal of the credit for the academic progress in this period is due to his quiet leadership. Much detailed work was effectively delegated to the Committee of Deans which Vick described more than once as a "first-class Committee." He noted: "Each Dean, of course, represented his Faculty but there was very little axe-grinding and the Committee had the interests of the whole university at heart."

Festival

The contribution of the Queen's Festival to the wider community was of great significance during the Troubles. Michael Emmerson resigned as Director in January 1971, and a new Director, David Laing, was appointed six months later. He staged two Festivals in 1972, but resigned in March 1973 to become Director of the Newcastle-upon-Tyne Festival. Michael Barnes, a senior lecturer in Modern History and Chairman of the Festival Sub-Committee, was appointed Acting Director for a November 1973 Festival. This was an artistic and financial success, with a surplus for the first time since 1969. Barnes was later confirmed as Festival Director and for over two decades the scope broadened enormously. With the financial help of the Arts

Michael Emmerson, the first Director of the Queen's Festival, with his wife, flautist Elena Duran.

Council for Northern Ireland it became a major highlight in the local Arts calendar and an event of national and international importance, being second only to Edinburgh in range and content. Michael Barnes, with the help of Deputy Directors Betty Craig and Robert Agnew and a willing team of helpers, made Festival not only an artistic and popular success while remaining solvent as a business operation, but also kept Festival as a beacon of cross-community co-operation and enjoyment despite the political and social upheaval and uncertainty created by the continuing violence and political deadlock.

The list of entertainers, from Emmerson's time and since, is literally too comprehensive to mention in detail but it ranged from Ulster's own Heather Harper, James Galway and Barry Douglas to the Leipzig Gewandhaus Orchestra with Kurt Masur and the Montreal Orchestra with Charles Dutoit, and not forgetting the talented Ulster Orchestra which played and still plays an important role each year. World-class performers have included pianists Nikolai Demidenko, Radu Lupu and Jorge Bolet, and from the theatre there were Siobhan McKenna, Laurence Olivier, Albert Finney and Ulsterman Colin Blakely (always a hit in his native Province), while Michael Palin performed his unique one-man show every two years, partly as a personal tribute to Barnes. Other regular visitors included the Royal Shakespeare Company, the National Theatre, the Abbey Theatre Dublin, and there were jazz greats including Buddy Tate, Benny Carter, Dizzy Gillespie, Zoot Sims and Art Farmer, and popular entertainers such as Ralph McTell, Barbara Dickson, and many others. Another regular guest was Seamus Heaney, paying his respects not only to Festival but to his Alma Mater and his native Province. Some of the best tributes came from those who took part – Sir Anthony Quayle, the actor, said: "I found Belfast, with all its hideous problems, stimulating and exhilarating. I never expected such humour, such a passion for life." Michael Palin noted: "I find in the city and people of Belfast an energy potential, a reserve of wit and intelligence and unaffected enthusiasm which I haven't found on the same scale anywhere else." Queen's has contributed much to Festival and thereby to the whole community, and in return the university has received a great deal of thanks and recognition, much of which is also due to Michael Barnes who so courageously stepped into the breach in 1973, and served with distinction until 1994.

Queen's Festival – two weeks plus of enjoyment to invigorate the mind and refresh the spirit during the grey November days.

Queen's Film Theatre, originally a converted lecture theatre with wooden seats, developed into one of the most advanced small auditoria in Ireland, with Italian "Cinemechanica' projectors, Dolby sound and high-quality French seating, 1994.

Changing times

The move from the old Students' Union to the new premises across the road from the Lanyon Building (symbolically a move to the 'front window' of the university) emphasised the role being played increasingly by students in running their own affairs. The earlier election of two Queensmen, Bill Savage and Geoff Martin, to the Presidency of the National Union of Students for successive terms, had underlined the calibre of the best student leaders from Belfast. Queen's has always been a rich training ground for budding politicians, some of whom in recent times have made their careers as professional politicians including Government Ministers and in one case as Premier of the Province of Nova Scotia in Canada. Dr John Savage, who graduated from Queen's with a medical degree in 1956, was President of the Students' Representative Council for two years. He was born in Newport, South Wales, where his father, an Ulsterman and also a Queen's medical graduate, was a family doctor. His mother, a nurse, was Welsh and John Savage still retains a strong Welsh accent. He and his family emigrated to Canada in 1966, and on May 25, 1993 he was elected Premier of Nova Scotia, the first Premier since Confederation who was not born in Canada.

Dr Savage looks back with affection to his time at Queen's:

Dr John Savage.

I was the first Roman Catholic President of the Students' Union, to my knowledge, though I don't think that people cared very much in those days whether you were a Roman Catholic or a Protestant when voting for the Students' Representative Council. Significantly, a large number of ex-service people were still around Queen's and this had a maturing influence on us. People had gone through a war when so many had been killed and we were looking for an era of tolerance and openness. More than anything, I learned a sense of tolerance, and there was a feeling that things did not have to be as they always had been. There was an openness to other views which some of the older generation, including my father, found strange but which we felt important. If it had continued it would have helped to bring about those changes which people in Northern Ireland now want.

John Savage also had time for sport at Queen's, and as a rugby 'Blue' he trained with the great Jack Kyle. "He led such a good, clean life that he did not have to train like the rest of us. He used to appear when we had done most of our training and he would trot around after us in his very distinctive 'jog'. Jack said he always kept himself for 'the game'. He was always in better shape than the rest of us!"

A decade later, another medical student detected a different political mood in the Province. Dr Lim Keng Yaik, a Malaysian, graduated in 1964 and returned home where he practised as a doctor for only three years before entering politics. At the age of 32 he became a Cabinet Minister in the Malaysian government with responsibility for around one million people who had been settled in 452 new villages as part of a counter-insurgency movement against Communism. Later, from 1986, he held the key post of Minister for Primary Industry, in a coalition government representing 11 parties in a country which has a complex ethnic and cultural mixture, including 52 per cent Malays, 35 per cent Chinese and 10 per cent Indians. He says:

> Queen's gave me a good, open education where students from developing countries not only received an excellent 'First World' education, but where we were also able to mix with Third World students, and I still stay in touch with friends from Ghana, Nigeria and the Seychelles. I was aware also that beneath the surface in Northern Ireland there were political tensions and that little or nothing was being done to bring the communities and the cultures together. My time at Queen's gave me an opportunity to observe divisions in a society which made me aware politically of the need for integration and sharing between the races and the cultures in my own country.

Dr Lim, however, also had time to sample the extra-curricular delights of Queen's. He played table-tennis and captained the basketball team, gaining a 'Blue', and he knew his way around the local watering holes. "I remember the 'Egg', the 'Botanic' and the 'Club Bar', and also dance halls like 'Romanos' and the 'Floral Hall' near the Cave Hill." He also recalls coming off the Liverpool ferry on his first day in Belfast and, with Malaysian friends, attending an international soccer match at Windsor Park that afternoon. In doing so he bears witness to the strong connections, indeed family links across the generations, between Queen's and Malaysia. Significantly, since 1972 there has been a Queen's graduate in successive Malaysian governments.

Dr Lim Keng Yaik

Nearer home, a number of former Queen's students also made their name in national and regional politics. Dr Brian Mawhinney, who graduated in Physics in the mid-Sixties, served as a Minister in the Conservative government of Margaret Thatcher with responsibility for education and other matters in Northern Ireland, and subsequently he became a Minister in the Department of Health and later Transport Secretary holding a Cabinet post, under the Premiership of John Major. Civil Engineering graduate John Taylor was the youngest Stormont Unionist MP when returned for the South Tyrone seat in 1965, and later he became Minister of State at Home Affairs and a Member of the European Parliament.

Austin Currie, who graduated in History and Politics in 1963 was the youngest MP ever returned to Stormont when elected, in the next year, as a Nationalist for East Tyrone. Currie was a leading civil rights campaigner and staged a much-publicised sit-in at a council house in Caledon to protest against its allocation to an unmarried Protestant woman. Currie became a founder-member of the Social Democratic and Labour Party, and was head of Housing, Planning and Local Government in the short-lived power-sharing Stormont Executive. He later became a member of the Fine Gael Party in the Irish Republic and represented Dublin West in the Dáil. A skilled politician, Currie learned much about the art of politics at Queen's, and he represented the new breed of articulate Roman Catholics who were not prepared to accept the largely passive role of many former Nationalist politicians. At Queen's he was a founder-member and later President of the New Ireland Society which had the stated objective "To bring together all those interested in the eventual unification of Ireland and in the political, social, economic and cultural advance of the country." He recalls:

Roger Young, who graduated with a Dentistry Degree in 1968, won 26 caps for Ireland from 1965 to 1971 and toured with the British Lions to Australia and New Zealand in 1966, and to South Africa two years later. He had the 'dubious' distinction of playing for Queen's 2nd XV while being picked for Ulster, and was promoted to the 1st XV in 1964 when given an Irish trial! Roger Young was one of the most distinguished of a long line of Queen's rugby players including fellow Irish internationals and British Lions Ken Kennedy and Dick Milliken.

When I came to Queen's it did not seem to cater for people like me. Like Stormont, all the traditions were Unionist – the portraits were of people like 'Lord' Londonderry, buildings were named after people like 'Sir' David Keir . . . I did not feel at home. One advantage was that I met more and more people from different backgrounds at Queen's. I took part in the Literific and I realised that I was just as good as people from other traditions, Queen's gave me confidence, and it was a most enjoyable period in my life, as well as a time of great personal growth. I owe a great deal to Queen's and to the educational system.

Queen's had long maintained a political tradition, and indeed the somewhat archaic practice of maintaining university constituencies at Stormont and earlier at Westminster elections was eventually abolished; but some of the budding student politicians of the Sixties were to make a particularly significant impact later (as constituency representatives) on the wider political scene.

Student power

In the Sixties there were also subtle but significant changes in the attitudes of students themselves. Sir Alwyn Williams, a Welshman who became a most distinguished servant of Queen's, had been appointed Professor of Geology in 1954. He later became Dean of Science, Secretary to the Academic Council and a Pro-Vice-Chancellor, and eventually Principal of the University of Glasgow. He recalls: "Some of my best students in the Fifties were scholars, but in the Sixties the good students were entrepreneurs as well. They became involved in student politics, or student magazine or newspapers, or other projects requiring initiative and drive, and they were prepared to 'think' outside their subjects." Alwyn and Joan Williams came to Queen's in 1954 when there was still a genteel quality to life in the Province and the university. Joan Williams recalls arriving off the Glasgow boat with the family and being met by Professor Estyn Evans and his wife who looked after them royally, and she remembers later in the day Professor Arthur Muskett "Coming up Richmond Park with an enormous silver salver bearing a tea service and the best china. That was our first example of Ulster hospitality!"

However, Sir Alwyn gradually began to note a change – particularly in the attitudes of some students in the Sixties: "There was a sense of disrespect which I fully understood, that students felt they had to strip the mystique from structured authority, but there was another foundation to this which I disapproved of, because it was becoming loutish in parts." Geoff Martin, President of the NUS from 1966–8, also saw a change: "There was a desire among students to enquire more deeply, and a greater degree of hostility to established values and institutions. Careerism, which was frowned upon, was also an element based on the need for people to succeed through their own qualities, and on the basis that 51 per cent of the vote actually meant something. There was no feeling of consensus – 51 per cent meant you won, 49 per cent meant that you lost."

Sir Alwyn and Lady Williams at home in Glasgow following his retirement as Principal of The University of Glasgow.

The Troubles

The late Sixties was a time of student protest in many countries. Pitched battles took place in Paris and elsewhere; there were sit-ins at British universities; and in Northern Ireland the Civil Rights movement gained momentum from 1968, in a campaign of protest and marches which students and a number of staff were ready to support. Back in the early Sixties Bowes Egan, Eamonn McCann, Michael Farrell and others were consistent and highly-articulate critics of the Establishment. And there were others, not all Nationalists, who felt that there were genuine grievances to be redressed. An important development took place in early October 1968 when some 3,000 marchers including a large number of Protestants and around 20 university staff converged on the City Hall and staged a three-hour peaceful sit-down protest. This in turn led to the formation of a political pressure group known as the People's Democracy which accepted a six-point reform programme broadly in line with Civil Rights demands. Its leaders included Bernadette Devlin (now McAliskey), a psychology student whose fiery advocacy of civil rights objectives made her a national figure in the British and Irish media. In 1969 she was elected to Westminster, the youngest woman ever to be elected there and the youngest M.P. for 50 years. Her maiden speech made headlines, as did her stance at the 'Battle of the Bogside' and her dramatic slapping of Home Secretary Reginald Maudling in the House of Commons later on. A major turning point in the civil rights campaign was the decision of the People's Democracy to embark on a four-day march from Belfast to Londonderry starting on New Year's Day 1969. The marchers were attacked by loyalists – at Burntollet – and the march considerably heightened an already tense situation. Although the People's Democracy had its origins in the Students' Union at Queen's, it eventually developed a life of its own beyond the university but it reinforced the suspicion in many people's minds that Queen's was a hotbed of Republican revolt.

The Vice-Chancellor and his senior colleagues were at pains to point out that only a minority of students were directly involved in political activities. There were disturbances around the campus and disorder among a small number of political societies as rivals tried to break up meetings. The general unrest inevitably affected students and staff as individuals and as citizens and a small number of undergraduates, particularly later on, became directly involved in and affected by the Troubles. But the university, despite a degree of polarisation, remained an oasis of relative calm in a deeply troubled landscape. Professor Alwyn Williams, in a keynote graduation speech on July 7, 1970 stated that Queen's was a microcosm of the Province: "Yet its ever-changing members seldom fail to acquire the art of living together, of tolerating one another's religious and political persuasions, and even of defending the right of anyone to hold opinions at cross-purposes with their own."

Dr Joan Holland, who graduated with a 'First' in English in 1968 and currently is on the full-time Faculty of the University of Toronto, recalls with affection the enriching environment of Queen's in the Sixties. "For many of us it was the first real opportunity for meeting with people from all around Northern Ireland with different viewpoints, different backgrounds and different visions of the future. I loved it." The second-year medical student she met at Queen's is now her husband, Dr Jack Holland, Professor and Chairman of Pediatrics at McMaster University, Hamilton, Ontario. "Queen's was terrific. Not only did I get a first class education but I learned a lot about life, about values and about myself. When I arrived I was fairly apolitical but university life changed that, and it was not possible to emerge from university in Belfast in 1969 without being influenced by the political wind of change." On looking back, Jack and Joan Holland see Queen's as "perhaps the only place in Northern Ireland in which there was a free exchange of thoughts and ideas across the political and religious divide and where lifelong friendships could be established despite the existence of the 'two solitudes' within the community."

At the height of the Troubles in 1972 the then Most Reverend Dr Cahal Daly (now Cardinal Daly), himself a Queen's graduate and a former Queen's lecturer, told a Social Study Conference at Falcarragh, Co Donegal: . . .

Few universities in these islands have so much to teach us in this time of explosion in third-level education as Queen's, about univer-

Andrea Jean Main (Née Leach), a Canadian student, typified the enrichment of Queen's life by overseas students. She came to Queen's in 1964 and majored in Psychology. She became the first President of Ogilvie Hall, but her education was interrupted by a serious car crash and after 18 months back in Canada she decided to return to Belfast to complete her degree. By this time she had married David Main, a teacher. They returned to Belfast in the early part of the Troubles, and their only child was born in November 1969.

During 25 years of marriage my husband and I have had constant friendly arguments about the 'better' Queen's (David graduated from Queen's University at Kingston, Ontario). Our son, David, after beginning his educational experiences at Queen's, Belfast, recently graduated from Mechanical Engineering at the 'lesser' Queen's at Kingston. I still wear my Queen's scarf and crest with every bit as much pride as I did while I was in Belfast. Occasionally people in Canada actually recognise these symbols and, when they do, it usually means a long discussion about my Alma Mater and the wonderful people in Ireland. Because of my experiences of going abroad for my education and because of the excellent education I received at Queen's, I feel I am able to guide the young people of today with the utmost ability and confidence.

149

sity expansion, administration, staff-student relations, student self-government and student participation in administration. Queen's University's success in maintaining through these bitter years of violence, not only a balanced but a courageously liberal stance, deserves to be studied by other sectors of society in Ireland, North and South.

The large majority of students and staff simply concentrated on the university's primary role of teaching and research. Queen's chose not to involve itself directly in the party political process. Lord Ashby reminded everyone that "universities stand for a wider commitment still – not solely to defend British or Irish values, but to defend human values." He also warned: "Universities which have corporately dabbled in politics have lost their influence and their liberties." Yet Queen's was no "ivory tower". For example Professor Williams courageously made a strong plea for integrated schooling, during a graduation speech on 6 July 1972: "In terms of its educational system . . . Northern Ireland . . . is the Alabama of Europe, and if desegregation of schools is accepted elsewhere in the world as one of the cures for racial discrimination and social injustice, it is time we started thinking about it here."

Life was not easy for student leaders in those years. Dr Ian Brick, President of SRC from 1967–8 and now a successful businessman in the United States, says:

> It was a very difficult time for student Presidents. It was an open secret that there were well-known trouble-makers from outside who were becoming involved in student bodies. The dilemma for any student President was to decide whether his or her main role was to serve the students and help them to obtain better facilities, or was there a wider role for a President in helping to 'improve' society. I believe that my role was to get the best deal possible for the student body. I learned a great many political skills in trying to maintain a balance – in many ways it was one of the best years of my life, and it gave me great experience.

Rory McShane, Student President from 1968–9, recalls that in the early part of the Civil Rights campaign in 1968, there was wide support from Protestant and Catholic students, but by early 1969 after the Unionist government had announced reforms, splits began to emerge among the student body. He reflects: "The trick was to hold people together and to try to prevent sectarian attitudes being taken. The situation slowly began to slip away during 1969 and the student body became like the community, quite polarised. I think it is a tragedy that Protestant support for Civil

THE PHYSICAL EDUCATION CENTRE

The swimming pool in the new Physical Educational Centre in the Botanical Gardens, 1986

When the Queen's Physical Education Centre was officially opened in December 1971, it was considered the finest university indoor sports complex within the British Isles. Its facilities include 10 squash courts, 2 handball courts, 3 modern weight-training and conditioning rooms, a large martial arts area, 12 badminton courts, main and minor hall areas, sauna, solaria, a mountain wall, aerobics rooms, a sprint track, lecture rooms, a laboratory, a swimming/diving pool complex, and a snackbar.

Its central purpose is to provide recreational and sporting opportunities for the university and the wider community, and some 7,000 visits to the PEC are recorded each week. Membership is also open to the public and their families, and approximately 3,000 individuals avail themselves of this opportunity each year. Facilities may also be reserved by outside bodies such as schools, colleges and businesses, and over 150 such organisations made use of the PEC last year. These figures contrast strongly with the early 1970's, when just 42 outside organisations used the PEC, and the number of visits by non-university users was one-third of what it is today.

The Physical Education Centre has a long history of promoting sport and exercise in the academic arena. The first lectures on sport were delivered in 1952 to Diploma of Education students by the First Director of Physical Education, Alistair MacDonald, who played a major role in planning the new PEC and transferring from the old and cramped gymnasium at Sans Souci Park. The original links with the Faculty of Education remain, with an expanded range of options on offer by PEC staff, including Master of Education, Diploma of Education and Post-Graduate Certificate of Education courses. Many of the cours-

es reflect a growing awareness of the relationship between activity and health, and supervised research degrees in this field are also offered to Ph.D. level in the Faculties of Education, Science and Medicine. Community and academia are brought together in the hugely popular "Fit for Life" courses, run in conjunction with the Institute of Continuing Education. Aimed mainly at the retired section of the community, these activity and educational classes regularly attract over 200 participants per week.

Two other aspects of the PEC are worthy of note. The Human Performance Laboratory, which provides a resource base for much of the teaching and academic activities of the PEC staff, is one of only nine such laboratories within the UK accredited by the British Association of Sports and Exercise Sciences. A considerable amount of fitness testing is carried out within the laboratory, as part of the "Bodycheck" health screening service, for elite athletes up to Olympic level and for the Irish Rugby squad. In addition, the PEC library provides the finest collection of sports books and journals on recreation and sports science to be found in the Province. A legacy of the National Centre for Documentation in Sport, originally housed in the PEC from 1969–72, it is a major resource for students and sports scholars alike.

The current director of the PEC, Dr Colin Boreham, shares with his predecessors (Mr Alistair MacDonald, 1949–77, and Mr Alan Nichols, 1977–89) the objective of promoting sport and recreation amongst the university community and the wider populace. The achievements, facilities and growing popularity of the PEC are evidence that this objective is being achieved.

Dr Colin Boreham, Director of Physical Education, joined Queen's in 1977 as a lecturer in the Department. For the next seven years he successfully managed to combine his career with his sporting interests, the latter culminating in selection as a Decathlete in the British squad for the 1984 Olympic Games in Los Angeles. After retiring from athletics, he completed his Ph.D. at Queens (1986) and was appointed Director in 1990. The photograph shows Colin Boreham in 1992, measuring the body composition of double Olympic Decathlon champion Daley Thompson in the Human Performance Laboratory in the Physical Education Centre.

Rights was largely lost and that there was no longer a broader base." McShane became a solicitor and businessman in and around Newry. "Queen's gave me an insight into dealing with government ministers. I began to realise how badly represented the community was by some of the people in authority and I also had the feeling that people at Queen's had a lot to give in terms of community representation. The old style Nationalist and Unionist politicians really weren't up to it."

One of the casualties of the early Troubles was Pro-Chancellor Lord MacDermott who was also Lord Chief Justice. He resigned from Senate following a meeting on February 25, 1969, when a motion put forward by him was defeated. He proposed that the buildings and other property of the university should not be used for any party political meeting or demonstration other than an indoor meeting held by an approved student society in accordance with Academic Council regulations. This was clearly an attempt to keep outsiders from taking decisions at meetings under the auspices of recognised Queen's societies. Later on, a general and somewhat stormy meeting of some 2,000 students on 22 April 1969 passed several resolutions, including one stating: "until further notice, participation in and attendance at meetings of a political nature in the Students' Union Building shall be restricted to those who are enrolled students or members of the university staff." Memorably, the students also resolved: ". . . never to allow religious differences to divide us. We call on all students to refrain from any militant activity in the present situation."

This set the tone for the attitude of the majority of the students. Despite the worst excesses of the Troubles there was an attitude at Queen's, as in the rest of the Province, of "business as usual." Sir Arthur Vick recalls the heroic spirit of staff and students during the Ulster Workers' Council strike in May 1974 which all but paralysed the Province:

> A lady who cleaned my office said to me 'I'm sorry that this area doesn't look as nice as it usually does, because the power goes off from time to time. I'm walking to the university now and I start an hour earlier.' That woman did everything she could to keep going, and that was typical of the whole place. The students, because there were no buses, got sleeping bags and camp beds, and during the exams they slept on the floor of the university. That gives some indication of the dedication and the loyalty of people during those troubled times.

With hindsight, it is remarkable how the university at large coped with the pressure of some of the worst years of the Troubles, as well as the increasing pressure of financial shortages and government cutbacks, and all the while with no diminution of standards or services to students and to the community. That achievement was summed up by Sir Alwyn Williams, reflecting later from his home in Glasgow on all that had happened: "We decided that the best way to serve the Province was to take in its sons and daughters from both sides of the divide and to give them the best possible education in the United Kingdom, and that's exactly what we did!"

7

Hurricanes of Change 1976–86

THE decade 1976–86, when Sir Peter Froggatt was Vice-Chancellor, turned out to be a period of major change for universities throughout the United Kingdom. Government concern with inflation and rising costs inevitably raised questions about the funding of third-level education, and hence the role of universities and their relationships with other institutions of higher education. Within Northern Ireland there was the added difficulty of developing relationships with the University of Ulster, which had been established in 1984 through the merger of the New University of Ulster at Coleraine and the Ulster Polytechnic. Queen's and the University of Ulster, like every university in the United Kingdom, had to compete for funds and for students. At the end of his Vice-Chancellorship, Sir Peter Froggatt told Senate in his final report for 1985–6 "all is now changed, changed utterly." The university world had indeed been turned upside down.

Management

In its search to make higher education more cost-effective, the government urged universities to re-organise their management structures to become more like business corporations. Doubts were expressed that universities could be managed in this way without having adverse affects on the cardinal principles of academic freedom and the integrity of scholarship.

SIR PETER FROGGATT

Sir Peter Froggatt, who was Vice-Chancellor from 1976 to 1986, was a former Dean of the Medical Faculty and the first Ulsterman to hold the post of Vice-Chancellor since Dr Hamilton who retired in 1923. Sir Peter told Senate in his first *Annual Report* for 1976–7: "Seldom can the financial situation have been so uncertain or so unpredictable . . . I must warn that the virtually uninterrupted expansion in numbers and resources which we have enjoyed over much of the past three decades is unlikely to continue, and in common with other universities we may have to operate from a reduced financial base."

His words proved prophetic, and there was much else besides a financial revolution, but Sir Peter presided over Queen's with characteristic good humour and stoicism. A man of many talents, he was a naturally gifted and often brilliant after-dinner speaker, and an outstanding golfer, who played for Ireland. He was, first and foremost, an academic with a solid background in Medicine. Born on 12 June 1928 in Glasgow, his family moved permanently to Belfast when he was 6 weeks old. He was educated at the Royal Belfast Academical Institution and the Royal School Armagh, and at Trinity College in Dublin where he graduated in Medicine. He took his Ph.D., and a Diploma in Public Health, at Queen's and after working in a Dublin hospital and later as Medical Officer at Short Bros and Harland in Belfast, he joined the Queen's staff in 1959. He was awarded a Personal Chair in Epidemiology in 1968 and during his career he produced many papers and articles, including studies on human genetics, occupational medicine, medical history and education, and epidemiology and smoking policies.

Few Vice-Chancellors, except perhaps his successor, had so many acute problems converging at the same time, but Froggatt kept his nerve and helped guide the university through a period of great upheaval. By his own admission he was more of an academic than a politician, but with hindsight he takes a not unjustified satisfaction in maintaining Queen's political neutrality during the Troubles, in fostering good relationships with students and minimising campus disruption, and in managing – with the help of senior financial officers – to keep the university financially "in the black" for the greater part of his period of office. He also had a good deal of success personally in making representations to the UGC, not least during the university's spirited and ultimately successful fight to save the Department of Architecture from closure. And he also found time to carry out the many and pressing social engagements of his office, very ably assisted by Lady Froggatt.

Sir Peter's main regret was the university's disappointing assessment in the first nation-wide research selectivity exercise.

Some would say that he was not ruthless enough in making radical changes earlier, though he has argued that the long period of deliberation by the Chilver Committee curtailed Queen's ability to plan and act strategically when this was badly needed.

One well-placed observer, not from Queen's, summed up Sir Peter's tenure as Vice-Chancellor in this way:

> During his first few years, Queen's, like many other universities, did not seem to see the need for great change which required an aggressive searching after greater excellence. After the trauma of the early Eighties, however, Peter gritted his teeth and did what had to be done. He can take credit for that, but nobody loved him for it. People found it expedient to blame him for the changes in circumstances which were none of his making. If Peter Froggatt had driven the university in 1978 in the way he was compelled to do in the mid-Eighties, he would have lost every friend and colleague in the place, because they would not have seen the need for it. No-one else saw what was coming.

The Bookshop at Queen's was established in 1958, moving to its present location at 91 University Road in 1972. It is wholly owned by the university and while concentrating on meeting the needs of the students and staff of Queen's, its' policy is also to provide a general bookshop for the wider community. The Bookshop has a particularly extensive Irish collection and regularly hosts book launches and signing sessions. Previous receptions for Seamus Heaney, Maeve Binchy, Michael Palin and Dr Garret FitzGerald have been highly successful. The Bookshop at Queen's has a stock range of some 50,000 general and academic books, a special order service and a mail order clientele in many parts of the world.

The United Kingdom universities and the UGC in the early Eighties made a pre-emptive strike and in 1984 established a working party under the distinguished industrialist Sir Alex Jarratt to enquire into university government and administrative (though not academic) efficiency. The Jarratt Report, published a year later, broadly encouraged universities to be more cost-effective, more efficient and to embrace the best corporate management methods. The UGC in effect had told universities to show evidence by October 1986 that they had moved significantly towards Jarratt or be penalised. Sir Peter told Senate in his final report that of the ten Jarratt recommendations aimed at universities, Queen's already practised seven, and that a working party had been established on what to do about the other three. Indeed in certain aspects Queen's had anticipated Jarratt. For example, the university's new Charter and Statutes (after a long and arduous review of Senate procedures with reference to the power and duties of Senate Committees, initiated in 1964), was given Royal Assent in July 1981, and made the governance of the university more relevant to the modern age. The university was also moving to a significantly different type of administration management, with the appointment of a Registrar, Mr Fred Smyth, in October 1985.

This system was meant to take much of the daily administrative pressure off the Vice-Chancellor, on the lines operating elsewhere in the United Kingdom. It must be said, however, that the previous system at Queen's had operated well in the hey-day of the University Secretary George Cowie and previous Vice-Chancellors, who had faced many problems but not to the same degree or intensity as in the Seventies and Eighties. The pressure on the university's management and the sheer pace of change was reflected in the vastly-increased bureaucracy and paperwork. During Ashby's time he had been involved in two major reports in 9 years, both to the University Grants Committee, whereas in 10 years Froggatt had been heavily involved in at least 40 to the UGC and other funding agencies and special commissions, some of which were very substantial. In the event, Fred Smyth's illness and untimely death in 1987 meant that the new system had insufficient time to prove itself, and the new administration under Dr Gordon Beveridge, the new Vice-Chancellor from August 1986, approached the matter differently.

Outreach

In other ways, the university responded to the increasing challenges to be even more outgoing in its relationships with the local community and with the world at large. A new part-time general degree was established through the Department of Extra-Mural Studies, now transformed into the larger and better-funded Institute of Continuing Education. Facilities were made available for a part-time Master's degree, and experiments were made with a modular system, designed to facilitate a wider choice within subjects, as well as the possibility of easier transfer to other institutions. It was all part of a growing awareness by Queen's and by universities in general of the need to remain competitive in a consumer-led society.

Other important developments in the mid-Eighties included the establishment of QUBIS and QUBIS Ltd to extend further the university's important links with industry, through the already-established Northern Ireland Materials Testing Station, the Northern Ireland Automation Centre and the Wolfson Signal Processing Unit. The role of QUBIS, (Queen's University Business and Industrial Services), established in 1983, was to liaise more closely with industry, and enable local firms to avail themselves of the university's considerable expertise in science and technology. QUBIS Limited, formed in 1984, has a mandate to identify research with commercial potential and to form equity-sharing joint ventures to exploit it to mutual advantage. A strong supporter of both was Professor Sir Colin Campbell, then a Pro-Vice-Chancellor and later Vice-Chancellor of the University of Nottingham, from 1988. Campbell, a dynamic and youthful-looking academic lawyer with a sharp political and entrepreneurial brain was closely involved with a number of outreach developments, including the establishment later on of a new and professionally-staffed University Information Office to develop further the interface with the public. During this period also, the university set up a Working Party under the distinguished academic, industrialist and mechanical engineer Sir Joseph Pope, a former Vice-Chancellor of Aston University. Sir Joseph had been an assistant lecturer in Engineering at Queen's from 1938–44 at a time when the Belfast College of Technology had provided most of the teaching facilities in the department. This led to the establishment later on of the highly successful Northern Ireland Technology Centre at Queen's. Sir Peter recalls: "The university

SIR BERNARD CROSSLAND

Professor Sir Bernard Crossland was appointed to the Chair of Mechanical Engineering in 1959. He recalls: "As soon as I accepted the Chair, the Vice-Chancellor Sir Eric Ashby announced his resignation. Perhaps he realised that his luck had at last run out, after a most distinguished series of appointments!" On the contrary, Bernard Crossland has made his mark as one of the outstanding engineers in the history of Queen's and as a loyal servant of the university.

Born in London in 1923 of Yorkshire stock, he was educated at Canterbury and after working as an apprentice in Rolls Royce he graduated from the University of Nottingham. He returned to Rolls Royce and then lectured at Bristol University before coming to Belfast. At Queen's he was Head of Mechanical and Industrial Engineering 1959–82, Dean of Engineering 1964–7, Pro-Vice-Chancellor 1978–82 and Research Professor, 1982–4

Bernard Crossland earned great personal credit and brought recognition to Queen's through his local, national and international service to engineering and to the wider community. He was awarded nine honorary degrees, and his distinctions included a Knighthood in 1990. His many academic distinctions included the George Stephenson Prize and Hawksley Gold Medal of the Institution of Mechanical Engineers, the Kelvin Gold Medal of the Institution of Civil Engineers, Honorary Fellowships of the Welding Institute and the Institution of Engineers of Ireland, and Vice-President of the Royal Society 1984–6.

He retired in 1984, but subsequently he maintained his high reputation as a consultant. In 1993 he was appointed Chairman of the public hearing and investigation into a major accident at Bilsthorpe Colliery in which three people died, and three were trapped and later rescued. At the age of 70, he was still a familiar figure around the campus, where he moved with the air of a man who still had much to do.

Pictured above; Professor Sir Bernard Crossland (left) at work following the Bilsthorpe Colliery accident in 1994.

was very much aware of what was happening nationally and in many ways we anticipated what turned out to be a Jarratt system, as well as the need to reach out even more to industry and to make ourselves more accountable to society in general."

Finance

The decade from 1976–7 to 1985–6 was a period of financial difficulty for the UK university sector as a whole. The quinquennial system of government funding, which for many years had provided a stable basis for long-term planning and development, was progressively abandoned. The aim of government was increasingly to reduce in real terms the level of resources for higher education and, within the reduced total, to fund individual institutions more selectively, favouring universities judged to have a record of achievement in high-quality research. For 90 years prior to the mid 1970's, the Committee on Grants to University Colleges in Great Britain and its successor body the University Grants Committee (which became an adviser to the Department of Education for Northern Ireland on funding Higher Education in the Province), had operated a quinquennial system of funding. Under this arrangement, and with Treasury approval, grants to universities were set for a period of five years, allowance being made for inflation each year. This system of forward planning began to disintegrate in 1977. In May of that year the grant for Queen's for the year beginning 1 August 1977 was announced, albeit hedged around with uncertainities, and with no information about future years.

In the following year the grant announcement was received only 10 days before the start of the financial year, again with no details of funding in the longer term. For 1979–80 things were even worse. On 14 July 1979 the grant was announced, but only for an 8 month period coinciding with the government's fiscal year ending 31 March 1980. This was the nadir of the system of forward planning, reducing the financial horizon from 5 years to a mere 8 months. During 1979–80 there had been an attempt by the UGC to re-establish some form of future planning based on a quadrennium but this was frustrated by plans for cost-cutting measures introduced by a newly-elected government and by the publication of UGC planning models for 1981–2 which held out the prospect of three possible financial scenarios for that year – 2% enhancement of grant, level funding, or a reduction of 5%. The combined effect of short-term funding and advance notice that future

STEWART PARKER

Stewart Parker, who graduated from Queen's with an honours degree in English in 1963, was awarded an MA in 1966, and became active in a group of young writers which included Seamus Heaney and Bernard MacLaverty. His first stage play, 'Spokesong', won him the Evening Standard Award as the most promising playwright of 1976. Later, his television drama, 'I'm a Dreamer, Montreal', won the Ewart Biggs Memorial Prize. His other critically-acclaimed plays include 'Catchpenny Twist', 'Northern Star', and 'Pentecost'. His work also includes an original cinema screenplay, 'Blue Money'. Stewart Parker died in London in 1988.

funding might be cut or increased or maintained at existing levels, left universities without the means to formulate reliable plans for the future.

Although the quinquennial system of funding began to disintegrate in 1977, the serious erosion of resources for higher education did not begin in earnest until 1980. Reflecting government policy, the Chairman of the UGC wrote to Vice-Chancel-lors on 30 December 1980 on the subject of the readjustment of the university system to changing resources and demands. The letter indicated that there was to be a 3½% volume cut in grant for 1981–2, plus another 2½% loss of income from other sources, a total of 6%. The government's philosophy on funding the universities was enunciated by Mr Mark Carlisle MP on 6 January 1981 when he stated: "I do not accept that a relatively small decline in resources must be precisely matched by a fall in provision. Human ingenuity is such that one is never tied to a fixed mix of buildings, staff, equipment and other materials to produce a given output of qualified students". The "small decline in resources" he proposed was a reduction of some 11 to 15% in real terms over 3 years. The Chairman of the Committee of Vice-Chancellors and Principals viewed the position somewhat differently and was prompted to issue a press release stating that "the government now intends to run down the British university system by about one-eighth over the next two years". By 1983–84 it was possible for CVCP to calculate that there had been a fall of some 12% in the nett general recurrent income of GB universities since 1979–80. To this general reduction in funding for all universities was now to be added a further difficulty for many institutions. In 1985 the UGC announced that selective funding would be introduced for the research component of recurrent grant. This was to

Following Mary Peters win of a gold medal at the 1972 Olympics in Munich, the athletics track at Queen's Malone Playing Fields was developed to international standards as the Mary Peters Track. The funds were provided through a public appeal in the Belfast Telegraph together with a government contribution. Subsequently many world-class athletes have appeared at the track including Mary Peters herself, Linford Christie, Colin Jackson, Steve Ovett, Butch Reynolds, Tessa Sanderson and (pictured here) Zola Budd.

PROFESSOR FRANK PANTRIDGE

Professor Frank Pantridge, a Queen's graduate and an eminent physician and cardiologist, created a place in medical history by the development of the mobile coronary care unit. He realised that speed was crucial in saving the lives of many heart attack victims, and was the first to develop the idea of bringing hospital treatment speedily to the patient. In 1965 Pantridge and Dr John Geddes (another Queen's graduate), at the Royal Victoria Hospital in Belfast, adapted a defibrillator – a machine that delivers an electric shock to the stricken heart and 're-sets' its normal rhythm – by hooking it up to two car batteries and manhandling it into an old ambulance. This became the world's first 'portable' defibrillator. Descendents of that bulky prototype are now used hundreds, if not thousands, of times daily throughout the world. Frank Pantridge has won many honours, including the Military Cross in the field.

become one of the most serious financial problems facing the new Vice-Chancellor Dr Gordon Beveridge, and is a challenge which continues to this day.

Throughout the decade up to 1985–6, Queen's managed its financial affairs with perhaps less need for draconian measures than any other university. There were a number of reasons for this, not least of which was the fact that Queen's entered the decade in an exceptionally healthy financial state. In his tenth and final *Annual Report* to Senate in December 1986, Sir Peter Froggatt explained that the cuts in grant which the university was to suffer from 1986–7 onwards were in part to correct the generous level of funding achieved in previous years. He paid tribute to the negotiating skills of his predecessor, Sir Arthur Vick, who had, during the 1968–73 quinquennium, "managed with DENI help to procure for Queen's one of the highest grants per student in the Kingdom". This generous baseline funding went a great way to ameliorate the effects of cuts in the period up to 1985–86. Sir Peter also acknowledged that the heaviest burden of the cuts would fall upon his successor, Dr Beveridge. In his final *Annual Report* Sir Peter stated:

> No matter how viewed, the outlook is bleak so long as the formula-funding is pursued; we may have to save something like £2m per annum for the next four years on recurrent account to balance our income and expenditure account, that is anything up to £8m on . . . [ultimate annual] base-line expenditure, an horrendous and unimaginable prospect. Money has been getting tighter since 1982, and this last year has been a particularly difficult one, but the reductions in grant now proposed represent a quantum leap into territory which we (and others) have not explored.

Sir Peter's words were to prove well-founded.

The cuts in funding for Queen's which occurred from 1981–82 to 1985–6 (5% in 1981–2, 2½% in 1982–3 and 2% in each of the following years) were dealt with pragmatically through a judicious mixture of applying the surplus funding which had been negotiated in earlier years by Sir Arthur Vick and then by applying a moratorium on the filling of vacant posts. By these means the university was able to achieve a small surplus of less than £0.5m in five of the years in the decade with a broadly corresponding deficit in the remaining five years. Overall, the nett financial result for the decade was a modest surplus of £0.2m on a total general income of £269m for the ten-year period.

PROFESSOR SIR DAVID BATES FRS

Professor Sir David Bates, who died in 1994, was one of the greatest scientists in the history of Queen's and one of the most distinguished of his generation, nationally and internationally. Born in Omagh, Co Tyrone in 1916, he went to Queen's in 1934 and graduated with a B.Sc. in 1937, and was awarded an M.Sc. the following year. At Queen's he developed a lifelong interest in Mathematical Physics under another outstanding scientist Sir Harrie Massey, whom he followed to University College London in 1938 as his research student. After the outbreak of the Second World War he went with Massey to the Admiralty Research Department and the Mine Design Department, where they successfully developed counter-measures to protect ships from magnetic mines – thus contributing significantly to a successful conclusion of the war.

In 1951 David Bates was appointed to the Chair of Applied Mathematics at Queen's, and for the next 31 years he built up an internationally-renowned Department which brought him great personal recognition and corresponding credit to Queen's. His honours included election to the Royal Society in 1955 at the age of 39, membership and a Vice-Presidency of the Royal Irish Academy, Honorary Foreign Member of the American Academy of Arts and Sciences, Foreign Associate of the American National Academy of Science, and no fewer than nine honorary degrees. In 1978 he was awarded a Knighthood for his contribution to Science and Education, and in 1990 he was nominated for the Nobel Prize in Physics.

He also was awarded the Hughes Medal by the Royal Society, the Chree Medal by the Insitute of Physics, the Gold Medal of the Royal Astronomical Society, the Fleming Medal of the American Geophysical Union and the Annual eponymous medal established by the European Geophysical Union. He was also Editor-in-Chief of Planetary and Space Science from 1962–1992. In 1993 he was awarded Honorary Membership of the European Geophysical Society.

Highly-respected and well-liked by his colleagues and his students, he was no 'ivory-tower' academic. He took a deep and keen interest in current affairs and the continued violence in his native Province pained him deeply. He was a founder-member of the Alliance Party and later Vice-President. Apart from his profound impact on international science, David Bates' lasting contribution to Queen's was his decision to remain at his old university throughout a long career when, literally, he could have gone anywhere in the world. His contribution was recognised and his memory perpetuated by the naming of the David Bates Building in his honour.

The Chilver Report

One of the most significant developments in higher education in Northern Ireland in the late Seventies and early Eighties was the publication of the Chilver Report. It was clear that the New University of Ulster was not attracting students at the rate envisaged by the Lockwood Committee in the mid-Sixties, so the government in 1978 set up a review group under Sir Henry Chilver, Vice-Chancellor of the Cranfield Institute of Technology. An interim report on teacher education and training was issued in 1980, and in 1982 the final report entitled *The Future of Higher Education in Northern Ireland* was published. Unusually, however, it was accompanied by a separately-published government statement which effectively overthrew the final report. The statement outlined the way in which the government intended to implement its own radical plan for higher education in the Province. Instead of shoring up the NUU, which Chilver had broadly suggested, the government in essence announced the merger of the ailing university with the thriving Ulster Polytechnic in a kind of 'Poly-Varsity' which became the University of Ulster, including the campus at Magee University College in Londonderry. It opened in 1984. Queen's was left to continue its mission as a highly-regarded traditional university with a long-established reputation within the United Kingdom network.

Partly because the Queen's response to Lockwood had been so poor, the university submitted no fewer than five formal written submissions to Chilver and two informal ones, involving a total of more than 300 pages with over 100 accompanying tables. Sir Peter Froggatt, reflecting several years later, wrote:

> In retrospect, the *recommendations* of the Chilver Committee, most of which were ignored, were far less damaging to Queen's than was the Committee's *existence* which effectively curtailed our ability to plan and act strategically at the very time when events required it. The Lockwood scenario was dead almost before its institutions were born; Chilver's advice was ignored, the time spent being cruelly wasted at least for Queen's. We have not done well out of "expert" committees!
>
> "Higher education in Northern Ireland: a Queen's University perspective" in R.D.Osborne, R.J. Cormack and R.C. Miller (eds), *Education and policy in Northern Ireland* (Belfast, 1987), p.224

There was much speculation by some, post-Chilver, about what might have been. The question is still mooted as to why the Government created yet another university when it already had

SIR ROWLAND WRIGHT

Sir Rowland Wright, who was elected Chancellor in 1984, followed a line of distinguished former Chancellors who, since the end of the Second World War, came from vastly different backgrounds – including an outstanding soldier, a world-famous theatre director, and an academic and educationalist of national and international prominence. Sir Rowland, a distinguished industrialist, came to Queen's at a time when universities were being required by government to take a more businesslike approach, and his knowledge of industrial affairs was a great asset to the university.

As a former Chairman of ICI and of Blue Circle Industries, he held several directorships of renowned companies, and his wealth of experience and contacts proved invaluable, not least as a member of the University's Development Appeal.

Sir Rowland had a particular interest in Queen's. He was an Honorary Graduate and a close friend of Pro-Chancellor Robert Hamilton, and his son John graduated from the University with a BA (Hons) degree in Geography in 1966. Sir Rowland was a charming and friendly man, and his visits to Belfast, with Lady Wright, were appreciated by everyone at Queen's and by friends of the University. He was a big man who cut an impressive figure in his Chancellor's robes at Graduation, where his speech showed evidence of careful preparation. At receptions, he always appreciated a special tipple of his favourite Scotch, supplied by an understanding member of the catering department.

Sadly, the latter part of his time as Chancellor was dogged by illness, and he died in 1991 at the age of 75.

HOCKEY CIRCLES

Terry Gregg, who graduated with a degree in Dentistry in 1976, was an outstanding hockey player and coach who played a major role in Irish hockey. He played for Ireland during his first year at Queen's, and went on to win 103 Irish Caps. He was Captain of the Irish team from 1975–79, and Vice-Captain of the Great Britain team from 1974–80. He did not compete in the Montreal and Moscow Olympics, due to politics, but played in every game for Great Britain from 1972–80, winning 42 Caps. He did play in the Munich Olympics, when the Great Britain team came sixth.

Terry Gregg captained Queen's in 1972, when the university team won the Irish Senior Cup for the first time in 16 years. He finally stopped playing for Queen's in 1974 to join Belfast YMCA, but a serious viral illness caused his early retirement at 29. However, he then began a remarkably successful career in coaching. Under his guidance, Team Volkswagen Indoor team won the All-Ireland Championship seven years in a row, and he also coached the Ireland Indoor Team from 1983–86. He then switched to outdoor hockey with equal success and coached Lisnagarvey to six Irish Senior Cup wins in a row. He made yet another switch and successfully coached the Ireland Ladies team which took part in the 1994 World Cup Finals in Dublin.

Terry Gregg (right).

The Queen's club produced a long line of internationals, including Billy McConnell who played for the Great Britain team which won a Bronze medal in the Los Angeles Olympics. He won 50 caps for Great Britain and, in mid-1994, he still held the record number of Irish caps, with a total of 135. Jimmy Kirkwood, another Queen's man, won a Gold Medal in the Seoul Olympics with the Great Britain team. In all, he won 40 Great Britain and 114 Irish caps.

Women's hockey also flourished at the university, and the Queen's club produced a number of outstanding players. In the Fifties they included Thelma and Moira Hopkins (See Chapter Four), and more recently there were a number of Irish internationals including Margaret Hunter (nee Brown), Adele Sloan (nee Scott), Joan Menown who also played for Great Britain, and Margaret Gleghorne who played for Great Britain and captained the Irish team.

one of the best polytechnics in the United Kingdom. Others ask why Queen's and NUU were not merged. Even with hindsight there are no definitive answers. It would appear, however, that the government having decided against creating one large university by choosing not to expand Queen's in the period post-Lockwood was reluctant to move down that road again. In the early Eighties there was a significant movement towards more technology-based universities, and in Northern Ireland this seemed to be an ideal opportunity to create a radically new breed by merging a traditional institution with a polytechnic. However, there was an added obligation on the government to ensure that the new institution worked, in contrast to the Lockwood blueprint and the NUU which clearly had not. Froggatt reflected the views of many when, with characteristic forthrightness, he spoke of "the certainty of the new institution receiving 'favoured child' treatment simply because government, denied any scapegoat since it acted on its own advice, could not allow it to be yet another expensive failure, though it seemingly could tolerate it being an expensive success!" (op. cit., p. 225) Government sources, naturally, deny this scenario, but the folk-memory lingers on.

A Civil Service view from someone close to the deliberations at the time suggested that it would have been difficult for Queen's to alter the course of events, at that stage.

> No one was indicating that there was anything "wrong" with Queen's. They were saying that here is an excellent institution doing a very good job, but what are we going to achieve simply by making it bigger? It had grown significantly and it was still a manageable size. We originally had set up two universities and had chosen not to expand Queen's, so by simply enlarging it were we not marching backwards rather than marching to the future?

The die was cast and the Province was to have two universities each conceived by government as having a different role. The challenge remained to harmonise relations and policies between the two institutions, and a Northern Ireland Working Party was established in 1983 to encourage "complementarity" – not always easy for two hungry and rather large fish in a diminishing pool of resources.

In retrospect, however, it would appear that the major crossroads on higher education in Northern Ireland occurred in the Sixties when the Lockwood committee was deliberating. In the long-term, however, it can hardly be argued that Queen's, or the Province, has suffered unduly in the provision of higher education. Sir Peter Froggatt makes the point: "A factor rarely mentioned is that one of the reasons why the NUU was a failure was that Queen's was a success, certainly in the eyes of school-leavers. Some 25 years on, despite all the Troubles, Queen's is still highly-regarded for its educational record." A contemporary, with an inside view of the Chilver Committee's deliberations, agrees.

> I think that Queen's has done well since Chilver. It has adapted to the increased demand for higher education, it has increased access and developed part-time degrees, and it is still regarded as the 'main' Northern Ireland university. If Queen's had shown the same openness and initiative before Chilver that it did afterwards, the outcome of the Report might have been very different.

The Troubles

Inevitably, the Troubles impinged upon the university, as they did on almost every aspect of life in Northern Ireland. The physical fabric of the university was damaged by a bomb in the Computer Centre, and by a fire which was started by incendaries in the Great Hall on 5 May 1981 at the height of the Provisional IRA hunger-strikes. Fortunately, damage to the building was limited due to the vigilance of a student who raised the alarm, and the prompt action of the Queen's security staff, the Fire Brigade and the Army. There was some scorching of the walls and ceiling, and the portrait of R.M. Henry was damaged beyond repair. In keeping with the 'Business as usual' spirit of the Province, the Great Hall was open next day to provide a mid-day meal. During the early Eighties two staff members – Miriam Daly, from the Department of Economic &

The university's historic Great Hall was damaged by fire in 1981. Although there was no structural damage, one side of the Great Hall was a picture of devastation with panelling, curtains and paintings destroyed and smoke damage in evidence on the roof. Skilled restoration work has left no trace of the fire. The oil portrait of R.M. Henry, which was totally destroyed, was replaced by its photograph, the unveiling being performed by Mrs Kathleen Henry, R.M. Henry's widow.

ON THE WATER

The Queen's University of Belfast Boat Club was founded in 1931, due to the work of four 'founder' members:– J.W. Rigby, D.B. McNeill, F. Maunsell and J.F. Doggart. Towards the end of January 1932 the newly-formed Club signed an agreement with Belfast Commercial Boat Club (BCBC) for accommodation that was its home until 1951. Membership rose from a dozen or so in 1932 to a maximum of 65 by 1937. The Club competed regularly in regattas in Ireland and Scotland. Rowing was maintained at a low level throughout the war years; however, after the war the Club really started making an impact, and under the vigorous Captaincy of F.J. Boyle (1944/45) it won the Wylie Cup (Irish University Championships) for the first time. Success continued under H.F. Jackson in 1945/46 when the Club retained the Wylie Cup, and next year went to Henley Royal Regatta for the first time. In 1947 a Queen's four won the Metropolitan Challenge Cup (the 'Blue Riband' of Irish Four rowing) and many other trophies. In 1951 the university provided a "temporary wooden structure" on the site of the present Club House, which was officially opened during the Captaincy of John Gorman, when the Club went to the Putney Head of the River and came 13th.

The Men's Rowing Eight competing in the final of the Ladies' Plate at Henley Royal Regatta in 1976.

1952–1967

From their newly-established Club House, Queen's came to be a dominant force in Irish Rowing and a major Club in the university. Under John Alexander's captaincy Queen's won the Wylie Cup and the Irish Senior Championship (the 'Big Pot') in 1952. The Club won the 'Big Pot' five more times – in 1953, 1956, 1957, 1959 and 1962. The victory in 1957 was remarkable because it was won by a 'second' Queen's crew, as the Championships were held during Henley Royal Regatta. In 1958 the Queen's Senior Crew represented Northern Ireland in the Commonwealth Games Regatta instead of attending the National Championships. That crew reached the third round of the Thames Cup at Henley, as did the crew in 1959. Other divisions of the Club did well, as the splendid record in the Wylie Cup shows: the only years Queen's failed to win the Cup were 1958, 1959, 1961 and 1966. Queen's Junior (now Intermediate) crews won the National Championships in 1958, 1960 and 1962 and the Maiden (Novice) crews in 1953, 1955, 1961, 1963 and 1969. Membership of the Club was usually about 100 at the beginning of each year, and frequently 4 or 5 'eights' rowed right through the season from October to July. The social side of life was not neglected, and the Boat Club Dinner and Formal Dance were among the highlights of the Queen's year. In 1967 Queen's held a regatta on the Lagan; this became an annual event and eventually transferred to its present venue at Castlewellan Lake.

1968–1983

Despite the success which Queen's had enjoyed for the previous fifteen years, there were developments in Irish Rowing which left these years rather bereft of trophies for the Club. And yet there were still great efforts made at Queen's, such as in 1976 when the Senior crew reached the final of the Ladies Plate at Henley. In 1976 also, the "temporary wooden structure" was at last replaced by a proper Club House. J.W.F. Boyd was Captain when the Club's new home was opened and three 'eights' made up of past Captains and members rowed a short race to celebrate the occasion. After graduating many members rowed for Lady Victoria Boat Club or the newly founded Belfast Rowing Club (BRC). John Armstrong, Captain 1982/83, won both Open and Lightweight National Sculling Championships and went on to win the titles many more times for Lady Victoria, most recently in the Lightweight Championships in 1993.

Ladies' Boat Club

Perhaps the most significant development of these years, however, was the formation of the Queen's Ladies Boat Club in 1969. The first Captain was Lydia McKinnon and the Club began with just four members. Over the last 25 years it has developed into one of the most vibrant and successful women's sports clubs in Queen's. After initial embarrassment, the ladies used a caravan parked at the back of the "temporary wooden structure" until 1976, when they obtained a share in the new boathouse. Crews competed at local, national and international level, notching up an impressive array of wins in the Irish University Championship (in 1983 for the first time), the Irish Championship (in 1978, 1980, 1981, and 1982), the Home Countries Internationals in 1977, and European and American regattas. The Club has represented Irish women's rowing at the highest levels. Cathy Buchanan, who helped QUBLBC to win in 1980 and 1981, went on to win 10 Irish Championships, mainly for Belfast Rowing Club. The strength of the Club's rowing is matched by a strong sense of its own history, reflected in its traditions of an annual dinner attended by present and past members, an annual rowing challenge between novices and 'old girls' and in the formation in 1992 of a graduates' club to maintain links with the past and help the Club move forward into the 21st century.

1984–1994

Women's rowing has remained strong over the last decade with a good record of wins in the University Championships in 1984, 1985, 1986, 1987 and 1990. Both women's and men's Club have had to come to terms with the fact that even Novice Championships were being won by crews which had been together for two

The Queen's Ladies Senior Four who were selected to represent Ireland in 1977 at the Home Countries International on the Serpentine in London and became the first Irish team to win the championship.

or even three years. Both clubs therefore concentrated on building up strong Novice and Intermediate divisions, and resigned themselves to the fact that gifted individuals would be lost to the Irish National Squad or Belfast Rowing Club which had a strong Senior section. For the men, success came with a win in the Novice Eights Championship in 1990 (an emotional occasion for old supporters who had last seen this event won by Queen's in 1967!) and the Intermediate Fours in 1991. In 1993 the Queen's crew reached the third round of the Temple Challenge Cup at Henley. Both men's and women's Clubs will continue to attract many recruits to the sport and will be able to hold their own in the Novice and Intermediate divisions. There are now many Queen's men and women of past years around to give encouragement, including Dr D.B. McNeill, one of the 1931 founding members, who in mid-1994 was still taking a keen interest in Queen's rowing.

Social History, and Edgar Graham, a law lecturer and noted Unionist politician, were shot dead. There were attacks also on students; an off-duty policeman was shot while sitting his finals in 1982, but recovered to graduate the same year with an honours law degree, while another student was shot dead in a separate incident. There was also an attack on the Lord Chief Justice, Lord Lowry, who was visiting the campus, and a member of staff was injured.

Such horrors and personal tragedies scarred many families in the Province, but Queen's as an institution continued to face the challenge of determining its role in a deeply-divided society. As always, there were differing views – some felt that Queen's should become more involved, while others argued the opposite. Peter Froggatt maintained the clear line, in the tradition of the Vick era, that "Universities who play politics can have politics played on them." He argued that a search for consensus on any large social or political issue would end in failure, and to try to force through decisions on majority votes, perhaps narrow ones, could split the University. He continued: "Vigorous debate on the distribution of power and wealth, the rights and wrongs of a political issue, even on the sovereignty of a country, should have no place in the insititutional university, only in relevant parts of the academic university such as seminars in economic or political theory." (In a lecture *The university as an instrument of social change: a dangerous or desirable concept"* to the Conference of Queen's university and schools, 14 May, 1977).

Froggatt eschewed the creation of new high-profile Departments of Peace Resolution or Conflict Study, which he thought would be gimmicky, and instead steered financial resources to Departments such as Sociology, Political Science, Economic & Social History and other important areas where research was contributing to an understanding of what was happening in the world at large. In that sense it could be argued that Queen's academics have made a more significant and lasting contribution to the ultimate resolution of the conflict than by taking sides in a still complex and volatile situation. Queen's also administered large grants from the Ford Foundation for Irish institutions of higher education working broadly in the field of conflict resolution. Like Sir Arthur Vick in his day, it is to Sir Peter Froggatt's credit that, by and large, he steered a steady course through a sea of troubles.

Behind the headlines

Behind the headlines, life went on as normally as possible, though even that "normality" was qualified. For example, on Rag Day – March 3rd 1978 – a soldier and a civilian woman searcher were murdered near the centre of Belfast by terrorists masquerading as students in Rag Day disguise. Later on most of the student body and many staff – some 7,500 in all – walked in silent protest to the centre of the city where the student President spoke briefly, and returned to Queen's. The Vice-Chancellor noted in his *Annual Report* for 1977–8 that the protest had attracted "very wide admiration, sympathy and respect, and universal support: as stirring and moving an event as that which prompted it was sordid and squalid".

Students, like members of staff, faced many other difficulties in these years, not least with finance. The Students' Union campaigned against the inadequacy of student grants, the cut-back to three-year instead of four-year degrees, the need for more student accommodation, greater student representation in the governance of the university, and other matters. A re-constituted Academic Board, established in Vick's time, allowed for greater student participation in decision-taking, though still below their aspirations. The Students' Union was also granted a second seat on Senate, a not insignificant development in that students could then produce a seconder for any proposal they might wish to put to the governing body. Despite the difficulties facing students and the university authorities, and some potentially ugly confrontations between students during the hunger-strike crisis, Queen's largely managed to avoid the massive disruptions and student sit-ins which virtually paralysed some other universities in the United Kingdom. Sir Peter Froggatt had the ability to maintain good personal relationships with student leaders, whatever the problems, and he was made an honorary life member of the Students' Union. This privilege allowed him the right to drink in the main students' bar and to play snooker, if he so wished!

Tom Lynch, President of the Students' Union 1978–80.

Tom Lynch, who was President of the Students' Union for two terms, from 1978–80, graduated in 1978 with an Honours Degree in Economics and is now Chief Financial Officer with a leading Irish company based in Athlone. He recalls:

> One of the great problems facing the Union, like the university itself, was keeping a balance amid all the conflicting pressure at a

time of great community breakdown in Northern Ireland. It was also vitally important to maintain a focus on issues which were relevant to students – grants, accommodation, in fact all aspects of student welfare. On a wider scale it was also important to try to maintain, in the United Kingdom and Ireland student bodies, a consensus on Northern Ireland which was in danger of being eroded.

Tom Lynch recalls the student protest march following the Rag Day murder of the soldier and the civilian.

It is the only time I can recall the entire student body marching with a unity of purpose. We felt that somehow this would make a difference, but the end of term came, a new body of students entered the university, and that feeling of solidarity somehow ebbed away. Maybe we could have done more as student leaders, or maybe we had done all we could.

Lynch, like other student Presidents, looks back on his years of office as a learning experience.

I learned to operate at a high level and also to deal with government bodies. I also learned that politics, even student politics, is a thankless task. Before I became President I believed that the university's Senior Management, or 'Front' as we called them, was not over-friendly to students, but in my dealings with Senior Officers I found nothing but concern for the well-being of students. On the negative side none of us at Queen's had any idea of the dramatic changes that would take place in further education, but I ended up with a profound liking for the university and for what we had tried to achieve at a very difficult time for Northern Ireland.

A team from Queen's won the popular television quiz game University Challenge in the early 1980s. So prolific at answering questions was Peter Jackson, that he was known for years afterwards as 'Queen's Jackson', the phrase used by quizmaster Bamber Gascoigne to invite his answer.

Entertainment

The Students' Union continued as a centre of evening entertainment at a time when such venues were scarce in Belfast; and a team from Queen's won the nationwide ITV University Challenge, beating Edinburgh in the final. On the wider entertainment front, the Queen's Festival continued to flourish. The celebrated pianist John Lill, following a superb Beethoven recital in the Elmwood Hall, said that the new Queen's Steinway was one of the best three pianos he had played in his life, while the London *Times*

ran a major article with the banner headline "Belfast Festival excelling under a broad umbrella" after Festival '82, which was a considerable artistic and financial success. Several years earlier, a man from New York had flown to Belfast for the weekend simply to attend a performance of Mercandante's Virginia for its first-ever British Isles performance, as part of Festival '76. When asked by an unbelieving television interviewer whether such a performance could be worth the then sizeable sum of $300, he replied that he would be happy to return for such a splendid performance!

University life

Academically the university continued to build on a solid base, with a voluminous list of research activities each year – ranging from papers on the history and development of the heat pump and computer-based genetic counselling to Irish political parties and European integration and even a dissertation by the Vice-Chancellor himself who found the time to produce a paper on the first medical school in Belfast 1835–49. The university continued to consolidate its considerable reputation in the world of science, while disciplines such as medicine, law,

Performances on the Balinese gamelan by staff and students of the Social Anthropology department add a resonance to university life.

dentistry, education, engineering and others turned out first-rate graduates, many of whom contributed to the wider life of the community. However, the university, like all others in the United Kingdom, was reminded that continued excellence could not be taken for granted and the results of the first-ever research assessment exercise, published in 1986, – and calculated by a process of Byzantine complexity – were disappointing for many universities, particularly Queen's, which had been expected to do much better overall – although Social Anthropology, under the late Professor John Blacking, received top ranking. For all universities the quality of research was to become a crucial factor, as part of a complex funding formula, and Queen's research profile had improved significantly by the early Nineties.

Universities, happily, are not measured by research activities alone, and the richness of life around the campus is a reflection also of the individuals who have contributed in so many different ways to the life of the institution. During Sir Peter Froggatt's time, a number of university stalwarts, and not a few characters, retired. They included the redoubtable George Cowie, the university Secretary for nearly 30 years; his successor Roy Topping; the ebullient Desmond Burland, who had been Bursar for nearly 30 years; his successor Robert (Bobby) Brown; and Desmond Neill, the first full-time Secretary of the Academic Council (1966–78) and previously first lecturer and Head of the Department of Social Studies.

Others who had given outstanding service died during the same period. They included Professor Sir John Henry Biggart, Dean of the Medical Faculty from 1944–71, professor of Pathology for 34

DR GEORGE COWIE

Dr George Cowie, a Scot who took up the post of Secretary of Queen's on 1 January 1948 and retired on 30 September 1977, was one of the great characters of the university. In his hey-day, he was a considerable power in the land, and although a disciplinarian he was greatly respected and held in affection by his staff and by many in the university at large. By all accounts he inherited a somewhat antediluvian filing and indexing system from his predecessor, the colourful Dr R.H. 'Dicky' Hunter, who ran a circus in his spare time, but Cowie soon stamped his mark on Queen's and established a first-rate administrative system. He provided valuable continuity for a succession of Vice-Chancellors who came to appreciate his pragmatism and commonsense. He was awarded an Honorary LL.D in1979 for his services to the University and on his retirement, his service to Queen's was summed up by the then Vice-Chancellor Dr Peter Froggatt in his first *Annual Report* 1976–7:

> George Cowie, your invaluable Secretary, retires on 30 September after 29 years and nine months of single-minded and devoted service: loyalty and a transcendent love of Queen's in all its parts were

his main dynamics; thoroughness, administrative facility, and complete integrity of purpose and action his main qualities. When he assumed the Secretaryship there were 2,000 students, a recurrent budget of less than £250,000, and hardly more than the central site property with total rents and rates of £800. Today there are four times the number of students, and (in real terms) more than ten times the budget, and some 150 times the rent and rates. Over all this growth George Cowie has presided with great skill, and during the year he served his fifth Vice-Chancellor as loyally as he served his first four.

On his 80th birthday, Dr Cowie was entertained to a special lunch at Queen's by a number of his former staff, who presented him with Tyrone Crystal – a gesture of affection and respect which moved him greatly.

years, and a Queen's Pro-Chancellor; professor of Anatomy Jack Pritchard; Sir William McKinney, a successful businessman and great character, and an outstanding Honorary Treasurer of Queen's who, according to the Vice-Chancellor "did not read academic tracts on how to run a university but knew how many beans made five!"; Monsignor Arthur Ryan, a former staff member, Senator and Senior Pro-Chancellor; Max Freeland, an

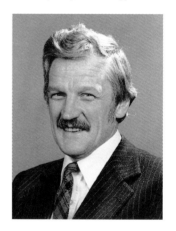

administrator with responsibility for admissions who was helpful to generations of students; and the popular Alan Graham, a former senior lecturer in Modern History and latterly Secretary of the Academic Council, whose untimely death stunned his many friends and colleagues around the university.

Buildings

Despite the pressure on funds, the university continued its programme of planning for new buildings or refurbishing and developing those which required attention. The new projects included facilities for Paleoecology and Pharmacy; a teaching floor in the City Hospital (at great expense to government, through the insistence of the UGC); a novel fluid-bed boiler heating system for the Keir Building; a major upgrading of the Marine Biology Station; the beginning of restoration of the spire and tower of the Elmwood Hall; and a rationalisation plan for the core of the main campus around University Square. Two of the most important projects of all were a new student residence at Sans Souci Park providing 60 places, and the extensive re-furbishing of the main

The Canada Room.

Lanyon Building of the university. Both projects were part of the University Development Appeal which was launched in 1981 and which raised £1.3m. The student accommodation – Sir Arthur Vick House – was opened, appropriately, by Sir Arthur himself on 4 June 1987; equally appropriately, Sir Peter Froggatt was still Vice-Chancellor when the Lanyon refurbishment was completed. It comprised a suite of new offices and ancillary rooms, a new Academic Council Chamber where the furnishings continue to out-do the accoustics, and a splendid Canada Room which is both a conference room and an attractive reception area for official functions. It was opened officially on 28 January 1986 by R. Roy McMurtry, the Canadian High Commissioner in London – denoting not only Queen's major role in Canadian Studies in the United Kingdom but also the financial contribution to the Canada Room and the Development Appeal by Queen's graduates in Canada and by the Canadian Central and Provincial Governments.

Farewell

After nearly 10 turbulent years Sir Peter Froggatt retired as Vice-Chancellor from the end of July 1986, and noted in his final *Report* to Senate: "Some things have been shaken up; nothing I hope has been shaken to pieces." He had grappled with formidable problems, not without success, and equally formidable problems, if not more so, were to face his successor. Things were being shaken up, and almost – but not quite – to pieces. Queen's, however, had survived much upheaval in its long history, and a typically philosophical view taken by Sir Peter Froggatt in his 1981–2 *Annual Report* put many current problems in perspective. He wrote: "Political instability is unstabling no doubt, north and south, but there is more to life than politics, and the Irish universities can take pride in the role they have played, especially this century, in ensuring that Ireland, despite its outrages and its intolerant and violent groups, provides no less a civilised, safe, and cultured environment than the rest of the developed world, adding its share to the rich endowment of nature." Indeed.

8

"The Old Order Changeth ..." 1986 –

THE pace of change which had so characterised the first half of the Eighties gained momentum during the Vice-Chancellorship of Sir Gordon Beveridge who took office in August 1986. The government cut-backs on funding became more drastic, while the numbers of students increased dramatically – a parallel development which led to a considerably increased work-load on staff, and which forced the universities in general to seek even greater economies. The structure of higher education itself changed further with the disappearance of the old Universities Grants Committee to make way for the Universities Funding Council and later the three Higher Education Funding Councils for the main regions of Great Britain. Locally the Northern Ireland Higher Education Council was established as an advisory body to DENI. During this period the so-called binary line between universities and polytechnics disappeared and, at the stroke of a pen, the government virtually doubled the number of universities simply by granting university status to the former polytechnics.

Within such a rapidly-changing national framework, Queen's had to maintain and enhance its reputation as one of the largest civic universities in the United Kingdom. It faced the challenges resolutely, and not without success. The quality of its research improved considerably, while its research income from outside sources also increased significantly, though there was still a shortfall. Internally there was a radical re-organisation of academic management, accompanied by the rapid implementation of modularity in the course structures. This, in turn, led to the disappearance of the three traditional university terms which were replaced by two semesters – a symbol in itself of the radical

*Sir Gordon and Lady Beveridge
at a summer graduation garden
party in 1993.*

SIR GORDON BEVERIDGE

When Dr Gordon Beveridge came to Queen's as Vice-Chancellor in August 1986, he was hailed widely as the right man for the job. As one of the new breed of Vice-Chancellors chosen by universities in the Eighties for their financial and managerial expertise, Beveridge was well-equipped to tackle the considerable challenges facing Queen's. He quickly won a reputation as a tough operator who led a small and able team and took the necessary measures to keep the university not only financially viable but in better shape than many had dared to hope, compared to some other well-known universities in the United Kingdom.

Born in St Andrews, Fife, in 1933, he was educated at Inverness Royal Academy, the University of Glasgow, the Royal College of Science and Technology in Glasgow, the University of Edinburgh (PhD), and the University of Minnesota, where he was a post-doctoral Harkness Fellow. Before coming to Queen's he was professor of Chemical Engineering and Head of the Department of Chemical and Process Engineering at the University of Strathclyde. He was knighted in June 1994 'for services to higher education'.

The pressure of work at Queen's has meant that he has had little opportunity to pursue his hobbies including "Scottish and Dutch history, Marlburian War games, and family golf and hill-walking"; but he has found time to contribute effectively to a large number of outside bodies, including the leading professional engineering institutions, and most notably to a wide range of local organisations ranging from Navan at Armagh to Opera Northern Ireland. Gordon Beveridge and his charming wife Trudy, who comes from the Netherlands, have achieved a reputation as excellent hosts, and within eight years some 3,500 people have been entertained at the Vice-Chancellor's residence. Sir Gordon and

Lady Beveridge have also worked extremely hard at representing Queen's at a multiplicity of functions in Northern Ireland and further afield.

Gordon Beveridge is a man of considerable presence, and despite a sometimes formal exterior, those who know him well can testify to a caring and courteous human being, who is not without a sense of humour. Others, however, mistake his formality for a certain aloofness, and complain about the layers of management between the top and those at the chalk-face. Beveridge himself expresses regret at being unable to meet as many staff as he would have liked and he has indicated that the pressures have been such that he has felt that he has been in the job for 30 years instead of eight: "The post of Vice-Chancellor can be a lonely position, and especially in a time of great change it is not always easy to relax in the totality of the academic community."

One colleague says: "He has a tremendous grasp of detail and an impressive ability to sort out technical and financial problems, but he has had less time than perhaps he would have liked to deal with problems concerning relationships between people or in providing more leadership vision in times of great change."

One outside observer notes:

Sir Gordon has demonstrated the right qualities for his time and he has made real progress in stabilising Queen's and giving it a sense of cohesion. He has brought the university to the point where it can begin to make decisions about where it wants to go and how it will get there, without pre-occupations about financial survival from year to year in times of tremendous pressure and upheaval. There has been a need for someone with strong visionary leadership, but a visionary alone might not have had the detail and the scope to get the funding, the manpower and the organisation right. Beveridge has brought the university through very tough times and the evidence is there for all to see. He has helped to change some of the attitudes and the culture, and Queen's increasingly has come to recognise its strengths and it is beginning to play to those strengths. Gordon Beveridge deserves recognition for what he has done. His is no mean achievement.

The British Association for the Advancement of Science held its Annual Meeting in 1987 at Queen's. The lectures and discussions, which receive wide coverage on the media, represent the latest thinking on a wide range of issues in the scientific world. The meeting at Queen's was one of the first occasions when the 'hole in the ozone layer' and 'global warming' were brought to the attention of the public.

(Above) A press briefing on the 'hole in the ozone layer'.

(Right) Dr Beverley Halstead, whose lecture on dinosaurs with his assistant Helen Haste made the front page in most of the national tabloid press.

A special phonecard was issued by British Telecom to mark the event

Queen's administrative staff unfurling the banner for the Annual Meeting of the national Conference of University Administrators at Queen's in 1991

nature of the changes taking place. The university's wider outreach accelerated in a variety of different ways through technology transfer, an even greater liaison with industry, the development of closer ties with Europe, and continued service to the local community. Queen's further enhanced its reputation as a conference centre, and hosted a large number of prestigious national and international gatherings including the 1987 Conference of the British Association for the Advancement of Science, and the 1991 Conference of University Administrators, which by any standards were spectacular successes. There were many other successes ranging from world-beating technology to outstanding sporting achievements, while on the other hand the university, like all other institutions and indeed individuals in Northern Ireland, had to cope with the continuing challenges and controversies of life in a deeply-divided society.

180

Overall, however, the years approaching the Second Millennium were a period of achievement for the university, in the very difficult circumstances of managing rapid change. Sir Gordon, a determined, no-nonsense Scot who needed all his considerable reserves of character and resilience to pilot such a large vessel through often mountainous seas, reflected after eight years at the helm: "The pressure of change was very intense, and it did not decrease at any point. If anything, it became worse and worse." He often quoted the words of Tennyson: "The old order changeth, yielding place to new . . ." The old order was changing indeed, though it would have been a brave observer who would have hazarded a guess as to what the eventual 'new order' might be.

Finance

The year 1986–7 was financially traumatic for Queen's, which had been judged by the funding authorities to be a high-cost university, in relation to its numbers of students and range of subjects. Secondly the research ratings, on which part of the recurrent grant from public funds were to depend, had been disappointing. In September 1986, it appeared that the university would be facing a deficit of £7 million by 1989–90. Beveridge noted later: "We believed that we had been funded some 10 per cent above the national average, but this was not so. It was something which emerged only after days and days of probing. It gradually became clear that our future recurrent funding would be well *below* the average, to the order of more than 10 per cent." Queen's faced a reduced level of public funding over the next four years, compared to the university sector as a whole, with an overall reduction of some 13 per cent in its recurrent grant. The university was now facing the swingeing cuts suffered by universities in Great Britain in 1981. The Vice-Chancellor and his senior officers moved swiftly to deal with this threatening situation. Some 250 members of staff accepted voluntary retirement at a cost to the university of £5.5 million. However, the honorary Treasurer, Sir Ewart Bell, the clarity of whose reports was exemplary in this difficult period, indicated that with government compensation the net cost of the scheme was more than £2 million. In return, the annual savings on staff costs amounted to over £3 million.

Despite "arbitrary" cuts in expenditure of £1 million, the university had a deficit of £2 million in 1986–7. The next year it had bounced back, however, with a surplus of £2.13 million. This resulted from the much higher than expected government reim-

One of the most striking sights at Queen's in the Spring of 1991 was the appearance of the Discovery Dome on the front lawn of the university. Over 10,000 schoolchildren visited the exhibition to learn about scientific principles in a practical and entertaining way. The event was organized by the Department of Pure & Applied Physics and sponsored by British Petroleum.

Pictured at a meeting of the Physiological Society at Queen's in 1990 are four 'generations' of Professors of Physiology: Dunville Professors Sir Henry Barcroft 1935–47 (second left), Archibald Greenfield 1948–64 (second right) and Ian Roddie 1964–88 (left), together with Professor of Applied Physiology William Wallace, appointed 1978.

bursement of premature retirement and severance payments, and the effect of a variety of measures to reduce costs and to enhance income, including the additional tuition fees from more overseas students. Though financially successful, the premature retirement scheme had two drawbacks – it led to the departure of some able staff who took the opportunity to leave with a nest-egg and to carve out a second career elsewhere. Secondly, it led also to the departure of some of those who were needed to deal with the administrative results of such surgery.

By 1988–9 the Vice-Chancellor felt secure enough to declare: "We no longer fear that the light at the end of the tunnel is that of an on-coming train." But he warned, in his *Annual Report* for 1988–89: "We are required to maintain a tight hold on the purse strings, and the coming financial year will require the same kind of discipline which we have demonstrated so far." Members of staff who were by now familiar with the uninspiring language of cost-cutting, efficiency and effectiveness surrounding higher education in general had little option but to comply. Through a prudent policy of good housekeeping and investment, the honorary Treasurer was able to report that in 1989–90: "the financial affairs of Queen's University proceeded in a relatively calm and uneventful manner", a remarkably encouraging statement in the final year of the reduction in the recurrent grant which had caused such anxiety in 1986. Instead of a feared deficit of £7 million, the university had balanced its books to within 1 per cent of turnover, with a surplus of £597,000 and reserves of £6.7 million.

When Sir Ewart Bell presented his last financial statement for the year 1992–3, he could point to a surplus for the sixth year in succession, in running what was by then a business with a turnover of £100 million. Due to greater income, significantly higher fees from larger student numbers, an increase in research grants and contracts, the further development of university services, and continued economies and other measures, the university was in a sound financial position. Not only that, the university had used

what resources were available to further an imaginative building and refurbishment programme and to assist academic and other areas where possible to meet the challenges of a rapidly increasing student population. This was a considerable achievement not only by the Vice-Chancellor who demonstrated tight leadership in financial matters but also by Sir Ewart Bell and by the Bursar, Mr David Gass, and his staff.

By December 1993, however, the financial outlook began to darken again with the announcement by government of a 2 per cent cut in student intakes. Several successive years of record intakes were followed, in 1994–5, by a 2 per cent reduction. In broad terms this would mean that Queen's would be unable to use the income from what had been ever-increasing student admissions to compensate for a shortfall from research income and contracts and other sources, and the university faced a possible £1 million deficit in the year 1994–5. The Vice-Chancellor's exhortation to further stringencies was already being anticipated by staff who had noted how the government earlier had thrown away millions of pounds in a fruitless effort to protect sterling in the European Exchange Rate Mechanism. As one Queen's observer of long-standing noted: "The universities may have needed a shaking up, but they found it hard to cope with a government which seemed bent on delivering a kick in the solar plexus every other week."

Management

The management of the university in the widest sense was a major priority of the new Vice-Chancellor, including the broad control of the complex academic structures. Gordon Beveridge argued that while a university could not be a business in the true sense of the word, it ought to be run on business-like lines. He believed that the structure of nine Faculties comprising nearly 100 Departments was unwieldy and that a simpler system run by fewer people was necessary. Accordingly, the 97 Departments were re-organised into 25 larger Schools, each with its own appointed Director, and the process was later completed with the appointment of five Provosts who were responsible for five main areas of academic administration and management. This created some confusion at grass-roots level while the implication of the changes from Departments to Schools and ultimately to areas controlled by Provosts worked themselves out, with question-marks over the long-term future of Faculties. But the university continued to demonstrate its commitment to the principles of

Dr Edith Devlin, whose Wednesday morning classes on English Literature became phenomenally popular, symbolised the community outreach of the Institute of Continuing Education. Her classes began in the late Sixties with 56 members, in a small lecture room, but by 1993 the class had grown to 450 people in a large lecture theatre in the David Keir Building. Her pupils covered a wide spectrum, from retired consultants and teachers, to former students and housewives, and they came from a large geographical area including Donegal, Derry and Dublin. She once confided: "People say to me 'Your classes have changed my life!' Literature has given them a wider perspective and a greater understanding of what it is like to be a human being. It helps them to discover the essential self that lies under the worry and fret of everyday living." In 1993 Edith Devlin was the worthy recipient of a Queen's Honorary Doctorate of Literature.

the Jarratt Report which had advocated a simpler management structure. Beveridge saw the role of senior management as providing: "an umbrella for staff to protect them as far as possible from the adverse winds of change and allow them to profess their disciplines and to advance in a positive way. The need to encourage the delegation of decisions in planning, budgeting and other matters emerged quite naturally out of a need for radical change which was being forced upon Queen's." He was clear about his role: "My job is to make sure that other people take responsibility for their own areas and that they generate the strategies and carry out the tactical solutions, and all the while looking after morale and trying to satisfy the expression of their staff."

That task was not easy at a time when the government's confusion over higher education and the financial cut-backs affecting relatively badly-paid staff deeply affected morale at all levels. Such a system also depended on the varying ability of individual senior managers to manage clearly and effectively – a process that is greatly inhibited by the bureaucracy, the consummate democracy and the often complex and prolonged process of decision-making which has been inherent in the university world in general. In 1987 the untimely illness of Fred Smyth, who had held the post of Registrar for only two years, led to a vacancy. (Mr Smyth died shortly afterwards) It was decided not to fill the vacant post and that added responsibilities be given to the triumvirate of Bursar, Academic Secretary and Administrative Secretary – a decision that came in for criticism later on from those who felt, rightly or wrongly, that a Registrar would have given more cohesion to the administration of the university.

Professor Mollie McGeown, one of Queen's most distinguished medical graduates, has made a major contribution to the research and treatment of kidney disease. She graduated with Honours in Medicine in 1946. Following the establishment of a unit for the treatment of acute renal failure in 1959, a purpose-built Dialysis and Transplant Unit was opened in Belfast City Hospital in 1968 and for the next 20 years, the kidney transplant programme, under the direction of Professor McGeown received widespread commendation for its outstanding success rates and for its pioneering advances in the clinical care of kidney transplantations. It has been estimated that Professor McGeown and her colleagues, over a period of 30 years, provided life-saving treatment for more than 3,000 patients, and established an outstanding record for medical care and research. Professor McGeown maintained the highest standards in her career, and she was ably supported for many years by her husband Max Freeland, the University's much-appreciated former Clerk of Admissions, who died in 1982.

Apart from a basic re-organisation of academic management, this period also brought important innovations to improve teaching and other skills and also the university's service to its students and the community at large. These innovations included the establishment of an Academic Audit Unit, a Centre for Academic Practice, and a Northern Ireland Educational Support Unit, as well as a highly-successful programme of Non-Specialist Language Teaching where students could rapidly learn the basics of a foreign language to enable them to further their careers. The Vice-Chancellor expressed the wish that by the year 2000 every graduate leaving Queen's would have a working competence in at least one foreign language. Dr Beveridge noted, in his *Annual Report* for 1990–91, the particular success of an engineering post-graduate who studied Beginners' German in the Non-

Specialist Language course and as a result was able to communicate meaningfully during a visit to the Hanover Trade Fair shortly afterwards.

One of the most significant achievements in the academic field was the improvement in the latest nation-wide assessment of research standards, following the university's disappointing performance earlier. The results of the National Research Assessment Exercise in 1992 indicated that some 80 per cent of the university's research was of national or international standard. The high-quality research was spread throughout the university, with Electrical and Electronic Engineering, Physics and Paleoecology scoring 5, the highest grade possible; Civil Engineering, Law, Economic and Social History, Sociology, the Institute of Irish Studies and Archaeology achieving grade 4; and a wide spectrum of other subjects being assessed at Grade 3. However, there was no room for complacency, and the university quickly put into place a strong research management strategy to ensure a continuing process of improvement.

In broad terms, the university had to make hard decisions to put more resources at the disposal of those areas and individuals where excellence had been demonstrated, at the expense of others where the performance had been poor. Because great emphasis was being placed by government on research excellence as one of the major factors in funding, Queen's had a choice of either supporting a broad number of categories with less impressive performances (with the resultant danger of encouraging a drift to lower standards), or on the other hand to back the high-flyers in an aggressive drive for excellence. The aim was to ensure that in the next National Research Assessment Exercise some 45–55 per cent of the academic areas would achieve the highest ratings of 4 or 5, with support also being given to first-rate individuals in certain other areas but not to all research activities in those areas. Emphasis was also placed on teaching standards, an area in which Queen's had long enjoyed a good reputation.

The long-term aim was to preserve Queen's place as one of the very good civic universities in the United Kingdom, on a par with other institutions such as Sheffield, Southampton or Newcastle, by maintaining high teaching standards across the spectrum of subjects and also by providing the best-quality research in selected areas. The Vice-Chancellor, in his graduation speech of 5 July 1993, left no-one in doubt as to his priorities: ". . . Queen's is about many things, and above all the university is about scholarship and excellence . . . Queen's remains a very good university, and we can demonstrate many illustrations of outstanding scholarship, but it is important that every single member of Queen's, whether staff or student, accepts that we must constantly strive for the best." His point was well-illustrated by the creation of a number of important posts and industrially-funded Chairs, including the Shorts Chair of Aerospace Engineering, the Northern Telecom Research Chair in Telecommunications Systems Engineering, and the Du Pont Chair of Process Engineering.

WAVE ENERGY

Queen's was in the forefront of attempts to develop a sea-borne wave-energy device during the 1970s. In the 1980s, the focus of the research at Queen's shifted to a land-based device, and the vision of our coastal waters dotted with wave-energy buoys receded. A completely redesigned device, based on the Wells turbine, was installed on the island of Islay and officially switched on by Energy Minister Colin Moynihan in July 1991. L-R: Energy Minister Colin Moynahan, Professor Trevor Whittaker, Dr David Cleland, and Professor Adrian Long at the opening of the wave-energy system on Islay.

Research projects

The range of research in the university was impressive in itself. The new, streamlined and attractively-designed *Vice-Chancellor's Annual Reports*, and the University's *Publications Reports* with more than 3,000 annual entries in the early Nineties, carried summaries of all kinds of work, ranging from a new two-stroke outboard motor developed by Professor Gordon Blair and a team from the School of Mechanical & Process Engineering, who were at the leading edge of such technology, to the development of wave energy, stemming from a turbine invention in 1975 by the then professor of Civil Engineering, Dr Alan Wells. Queen's Professor Trevor Whittaker established a world lead in this area, and in 1991 the university's wave energy device on the island of Islay in the Hebrides was officially switched-on by the Energy Minister Colin Moynihan.

Queen's successful research ranged widely, from work on potato growing in the Sudan by staff in the Department of Agricultural Zoology, to a study on child fitness by the Faculty of Education and the Physical Education Centre, and a ten-year World Health Organisation MONICA Project (MONItoring in CArdiovascular disease), run by the Department of Epidemiology and Public Health. Also worthy of note was the success of a multi-disciplinary research team of Queen's doctors and scientists who won a prestigious National Toshiba Year of Invention Competition in 1990, in which there were nearly 3,000 entries. The Queen's team won with its innovative computerised knee scanner, a non-invasive device which increases the accuracy of diagnosis of torn knee cartilages by measuring vibrations during exercise and movement.

There was also a wide range of important research work in the Arts and Humanities. For example, the Celtic Department – with substantial funding from the Central Community Relations Unit – was engaged in a major research project on the place names of Northern Ireland. By mid-1994 three volumes on County Down had already been published, and the series was expected to run to more than 40 volumes.

Sir Gordon Beveridge, in his 1992–3 *Annual Report,* noted that research was the life-blood of universities. He wrote: "It is the driving force for scholarship, it underpins the teaching process to keep students at the fore-front of new developments, and it brings an impetus and an immediacy to the learning situation, as students respond to being taught by the same academics who are involved on the leading edge of discovery." A year earlier the Vice-Chancellor noted that the university's income from research, some £12.5m, showed a net increase of 115 per cent on the 1987–8 figure. This placed Queen's 19th from the top of a national list of 86 institutions, with the University of Ulster in 45th place *(Universities statistical record: HEFC, SHEFC).* However, the shortfall compared to a similar-sized institution in England was still some £6m by 1994, which was partly due to the scarcity of significant research money from Northern Ireland sources.

The question of good working relationships between Queen's and the University of Ulster continued to be of significance to both institutions and to government. Another major development was the establishment of a Working Party on Research Selectivity, under the Chairmanship of Sir Clifford Butler. It was set up by the Department of Education for Northern Ireland to consider research provision in the light of UGC policy on the selectivity of resource allocation. The main recommendations were that emphasis on Physics and Chemistry should be concentrated at Queen's which would offer single honours courses in these subjects, and that Business Studies should be concentrated in the University of Ulster. This development caused considerable disappointment to many at Queen's who believed that its flourishing area of Business Studies had been dealt a savage blow, though Queen's management were at pains to point out that Business Studies was still part of the university's curriculum in association with other subjects. The Policy Research Institute, a joint venture between the two universities to provide an evaluation of policy issues, began by building a solid base in the mid-Eighties but its early promise was not sustained and it was eventually wound up. A policy of complementarity between the two institutions remained the ideal, though at a time of scarce financial resources it was inevitable that each university was also anxious to protect and to enhance its own interests.

Buildings and estate management

The rapid expansion in student numbers to some 13,400 by 1993–4 and the need for the continued refurbishment of halls, lecture theatres, and laboratories placed a heavy burden on the university which has responsibility for some 300 buildings. They range from the main Lanyon Building (arguably the finest architectural set-piece in Northern Ireland which cost £34,000 to build and had a replacement value of around £9 million by 1994) to a number of buildings of questionable architectural merit. By 1990–1 it was estimated that the replacement cost of the entire estate was approximately £250 million, and the university was spending some 16 per cent of its annual budget on maintenance and running costs. Despite the financial cut-backs, the university – through the prudent use of resources and by borrowing additional funds – embarked on a substantial building programme. Student accommodation was high on the list, and although there were approximately 1400 residential places available by 1987 there was a substantial shortfall in meeting the minimum target of 2300 places.

Shaftesbury Hall, one of three new halls of residence opened in 1991.

Such provision was extremely costly, but by 1991 another 218 study bedrooms had been provided on three locations, at a total cost of some £3 million – financed through private university funds and commercial loans. The official opening ceremonies took place on 23 May 1991 when the Earl of Shaftesbury opened **Shaftesbury Hall** in memory of his grandfather, the first Chancellor of Queen's 1908–23; Dr Michael Grant, who with his wife Anne-Sophie making a welcome return to Queen's, opened Grant House; and Mr John B. McGuckian, the Senior Pro-Chancellor opened Guthrie House in memory of Sir Tyrone Guthrie, the Chancellor from 1963–70.

On 27 November 1992, another student residence providing accommodation for 114 students was opened on the Queen's Elms site at a cost of £1.7 million. It was named after Sir Rowland Wright, Chancellor of Queen's from 1984–1991, and the opening ceremony was performed by Lady Wright, accompanied by her son John, a Queen's graduate. The opening of this Hall, plus the renovation of university properties by 1993 brought the total number of places available to 1900. Some 430 of these places, almost a quarter of the total, had been provided within four years, at a cost of £6 million. Another 130 places were scheduled through the rehabilitation of self-catering houses at Mount Charles, at a further cost of £2.4 million. Nevertheless, the pressure on student accommodation in the private sector remains intense, particularly because the Queen's area is desirable for many young professionals as well as students from the University of Ulster who commute to Jordanstown daily.

Other important projects were the restoration of University Square, probably the best example of three-storey Victorian terracing in the Province, to add lustre to the university's designation as a Conservation Area; the refurbishment of the Lanyon Building; the redecoration of the Great Hall in a delicate shade of pink which infuriated, amused or pleased equal proportions of staff; and the refurbishment of the Sir William Whitla Hall, as

University Square following refurbishment.

well as a terrace of listed properties opposite the Lanyon Building. A major reconstruction programme costing £3.5 million was completed on the Medical Biology Centre, to enhance the integration of Biology and Biochemistry into a single School. Other work included refurbishment in the School of Clinical Medicine at the Royal Hospitals site and in the Whitla Medical Building, in College Park to house the Northern Ireland Educational Support Unit, and also the School of Dentistry. Apart from such necessary work, the university had to deal with various letters of advice from government, (some of these offering somewhat inconsidered advice) including a directive that buildings not being used for academic purposes should be sold. Wisely, the university reacted with less than alacrity to such advice, which later became largely redundant when government decided to increase vastly the number of students; but Queen's did take the opportunity to rationalise its use of buildings and will continue to do so into the next century. This rationalisation stems from a need to move away from the repair, maintenance and constuction of buildings and to consider the overall management of the estate including the efficient and functional use of all space; to realise that the estate is not a "free gift"; and that there is need for economic management including procurement procedures, energy costs and environmental awareness.

The Vice-Chancellor praised all those who had the foresight to press on with new buildings and to refurbish others, despite the financial stringencies of the times. He noted in his 1990–1 *Annual Report*: "This expenditure has been carried out in a manner which has enhanced the physical heritage of our campus and which will continue to provide a quality environment for learning to all who use it."

Technology transfer

The significance of the interaction between Queen's and the wider community was emphasised by the developments in technology transfer. The important work of QUBIS continued over a wide range of activities, and a noteworthy innovation was the creation of a Chief Executives Club which provided an opportunity for senior figures in industry to meet and to exchange views with each other and with the university. QUBIS Ltd also flourished and by mid 1994 it had established no fewer than 14 companies, with a combined turnover of £6.5 million and 150 employees, mainly graduates, and many with higher degrees.

The 14 companies continued to reflect the full range of science and technology research in the university and the objective of QUBIS Ltd was to continue to commercialise such research, especially through joint ventures with local and international partners. Two of the best known companies are Kainos Ltd, and Audio Processing Technology (APT). Kainos Software Ltd is a joint venture between QUBIS Ltd and ICL and from its foundation in 1986 it expanded steadily to become one of Northern Ireland's most successful software houses. In November 1992 it was employing 63 staff when it announced a further expansion with the backing of the Industrial Development Board to create 23 new jobs in the next 3 years and was employing around 100 people by mid-1994. Announcing this expansion, Mr John Gardner the Chairman and Managing Director of ICL (UK) Ltd which owned a majority share in Kainos, cited the company as ICL's best example of a successful start-up venture.

(Above) Professor John McCanny and Dr Stephen Smyth and (below) Queen's Alumnus Liam Neeson in Schindler's List.

The success of APT arose from research undertaken by the Digital Signal Processing group, led by Professor John McCanny and Dr Roger Woods. During the past decade the group pioneered many new technologies and successfully transferred these to industry. These included families of high performance silicon chips for use in telecommunications, television and multi-media applications. Some of these were developed in collaboration with organisations such as GEC Plessy Semiconductors, Northern Telecom, the BBC and Snell and Wilcox. New digital filter chips, capable of performing over half a billion multiplications/additions per second made world-wide headlines when these were

191

The Northern Ireland Semiconductor Research Centre at Queen's, set up in 1992 with the help of a £2.5 million grant from the European STRIDE initiative and headed by Professor Harold Gamble, pioneers advanced silicon technology for high-speed and for low-power integrated circuits.

announced in 1991 and resulted in commercial chips being developed by GEC Plessey Semiconductors. Other research, undertaken by Dr Stephen Smyth, resulted in a new audio compression technique. This allows professional hi-fi quality sound to be stored or broadcast using only one quarter of the information needed on a Compact Disk. This led to the formation of APT, a joint venture involving the university and Solid State Logic, a Carlton Communications company. APT quickly established itself as a world leader and it became particularly successful in the competitive American and Japanese markets. APT's technology led to the development of a new digital cinema sound system, Digital Theatre Sound (DTS). This was first used for Steven Spielberg's films "Jurassic Park" and "Schindler's List". APT won a Queen's Award for Export Achievement in 1994.

Other important developments enhanced Queen's provision of sophisticated services which also benefited the rest of the Province. They included the Northern Ireland Technology Centre (See page 194), a Biotechnology Centre, a Northern Ireland Regional Transputer Support Centre (one of only five in the United Kingdom), Automotive Design Centre, an Institute of Advanced Microelectronics, a Northern Ireland Semiconductor Research Centre, a Rotational Moulding Research Centre and QUESTOR (Queen's University Environmental Science and Technology Research) Centre to increase university and industrial liaison on measures to eliminate or substantially reduce the deterioration of the environment through industrial causes. QUESTOR, incidentally, was the first centre of its kind in Europe and the first to be established outside the United States, with backing from the university, the International Fund for Ireland, and British and Irish industry.

To underline such a spread of excellence, QUBIS Ltd companies, by October 1993, had won 12 SMART Awards (Small Business

Merit Awards for Research and Technology, from the Department of Economic Development's Industrial Research and Technology Unit) over five years.

Queen's has also had an enviable record in the establishment of Teaching Company Programmes – partnerships between industry, the universities and government to assist technology transfer through the expertise of young graduates. To date Queen's has had 45 Teaching Company Programmes, the highest per university in the United Kingdom, and no fewer than 18 of these have been associated with the Department of Chemical Engineering.

Internally, as well as externally, the university developed a highly-sophisticated communications network using the latest technology. A £1.5 million Cray super-computer, funded by Queen's with a grant from the Science and Engineering Research Council and which became operational in April 1993, provided staff and students with some of the best facilities possible to support their research in a Cray network which included Great Britain, the United States, Japan and Australia. In 1994 the university further enhanced its computer provision by taking its place in the Super Janet network.

Such developments confirmed Queen's position among the United Kingdom leaders in the provision and support of computing for staff and students, partly through generous support from government departments and agencies in Northern Ireland and from funding sources further afield. One important initiative in the mid-Eighties, backed by the Department of Education for Northern Ireland and the Industrial Development Board was the comprehensive provision of computing facilities for undergraduates which made Queen's the United Kingdom leader in this field. An important element of this project was the help given to Schools to assist the use of microcomputers in the undergraduate curriculum, and to support this work the Northern Ireland Centre for Computer-based Learning was established by the Computer Centre and the School of Education. It was opened formally by the Rt Hon Dr Brian Mawhinney MP, the then Minister for Education, in 1988.

Tree-ring dating, an area in which the Palaeoecology Department has done pioneering work to establish one of the world's longest tree-ring chronologies – a year-by-year record of oak growth back to 5470 BC. Among the results of the work was the dating of the massive volcanic eruption of Thera, which had a profound effect on the ancient world, at 1627/8 BC.

THE NORTHERN IRELAND TECHNOLOGY CENTRE

The Northern Ireland Technology Centre at Queen's, which was officially opened by the Duke of Kent on 29 May 1990, is one of the university's most imaginative and highly-regarded initiatives to extend further its inter-action with local industry. Its rationale is "the effective utilisation of today's technology today", and a range of industrial and educational services exists to meet that objective. It was set up as the result of an Engineering Working Party chaired by Sir Joseph Pope, in the Vice-Chancellorship of Sir Peter Froggatt, and the Centre was funded by the European Regional Development Fund, the Department of Education in Northern Ireland, the Industrial Development Board, the Department of Trade and Industry, and the International Fund for Ireland.

The long-established and successful industrial service units for materials testing, automation and signal processing (which had existed for many years in the Civil, Mechanical and Electrical Engineering Departments) were integrated into the Centre, and two new units were established to cater specially for computer-assisted design and manufacturing. The Centre is a self-financing operation which employs 40 staff and has a turnover of more than £2.75 million per annum. The Centre maintains contact with 2,000 companies, and has 700 regular business clients. In a typical year the staff answer 1,500 industrial queries, undertake 20,000 tests and calibrations, and complete over 100 consulting projects. The educational services provide over 60,000 hours of training each year for more than 600 students, while around 900 industrial staff attend some 70 training courses per annum. Surplus revenue is used to off-set most of the educational services – which means that industry today is contributing directly to the further education and training of the industrial leaders of tomorrow.

The photograph of the opening ceremony shows the Duke of Kent being presented by the Vice-Chancellor, Sir Gordon Beveridge, with an inscribed brass paperweight, made by students using the computer-aided design and manufacturing facilities in the Centre. On the right is the Centre's Director, Professor Eric Beatty.

Community

Although technology was vital, the life of a university involved much more than the latest "hardware" or "software" or impressive technological and research developments. The Vice-Chancellor made the point, more than once, that a university is more than a collection of buildings, or a set of courses, or a complicated list of financial figures. It was, and is, a community of people – in Queen's case more than 20,000 people in what used to be called "term-time", which makes the university the size of Newry or Ballymena. Despite all the challenges of progressing in a period of rapid change and financial cut-backs, the university remains ever-conscious of its role at the heart of the local community.

The Belfast Festival at Queen's continues to attract major national and international performers as well as very substantial local audiences, and in 1994 its distinguished Director, Michael Barnes, retired from the scene. The university paid well-deserved tribute to his enormous contribution to the arts in Northern Ireland: "His major achievements have been to raise the Festival to acknowledged international status . . . and to keep Festival at this high standard in spite of the civil unrest which has affected much of the life of the Province."

Queen's continues to support the Arts in a wide variety of ways, through the Fenderesky Gallery at Queen's, by continuing to provide a suitable "home" for the Ulster Orchestra at Elmwood Hall, and through its own excellent School of Music, the University Orchestra and Choir and the Hamilton Harty Chorus, formed in 1994, all of which have staged well-received concerts on the campus. The university's role in the wider world is also reflected in its awards of honorary degrees to a wide range of people such as the writers Brian Moore, William Trevor, Brian Friel, and Jennifer Johnston; the industrialists Tony O'Reilly and Alastair McGuckian; the actor Kenneth Branagh and the artist Tom Carr.

Equal opportunities

The university has long been conscious of its pivotal role as a place where people from all backgrounds can meet, particularly students from the Protestant and Roman Catholic traditions – many of whom have found at Queen's their first opportunity to encounter others from a different cultural and religious background. Indeed, a number who became church, political, busi-

The fourth Rockwell Conference, on the theme 'Religious Conflict and Politics in Ireland 1885–1921' was held at Queen's in January 1994. Some 200 school pupils from all over Northern Ireland were welcomed by the Rt Rev. Dr Gordon McMullan, Bishop of Down and Dromore, here seen chatting to Assumption Grammar School pupils Anna Morrow (left) and Kirsten McKevitt from Ballynahinch.

Jack Kyle, one of the greatest rugby players of all time, won 46 international caps, then an Irish record, between 1947 and 1958. He played in the Irish team which won the Triple Crown in 1948 and 1949, and he was also selected for the British Lions. In July 1991, he was awarded an Honorary Doctorate of Social Sciences by Queen's, not for his rugby prowess which had brought him such credit and such reflected glory to his old university, but for his services to the Third World. A dedicated Christian, he worked as a surgeon in Northern Zambia for many years, bringing healing and compassion to a vast and needy population. In presenting Jack Kyle for his much-deserved honorary degree, the Dean – Professor Kenneth Brown – said: "It is entirely appropriate that today we honour one of our own. This university provided the training and skill. The man himself has given the commitment and the service to the under-privileged of Central Africa. In so doing, he has epitomised the real values on which humanity must ultimately depend."

THE UNIVERSITY CHAPLAINS

Presbyterian

Post-war chaplaincy at Queen's developed into full-time work for the four main denominations very largely through the pioneering impetus of the Reverend Dr Ray Davey who was appointed the first full-time Presbyterian Dean of Residence in 1946. Allied to this was the designation of a building with residential capacity for chaplaincy work, in this case the former dwelling of Principal Paul of Assembly's College. This pattern of a full-time chaplain operating from a residential student centre became the basic model to be followed by the Methodist, Roman Catholic and Church of Ireland in subsequent years. Ray Davey, who had served in the second world war as a YMCA chaplain to his fellow prisoners-of-war, began work in the College Park East site with a strong emphasis on a small, core community setting a programme of spiritual, ecumenical, educational and social interests, as a meaningful expression of living the Christian faith in a contemporary university setting. A new purpose-built centre containing 10 self-contained student rooms, a hall and a flat for the chaplain and family was opened in 1963 on the College Park site, imaginatively meeting the needs of the Presbyterian church until 1991 when the building was sold to Queen's in response to the changing patterns of student activities and life-style.

Ray Davey

Ray Davey was succeeded in 1970, on his appointment as first leader of the Corrymeela community, by the Reverend Dr Richard Gordon who had been engaged in Commonwealth Mission work in Kenya. Dr Gordon, who returned to Kenya in 1975, was succeeded by the Reverend Dr John Morrow who was installed in 1976, having previously been engaged in student work in Glasgow and Trinity College Dublin. Dr Morrow was appointed to succeed Ray Davey as leader of the Corrymeela community in 1979. The Reverend Noel Williamson, minister of Second Islandmagee, was appointed to succeed Dr Morrow in January 1980. By the middle of 1994, construction of a student hostel was under way at Derryvolgie Avenue near the main Hall of Residence, and a day-time drop-in centre was located in Elmwood Avenue alongside the other chaplaincy centres.

Roman Catholic

Until 1949, chaplaincy interests were carried out by a local priest working from home on a part-time basis, usually visiting student lodgings on a Friday evening. However, a legacy enabled the first Roman Catholic chaplaincy centre to be opened at 14 Fitzwilliam Street in 1949 with Fr Michael Kelly as chaplain. Facilities were expanded in 1951 with the purchase of 16 Fitzwilliam Street to provide lounge and kitchen facilities as well as a small oratory. In the late 50's, further adjacent property was purchased, though not integrated into the existing arrangement. Fr Patrick Walsh (currently Bishop of Down and Connor) was appointed chaplain in 1964, assisted by Fr Ambrose Macaulay.

Negotiations for the purchase of the present chaplaincy site in Elmwood Avenue began in the 1967–68 academic year and the splendid new building and magnificent chapel were opened in October 1972. Fr Macaulay took over as chaplain in 1970 and was assisted from then until 1975 by Fr Anthony Farquhar (currently Auxiliary Bishop of Down and Connor) who became chaplain at the New University of Ulster at Coleraine. Fr Macaulay resigned in 1984, moving to Rome to complete his historical research. He was succeeded in September 1984 by Fr Joseph Gunn. In recent years there has been a marked expansion in the number of Roman Catholic students at Queen's, with greatly improved and expanded facilities.

Methodist

A special link has long existed between the University Road Methodist congregation and the Methodist students of Queen's. The minister of the congregation served the needs of students until

1964, when full-time chaplaincy began. The Rev David Turtle, returning from missionary duty in Burma, was appointed full-time chaplain. This development coincided with the opening of an excellent student centre 'Aldersgate House' which was the brain-child and response of the University Road congregation to the increasing demands of student life. Unfortunately an IRA bomb effectively ended the use of the Aldersgate site in 1972.

In 1974 a substantial grant from the Rank Trust enabled the Methodist Church to purchase the present chaplaincy buildings at 24/26 Elmwood Avenue, providing family accommodation for the chaplain as well as a house fully equipped for 6 students. David Turtle retired from his long and distinguished career in 1988, and he was succeeded by Rev Donald Ker, then chaplain at Trinity College Dublin. Mr Ker moved to a lecturing post in Edgehill College in 1991 to be succeeded by the Reverend Henry Keys, formerly chaplain at Kingswood School Bath, and the Methodist College Belfast.

Church of Ireland

The appointment of the Reverend Edgar Turner in 1951, marked the commencement of full-time chaplaincy by the Church of Ireland. A committee was set-up in December of 1952 to establish a student centre, and a site at 22 Elmwood Avenue was purchased in March 1953. It opened the following year with six residents at a cost of more than £4,000. Throughout this period, the Apostolic Church in Cromwell Road was made available for worship.

The Reverend Maurice Carey became chaplain in October 1958 and planning began to build a new worship centre. When Mr Carey left for St Bartholomew's in Dublin in 1965, he was succeeded by the Rev Cecil Kerr. At this time 20 Elmwood Avenue was purchased for the chaplain's dwelling and incorporated six rooms for female students, a pioneering development at that time. The splendid new Church of The Resurrection was opened in 1967. Another expansion of the impressive chaplaincy was completed by the purchase of a house (16 Elmwood Avenue) from the Canon Theologian of

St Anne's Cathedral in the early seventies. The Rev John Dinnen succeeded Cecil Kerr in 1975, and a further purchase of 18 Elmwood Avenue in 1980 brought the residential capacity to 40 students, with very adequate facilities for self-catering, social, recreational and worship requirements. The Rev Harold Miller was appointed chaplain in 1984 and he was succeeded by Rev Stephen Forde in 1989. Mr Forde has overseen alterations to the Church of the Resurrection, which facilitated expansion of a coffee-bar and recreational area known as 'Oasis'.

The four main denominations retain the only full-time commitment to chaplaincy. Other churches, however, have a keen interest in the ministry to students and employ chaplains appointed by the Senate of Queen's on a part-time basis. Indeed the Reformed Presbyterian Church maintains an impressive student centre 'Renwick House' in Elmwood Avenue. At present some thirteen chaplains are listed in the University Calendar. The rapid post-war increase in student numbers resulted in an imaginative response by the churches, which represents their desire to meet the spiritual, intellectual and social needs of their young people in a setting and spirit of co-operation.

Monsignor Ambrose Macaulay

ness or community leaders later on have testified to the formative impact of such contacts at Queen's during their early years as undergraduates. The university has always been proud of playing such a vital role in Northern Ireland society and there was consternation and regret when it found itself caught up in the early Nineties in controversy, concerning fair employment and equality of opportunity. There arose a series of complaints to the Fair Employment Tribunal alleging discrimination on the grounds of religion or gender, or in some cases both. The university as one of the major employers in Northern Ireland became increasingly aware of its obligations to comply with the recent strict legislation prohibiting unlawful discrimination on grounds of religious belief, political opinion, gender, pregnancy or family status. In 1986, the Fair Employment Agency announced an investigation into the provision of equality of opportunity by Queen's, as part of its broader review of this aspect of the Higher Education system in Northern Ireland. Following a three-year investigation, in which the university afforded full co-operation, the Agency found that there were major areas of under-representation of Northern Ireland Roman Catholics on Queen's staff.

Dr Paul Hudson, a senior lecturer in Operational Research, is the only Queen's staff member to be elected National President of the Association of University Teachers. In 1989 he won the first contested Presidential election, and the university granted him leave of absence to serve as National President for 1990–91. The local branch of the AUT is noted for its independence, but it enjoys a strong national influence, particularly in winning elections to the National Executive of the AUT.

Accordingly the university strengthened considerably its structures, staffing and procedures for ensuring equality of opportunity at all levels, including the establishment of an Equal Opportunities Group and an Equal Opportunities Unit within the university, which increasingly play a key role in this area. Nevertheless the considerable publicity and resultant controversy over a number of complaints of alleged discrimination overshadowed the genuine efforts of the university to establish demonstrably fair equal opportunities policies and procedures. Its swift response was to commission outside consultants to carry out an independent review of its structures, procedures and practices relating to equality of opportunity and fair participation. Their report subsequently made 93 recommendations, the vast majority of which were accepted enthusiastically by the university's governing body, the Senate, in February 1993. One of the major results was the establishment of a high-powered Senate Committee to monitor the implementation of the recommendations and to oversee the provision of equality of opportunity. Within 12 months the Committee – to the warm approval of Senate – was able to report that more than half of the recommendations had been implemented, and that substantial progress was being made on the remainder. Senate had also set up another committee to encourage the promotion of a neutral social and working environment within the university, and to deal with the controversy over playing the national anthem at graduation ceremonies, and others matters.

Another important development was the programme of equal opportunities workshops for all staff. By October 1994, over 1,600 out of a total of 3,000 employees had taken part in more than 25 day-long sessions conducted by equal opportunities professionals and by volunteers from all parts of the university, who symbolise a widespread commitment to equality of opportunity and to the promotion of harmonious social and working relationships. It is intended that all members of university staff will take part in this series of workshops which is programmed to continue until 1996. This is one of the most ambitious projects undertaken by any large employer in Northern Ireland.

Following the signing in September 1994 by the Vice-Chancellor and Queen's trade union representatives of a joint declaration of protection against sectarian harassment, the Chairman of the Fair Employment Commission, Mr Robert Cooper stated on Ulster Television; "There are people at senior level in the Senate and on the staff who are very committed to putting their house in order, and among the unions as well. There is a good Equal Opportunities Unit which takes the issue very seriously indeed, and Queen's is working its way through to a situation where they will be able to be proud of what they are doing."

The statistics of employment within the university also underlined the substantial advances being made towards fair participation. The figures showed that the Roman Catholic proportional representation had increased from 21 per cent in 1987 to 29 per cent in 1994 – taking into account only locally-recruited staff. The most notable increase in local Roman Catholic participation could be seen among administrative staff, where it had risen from 11 per cent in 1987 to 23 per cent in 1992 (the latest figures available at the time of writing). Such figures were encouraging to Queen's staff, graduates and supporters and it provided firm evidence to its critics that the university had moved swiftly and effectively to deal with the situation, which had caused a great deal of heart-searching within the university itself. There was no doubt about its commitment to maintain the momentum which, in the words of the consultants' report would . . .."enable (Queen's) to become an example for other employers in

Northern Ireland, whilst not deflecting from its primary function to provide a high standard of education for its students."

Senior Pro-Vice-Chancellor Professor Leslie Clarkson, summarised Queen's all-embracing role in a Winter Graduation Speech in December 1993. He said:

> The Queen's University of Belfast exists to serve several communities. One is an international commonwealth of knowledge to whom we owe the highest standards of scholarship. But, more immediately, there are the local communities. Northern Ireland embraces at least two cultures differentiated by religion, political loyalties, history, language and traditions. Historically, Queen's has been identified with the Protestant culture. It is still so perceived, notwithstanding that half our students come from the Roman Catholic tradition. The publicity suffered by Queen's . . . arising from alleged discriminatory employment practices, has heightened the impression in some quarters that we remain a 'Protestant university'. On the other hand, the steps taken to ensure equality of opportunity, and changes occurring in the composition of the student body, has led to the perception in other quarters that Queen's is becoming a 'Roman Catholic university'.

> Both perceptions are misleading and unfortunate. The image to which Queen's must aspire is that of an integrated community with high scholarly standards. In order to achieve this the university must recognise that the Roman Catholic population of Northern Ireland has over the last three decades become better-educated, politically more articulate, and more self-confident. The university must also recognise that, not surprisingly, parts of the Protestant community are becoming apprehensive about the future of 'their' Province and even 'their' university. Queen's has a vital role to play in helping both communities to comprehend what is happening. . .

> How is this to be pursued? First, by having employment policies and procedures that are fair and seen to be fair. Secondly, by ensuring that for courses of study, entry and assessment procedures discriminate only on grounds of ability. Thirdly, by providing a truly 'neutral' environment in which people can work, study and socialise. Fourthly, by ensuring that among its academic programmes there are courses that address directly and objectively the nature of divided societies. Fifthly, by working, formally and informally, with all the universities in Ireland for the good of all its people. And, finally, by ensuring that in pursuing its academic mission the university is seen to be contributing to the well-being of all communities in Northern Ireland.

Wider outreach

While putting into place necessary procedures and policies at home, the university is also aware of the need to extend its considerable outreach overseas. Indeed, this point was emphasised by Sir David Orr, the Chancellor, in his installation speech in May 1992. His comments added impetus to the drive launched by Queen's to recruit more students from abroad. By the end of 1992 nearly 600 foreign students were enrolled from more than 50 different countries. Traditionally the majority of overseas students came from the Far East, with more than 200 from Malaysia alone. Links were also strengthened with Singapore and Hong Kong, with an increase in the small numbers from the People's Republic of China, and continental Europe. There was also a marked increase in the number of students from the Irish Republic. In 1985–6 there were 95 undergraduate and postgraduate students from the Republic, and this figure had risen to 632 by 1992–3.

Europe

The university was also conscious of the need to develop further its ties with the European Community. One of the most important initiatives was the establishment of an Institute of European Studies, at a cost of some £350,000, to take advantage of the cultural and other rewards offered by the EC and by developments in the wider Europe, following the end of the Cold War in the early Nineties. The main functions of the Institute, under the first Director, Michael Smith, include the co-ordination of teaching programmes in European Studies and acting as a focus for research on European Affairs. Queen's had been already involved in a number of important EC initiatives. They included ERASMUS (the European Community Action Scheme for the Mobility of University Students), the COMETT programme (Community Education for Training and Technology), and TEMPUS (Trans-European Mobility Programme for University Students). A major EC scheme in which Queen's was particularly successful was STRIDE (Science and Technology for Regional Innovation and Development in Europe) where the university received substantial funding, including – for example – £4.3 million during the 1992–93 academic year. Of the successful Northern Ireland projects under STRIDE, Queen's was awarded four – the largest of which, at £2.5 million, was used to establish the Northern Ireland Semi-Conductor Research Centre in the School of Electrical

Sir David Orr was installed as Seventh Chancellor of Queen's on 8 May 1992. Sir David graduated in Law from Trinity College Dublin and made his career as a distinguished industrialist, eventually becoming Chairman of Unilever, and Chairman of Inchcape plc. He was also Chairman of the British Council. Sir David, as a "captain of industry" carried on the tradition of Sir Rowland Wright, and he and Lady Orr were excellent ambassadors for the university. At the Chancellor's installation ceremony, the Vice-Chancellor Dr Gordon Beveridge, said that Convocation had shown extremely good judgement in presenting Queen's "with a man who is so obviously suited for the tenor of the times and the responsibility of such a distinguished office . . . We all need the kind of help and advice, to say nothing of guidance through the decision-making corridors of power, which an eminent Chancellor can bring to our deliberations." Sir David, in his reply, stated: "Queen's is a proud university, with a distinguished place in the community and a reputation which extends far beyond these shores. This is something which is close to my heart, and one of my main objectives as Chancellor would be to play a part in helping to increase the overseas contacts in this university."

Professor Phil Burke, Professor of Mathematical Physics since 1967 and a Fellow of the Royal Society, has been one of the most distinguished physicists of his generation, winning many national and international honours for his work. They include a CBE in the 1993 Queen's Birthday Honours List, and in 1994 the Institute of Physics Guthrie Medal and Prize. This is one of the Institute's two premier awards given annually to a physicist of international reputation. Professor Burke has made many outstanding contributions to theoretical atomic, molecular and optical physics. He developed a new approach – the Wigner R-matrix theory – for studying a wide range of atomic, molecular and optical processes and, with his collaborators, has written computer program packages which are now used world-wide to calculate atomic processes of importance in astrophysics, laser physics and controlled thermonuclear fusion devices. He has also made major contributions to the development of computational physics. In 1968 he established the international journal, Computer Physics Communications, and was its first Principal Editor, and for years he has been the Director of the associated International Physics Program Library.

Professor Burke has many academic honours and achievements to his credit, including an Honorary D.Sc. from Exeter University where he was an undergraduate student, and a Fellowship at University College London where he earlier took his Ph.D. He retains 'a considerable affection' for both universities. A modest and unassuming man, Phil Burke was singled out for praise by the Vice-Chancellor at the Graduation Ceremony on 5 July 1993. He said: "...Professor Burke epitomises the very best qualities of scholarship - dedication to his subject and to original thinking. He is a major contributor to his University, to his academic discipline in general and to the scientific world at large."

Engineering and Computer Science. Queen's also received substantial research funding under the EC Agricultural and Agro-Industry programme, as well as funding from the Jean Monnet Initiative, which was designed to develop university teaching on European integration.

Apart from such substantial and vital funding, these initiatives in Europe provided an exciting challenge for staff and students who, in exchanges and co-operation with their counterparts in Europe, brought a rich new element to the life of the university. The exchanges with Queen's developed even further afield through IAESTE – the International Association for the Exchange of Students for Technical Experience. Queen's had been involved with IAESTE for more than 40 years, but a three-year funding agreement from the International Fund for Ireland in 1989 led to a marked expansion in the number of local students going all over the world to continue their studies, and an increase in overseas students coming to Belfast. At one point Queen's was the most active participating institution in the United Kingdom, and received a plaque from IAESTE to mark such an achievement, and in 1994 it was the United Kingdom leader in this area of activity.

Students

The numbers of students increased dramatically, with record intakes every year from 1986, and with no diminution of the high standards required across a spectrum of subjects. The numbers of undergraduate and postgraduate students increased from approximately 8,800 in 1986–7 to some 13,400 by 1993–4, an increase of over 50 per cent, while the number of academic staff increased only marginally from 960 to just over 1,000. (These figures in themselves testify to increasingly efficient teaching methods).

The student body, perhaps more than ever, had considerable difficulties in making ends meet, in the face of continuing financial cut-backs. The government progressively cut grants, introduced an unpopular system of student loans, and tried to interfere, with limited success, in the running of Student Unions. The university recognised the continued need for co-ordinated and supportive welfare arrangements, and this important area was the direct responsibility of a Pro-Vice-Chancellor. The university also recognised the vital work being carried out by the Students' Union with regard to the welfare of students, ranging from the universi-

SPORTING TIMES

Despite the pressure of studies, Queen's students have always excelled at sport, with individuals and teams in the last two decades carrying on the traditions of many of the illustrious sportsmen and sportswomen of the past. The university has arguably some of the best sporting facilities of any educational establishment in the British Isles, and these include the Physical Education Centre, Malone Playing Fields, the Boathouse and the Mourne Mountain Cottage. There has also been a sound infrastructure to advise and to guide students in sporting matters, with help available from the students Vice-President of Clubs and Services, and from staff within the PE Centre itself.

There were many outstanding individuals in a wide range of sports and the late Seventies and early Eighties brought another crop of first-class Rugby players to Queen's – including David Irwin, Trevor Ringland, Kenny Hooks, Nigel Carr, Brian McCaul, Philip Matthews and Philip Rainey, all of whom played for Ireland. David Irwin and Trevor Ringland played for the British Lions in New Zealand and Philip Matthews went on to captain his Country. Former Queen's captain Jimmy Davidson was the Irish coach in the era 1988–1990.

Clive Beattie (Athletics) was a British International in 1977 and 1979 and was selected for the 1978 Commonwealth Games in Edmonton and the World Student Games in 1977. His brother Philip Beattie was a British International Athlete from 1983 to 1990. At the Commonwealth Games in 1986 he won a Gold Medal in the 400m hurdles and he was a member of the British Olympic Team in Los Angeles in 1984 and at the European Championships in 1986. Simon Baird (100m/200m) was a member of the Northern Ireland Commonwealth Team in 1986 and in the same year won a British vest. His teammate Mark Kirk (800m/1500m) competed in the 1986 and the 1990 Commonwealth Games and was a full British international (indoor and outdoor). In the ladies section, the two outstanding International Athletes were Debbie McDowell and Janet Boyle (both

competing in the High Jump). Janet won a Bronze and Silver Medal in the 1986 and 1990 Commonwealth Games respectively. She also finished 12th in the Olympic Games at Seoul establishing a new All-Comers NI High Jump record of 1.92m.

Ivan Anderson, a 1967 Honours Graduate in Pure Mathematics and a long-time member of the Queen's administrative staff, was one of the most accomplished players in the history of Irish Cricket. As a first-class batsmen and bowler he won 86 caps, taking 48 wickets for Ireland and scoring 3,777 runs. He scored seven centuries (the most scored by an Irish player) and he is the only Irish batsman to score two centuries in the same match – 147 and 102, against Scotland. He also recorded the highest innings by an Irish player, scoring 198 not out, against Canada in 1973. He was a member of the Irish team which sensationally beat the West Indies at Sion Mills in 1969, when the visitors were bowled out for 25 runs. Ivan Anderson played for the Queen's First XI in 1966 and 1967, gaining a 'Blue', and captained the side in 1967 which won the Senior League Section II. He 'retired' from top-class cricket locally in 1993, after 25 seasons with Waringstown, for whom he scored over 10,800 runs and took 750 wickets, winning 14 Senior Cup Medals and 16 Senior League Championship Medals.

(Left) James McCartan who starred in the successful Sigerson Cup team of 1993.

(Below) The Gaelic football team which brought the Sigerson Cup to Queen's in 1990.

Anthony Tohill, (right) affectionately known as the 'Swatragh Skyscraper', has a list of achievements and honours that other Gaelic footballers can only dream about! In the same year (1989) he won a medal in the Hogan Cup and the Mageean Cup (hurling) and helped the Derry minor team win the all-Ireland championship. He is the holder of Sigerson Cup and Ryan Cup medals with Queens and National League and senior All-Ireland medals (1993) with Derry. The same year he was the first recipient of the Sports Achievement Award at the University's inaugural Blues Dinner and won his second AllStar Award in two years, the highest accolade conferred on players by the Gaelic Athletic Association.

The Gaelic Football Club which consolidated its reputation as one of the strongest in the university had a number of outstanding individuals including 'All-Stars' Anthony Tohill, James McCartan and Gregg Blaney, while Ciaran Barr of the Hurling Club was also an 'All-Star'. (All-Stars are among the top players in Ireland elected by the sporting press in association with the GAA). Neil Darby of the Boat Club distinguished himself by his successes in Rowing, including appearances in international regattas in France and also Belgium, where he won two Gold Medals in Ghent, while in the world of Swimming Marion Madine and Brian Bell made headlines. Marion was the British 100m and 200m Butterfly Champion in 1993, and was nicknamed 'Madame Butterfly' by the local press. She was an Irish team member in the European Championships and a Northern Ireland Commonwealth Games representative. She is also an Irish multi-record holder. Brian competed at the

World Student Games in two successive championships at Sheffield and Buffalo, and in 1993 he was ranked No. 1 in Ireland in the 50m/100m front crawl.

While individual achievement was important, equally significant for the wider university was the continued success of Clubs over a great range of sports, including Volleyball, Archery, Water Polo, Basketball, Table Tennis, Camogie, Fencing, Golf, Racquetball, Sailing and Snooker. The Snooker Club became one of the most progressive in the university, and in the 1992–93 Season they won three victories in a row in the British Universities Snooker Championships, and also won promotion in the Belfast and District Premier League.

The growing importance of sport at Queen's was underlined by the instigation in 1993 of the Inaugural Blues Dinner to honour recipients of University Blues during the academic year – a 'Blue' being awarded by the university, under strict criteria, for sporting excellence. The university also presented the first 'Queen's Sports Achievement Award' which went to the outstanding Gaelic Footballer, Anthony Tohill. The list of runners-up bore testimony to the depth and breadth of sporting achievements at Queen's, and included representatives from Judo, Swimming, Cross-Country, Water Polo, Basketball, and Billiards and Snooker. Queen's graduates Dawson Stelfox and Jack Kyle, and Olympic Gold Medallist Mary Peters, were among the guests at the dinner which honoured the university's sporting luminaries, past and present.

Another important development in recent years was the creation of the much-prized Guinness Sports Bursaries for competition by students with a record of sporting and academic achievement. The essence of sport, however is not just in winning but also in participation; and throughout the world today there are many Queen's men and women who look back fondly on their student days when a place in the second or third-level team was the pinnacle of their achievement. But the memory of fun and the friendships has lasted for a lifetime!

Marion Madine - Queen's own 'Madame Butterfly (right).

ty's provision of adequate child-care facilities (for which two creches were provided) to suitable living accommodation. Queen's also remained aware of the need to help students in chronic financial difficulties, and by the middle of 1994 the university was administering a hardship fund of some £223,000 – a large proportion of which was provided by the Department of Education for Northern Ireland. Another important aspect of student life was the development of personal skills, in addition to academic qualifications, and Queen's became one of the United Kingdom leaders in the Enterprise in Higher Education Initiative, pioneered by government in 1987 and launched in Northern Ireland in 1990, with the support of the Training and Employment Agency. The Enterprise Initiative proved to be of great benefit to students in helping to develop personal skills advantageous both within and beyond university and affected a wide range of disciplines in Queen's, where staff also benefited greatly from the experience.

Another highly successful initiative was the Student Tutoring Scheme, administered by the Northern Ireland Education Support Unit, whereby undergraduates volunteered to work alongside teachers in local primary and secondary schools. Yet another important development was the continued success of the Careers Advisory Service, established in the Sixties, which provided seasoned advice on a wide range of career and employment opportunities – to the point where Queen's in 1994 topped *The Times* national league table for graduate employment and further studies. Despite the challenges of studies, financial survival and trying to start a career in a difficult jobs market, the students continued to enjoy themselves in the time-honoured ways, while Rag Week continued to raise very creditable sums for charity.

Paul McMenamin, the Student President for two terms from 1993–5, reflected:

> The work-load has increased considerably in recent years with the larger numbers of students, a greater turnover, more staff in the Students' Union and more services provided. It is now becoming a much bigger business. The students of the Nineties are walking a very thin tight-rope and trying to keep a balance between their academic work, their social life and their financial commitments. Students have to adopt a more structured approach than in the past. The pressure is such in a three-year degree that students really have to keep in touch with their studies. They can no longer miss several lectures and tutorials and expect to catch up.

Paul McMenamin, President of the Students' Union 1993–5.

The financial pressures were also intense, resulting from the introduction of student loans and a cut in student grants of 10 per cent in each of three years:

> In the Autumn of 1993 the Union carried out a random survey of 650 students and we found that 49 per cent were having to take part-time jobs in order to make ends meet, and that they were taking employment ranging from 5 hours to 35 hours a week. It is only a matter of time before such pressure will have a negative effect on the students' degree classifications on leaving the university.

Despite the tough challenges facing all students, there was still time for recreation:

> The vibrancy of 18–21 year olds will always be there, and I believe that today's students, despite the shortage of money and the pressure of studies, and in many cases of part-time employment, still know how to enjoy themselves. From my own point of view I am learning a great deal as student President. I am studying politics and I have had the opportunity to meet the main politicians and community leaders in a way that would not have been possible otherwise.

Alumni

At the other end of the spectrum, the university developed greatly its Alumni outreach. Queen's had been fortunate already with the quality of its Alumni support through the Queen's Women Graduates' Association, founded in 1923, the Queen's University Association, London founded in 1924 and the Queen's University Association, the central body, which was formed in 1930. In addition to three long-established Overseas Associations in British Columbia, Malaysia and Nigeria, newer branches were formed in Canada, the United States, Hong Kong and Norway. In the early Nineties an Alumni Office with full-time staff was established to further this important work, and in 1993 the university launched a new umbrella Alumni organisation, the Queen's University Society. Its role was to preserve and enhance the ties which bind together the Alumni, staff and a new category of "Friends of the University". The university also launched, in association with the Bank of Ireland an attractive 'Affinity' Visa Card with a picture of the Lanyon Building which was also carried on a new series of Bank of Ireland banknotes. Another particularly encouraging development was the establishment in 1993 of a new Queen's University Alumni Association for the Dublin area, as the result of a reception hosted by the then Lord Mayor, Alderman Gay

Mitchell, who took a Master's at Queen's in Irish Political Studies. Convocation, the graduate body, also played an important role – not least in electing Chancellors – and in recent years it took a particularly keen interest in the university's affairs.

People

The period from 1986 also witnessed the departure of a number of well-known Queen's people, either through death or retirement. On October 16, 1992 the University Air Squadron's Officer Commanding, Squadron Leader Rob Burge, was killed and a female student was seriously injured when their plane crashed, and later the same day Ms Sheena Campbell, a second-year Law student, was shot dead by a gunman in a Belfast hotel. In March 1988, Mairead Farrell, a mature student, was one of three people shot dead by the Army in Gibraltar; she was described by the Provisional IRA as a member of an active service unit. And in the early Nineties Adrian Guelke, a lecturer in political science, was wounded by Loyalist gunmen in a case of mistaken identity. The university lost a number of outstanding scholars through death, including Emeritus Professors Sir David Bates and Estyn Evans, Professor John Blacking, and former Pro Vice-Chancellors Professor Alan Astin, Professor Bill Kirk, Professor John Braidwood and Professor Roy Wallis, as well as the much-respected and much-liked Chancellor Sir Rowland Wright and Senior Pro-Chancellor Dr John Benn, former Bursar Desmond Burland and former Secretary Roy Topping. There were many others, including students, staff and friends of the university whose contributions were, to a greater or lesser extent, all part of the story of Queen's.

Among those who retired were Dr Robert Hamilton, a former Senior Pro-Chancellor who played a major role in establishing the new Information Office in the mid-Eighties to inform the world at large, and the university itself, of major achievements and initiatives at Queen's. Another notable departure was that of David Gass, the Bursar, who retired through ill-health. The Vice-Chancellor in paying tribute to Mr Gass said that "He faced many challenges as Bursar with skill and great personal dignity."

Professor Lewis Warren, who was appointed to the Chair of Modern History in 1973, was one of the most distinguished scholars at Queen's in the post-Second World War period as well as a gifted teacher and a superb communicator. He retired in 1993 and died a year later. Lewis Warren played an important role in the life of Queen's. He was a former member of Senate and the Academic Council, a former Dean of the Faculty of Theology, former Chairman of the University's Arts Centre Board and the first Warden of the new Halls of Residence. He also played a significant role in the wider academic world, and he became a member (and eventually Chairman) of the history panel of the former University Grants Committee. Professor Warren's vivid style and vibrant enthusiasm underlined his conviction that history should be accessible. His biographies on King John and Henry II became classics of historical scholarship, and he also communicated his enthuisiasm and knowledge to a wide audience through radio and television.

Professor Mary McAleese was appointed a Pro-Vice-Chancellor in 1994 and is the first woman at Queen's to hold this important post. Born in Ardoyne, Belfast, in 1951, she graduated from Queen's with an Honours Degree in Law in 1973 and later received an M.A. from Trinity College, Dublin. A barrister by profession, she is a former Reid Professor of Criminal Law, Criminology and Penology at Trinity and television presenter and journalist with Raidío Teilifís Éireann. She became Director of the Institute of Professional Legal Studies at Queen's in 1987 and was appointed to a Chair in June 1994. She has served on several Queen's bodies, including the Equal Opportunities Group, the Equal Opportunities Workshop Training Team and the Staffing Committee. A member of various professional associations, she has served on many bodies in the wider community.

Five distinguished graduates and post-graduates of Queen's University posing in September 1994 for an historic picture as part of the celebrations to mark the university's 150th Anniversary. All five hold, or have held, major posts of public importance - the heads of three main churches and the Lord Mayors of Belfast and Dublin.

They are, from left to right: Cardinal Cahal B. Daly, Roman Catholic Archbishop of Armagh and Primate of All-Ireland (B.A. in Classics 1937, M.A. 1938, Hon. D.D. 1990); Alderman Gay Mitchell, former Lord Mayor of Dublin 1994 (M.S.Sc. in Irish Political Studies 1990); Alderman Reg Empey, former Lord Mayor of Belfast 1994 (B.Sc. in Economics 1969); the Very Reverend Dr

John Dunlop, former Moderator of the General Assembly of the Presbyterian Church in Ireland 1994 (B.A. in Philosophy 1962) and Archbishop Robin Eames, Church of Ireland, Archbishop of Armagh and Primate of All-Ireland (LL.B. 1960, Ph.D. 1963, Hon. LL.D. 1989).

Sir Gordon Beveridge noted "We are delighted to welcome back such distin-guished former students who have con-tributed so much to public life across a wide spectrum. It is noteworthy that all five Queen's graduates held high office at the same time, a happy coincidence that is thought to be extremely rare, if not unique, in the history of the universities on this island."

Celebrating Queen's 150

As the university prepared itself to commemorate the 150th Anniversary of the founding of the Queen's Colleges in 1845, it was decided – appropriately – to make the Sesquicentenary ". . . a celebration of the university's long tradition of excellence in scholarship, its outstanding service to the community at home, its influence abroad and its promise for the future."

During its long history, Queen's has survived the major upheavals of two World Wars, the continuing turbulence and dangers of Irish history swirling down all the years and the considerable

Dawson Stelfox, who graduated with a degree in Architecture from Queen's in 1980, made history in May 1993 by becoming the first climber from Ireland to conquer Mount Everest and the first from Great Britain to do so by way of the treacherous North route. The photograph shows him on the way to the summit. He noted later: 'The view was absolutely breathtaking. When I reached the top the sky was a perfect blue and it was warm with hardly a breeze. I was above the cloud and down below, in places, I could see that it was snowing. It was the extent of the view that was most breathtaking. I could see most of the Himalayan mountain range stretching 300 - 400 miles. Looking over the peaks of other mountains I could make out the jungles and forest of Nepal and the high dry brown plain of Tibet. The immense contrast between all these terrains was unbelievable.'

In the 1990s, students still enjoy the fine spring sun-
shine in the impressive setting of the Quad.

financial and other difficulties created by not always consistent
government policies on higher education; and it has experienced
the set-backs, the controversies, and the human foibles and weak-
nesses that are part of the life of every large institution. More significantly, however, the university can point to many successes, to
brilliant technical and other innovations, to excellent scholarship, to significant contributions to the arts and to community
life, to outstanding sporting achievements, to extending its not
inconsiderable influence around the world, and perhaps, above
all, to its sheer staying power. Dr Dennis Kennedy, a Queen's
graduate and a former Deputy Editor of *The Irish Times*, brought
the professional journalist's cool detachment to his review of
Queen's recent past, for an article in *University Life* magazine. He
wrote in February 1994:

> (Queen's) . . . is already emerging from the most difficult days of
> the past 25 years. That it has survived a 25-year crisis during which
> it has had to cope with severe problems of finance, with much revi-
> sion of third level education policy, with its own doubling in size,

and all this against a background of bitter conflict and almost daily violence, not just on its doorstep but at times within its own gates, is already a far from modest achievement.

His words could well be applied to the story and spirit of Queen's, in all their rich variations, since 1845.

The future

All predictions about the future are hazardous, but it is almost certain that the Queen's of the future will be very much larger with a greater mix of part-time and full-time students building up their course credits, perhaps from several institutions in different countries. There will be an even greater emphasis in technology, with the possibility of "a paperless university", though books may still be available in special areas such as libraries. Distance-learning will almost certainly be further developed but there can be no adequate technological substitute for the person to person contact between staff and students and between students themselves, which is the life-blood of any great university. All such predictions may well be overtaken by time, in the same way that the quill pen and the typewriter are now obsolete. But the essence of Queen's will survive.

Perhaps the last word belongs rightly to the current Vice-Chancellor Sir Gordon Beveridge:

> From the very beginning, Queen's has had many trials and tribulations, and these have come and gone in waves. We all have had our day-to-day difficulties, and some no doubt have seemed so overwhelming that some people believed that the university would be irrevocably scarred. Despite all of that, the university has in fact flourished through a period of great change, and it will go on flourishing. With each generation we come increasingly to realise that, in the words of Tennyson, 'the old order changeth, yielding place to new'. Even at this very moment, the 'old order' is changing and what emerges is an exciting prospect for those of us who are challenged and privileged to pass it on, and a hopefully worthy legacy for the Queen's men and women of the future. Queen's will still be around long after those of us who read this book will have quietly passed away.

Presidents of Queen's College, Belfast

Rev. Pooley Shuldman Henry	1845–79
Rev. Josias Leslie Porter	1879–89
Rev. Thomas Hamilton	1889–1908

Chancellors of The Queen's University of Belfast

Anthony Ashley-Cooper, Ninth Earl of Shaftesbury	1908–23
Charles Stewart Henry, Vane-Tempest-Stewart, Seventh Marquess of Londonderry	1923–49
Field Marshall the Viscount Alanbrooke	1949–63
Sir Tyrone Guthrie	1963–70
Lord Ashby of Brandon	1970–83
Sir Rowland Wright	1984–91
Sir David Orr	1991–

Presidents and Vice-Chancellors of The Queen's University, Belfast

Rev. Thomas Hamilton	1908–23
Sir Richard Winn Livingstone	1924–33
Sir Frederick Wolff Ogilvie	1935–38
Sir David Lindsay Keir	1939–49
Lord Ashby of Brandon	1950–59
Dr Michael Grant	1959–66
Sir Arthur Vick	1966–76
Sir Peter Froggatt	1976–86
Sir Gordon Beveridge	1986–

(honours conferred later are included in list above)

Acknowledgments

The authors would like to thank the many people who helped in the preparation of this book. Some provided valuable background material. Others assisted greatly in the technical preparation of the manuscript. Special thanks are due to Daphne McNiece, Sarah Gardner and Mervyn Dinsmore who helped with the typing of Part One of the manuscript: Pauline Allen of the Information Office who devoted much time to typing the material for Part Two, ably assisted in earlier and later stages by Gwynne Donnell, Irene Martin and Lorraine McCallum: and Norman Russell, Michael Smallman and Mary Kelly of the Library who helped to provide a quiet room in which to peruse the voluminous research material for the book.

The authors wish to thank a number of editors, authors and publishers for the use of source material or illustrations, and in some cases both. They include the editors of the *Belfast Telegraph*, the *Newsletter*, and the *Irish News*, the *Independent*, the *Irish Times*, the *Economist*, *Images*, and *University Life*. For permission to quote from articles or books, we are grateful to Dr David Hadden *(Ulster Medical Journal)*, Miss Mollie Martin, Dr Frank Pantridge and Mr John Boyd.

We would also like to express special thanks to the Vice-Chancellor, Sir Gordon Beveridge, who first mooted the idea of a book, and to Professor Ronnie Buchanan, Mrs Gwen Buchanan, Ivan Strahan, Bryan McCabe and Rodney Miller and his colleagues, Arnold Gormley and John Hamill, all of whom played an important role in the editing, visual design and printing process.

The following is a list of other people whom the authors wish to thank for their help, and in so doing we acknowledge all those individuals whose names have been inadvertently left out.

Mr James Anderson
Dr Colin Boreham
Mr Paul Browne
Dr George Cowie
Cardinal Cahal Daly
Very Rev. Dr John Dunlop
Archbishop Robin Eames
Alderman Reg Empey
Mr Bill Gardner
Mr David Gass
Mrs Florence Gregg
Father Joseph Gunn

Dr Robin Harland
Dr Myrtle Hill
Dr Greta Jones
Dr David McClean
Mr Hubert Martin
Miss Mollie Martin
Alderman Gay Mitchell
Mr Raymond Patterson
Mr Norman Russell
Mrs Maureen Strain
Dr John Weaver
Rev. Noel Williamson

The authors would like to express their gratitude to the many people who gave the time for lengthy interviews about their years at Queen's. Finally, our thanks are due to Hilary McCreary and Evelyn Walker and our families for their continued support during the writing and production of this book.

Notes on sources

A wide range of sources was consulted during the research for this book. Much valuable and hitherto unpublished material was obtained by lengthy conversations with Queen's former and current staff, including interviews with every post-war Vice-Chancellor, and with former students, dating back to the early decades of the century. The university archive in Queen's library provided an important collection of the principal records, both manuscript and printed, relating to the history of Queen's, 1845-1995.

Among the material in the university archive special mention must be made of the minutes of the Senate and the Academic Council. Printed primary sources of value included the Presidents' and Vice-Chancellors' *Annual Reports* and the *Annual Review* (later *Record*) of the Queen's University Association. Government reports and enquiries into higher education in Ireland and later Northern Ireland were important: these include the Lockwood Report (1965) and the Chilver Report (1982).

The two volumed *Queen's Belfast, 1845 - 1949: the history of a university* (London, 1959) by J.C. Beckett and the late T.W. Moody was an indispensable source of information for the first part of this book (referred to as *Queen's history* in the text). Amounting to almost a thousand pages, their history, in the words of F.S.L. Lyons, constituted "a monumental task", which was "not only a model for all historians of universities, but also a major contribution to the history of modern Ireland". Other general histories of value were J.C.Beckett, *A short history of Queen's College, Belfast, and The Queen's University of Belfast* (Belfast, 1984) and David Kennedy, *Towards a university: an account of some institutions for higher education in Ireland and elsewhere, and of the attitude of Irish catholics to them, with special reference to Queen's College and Queen's University, Belfast* (Belfast, 1946).

A considerable number of biographies and autobiographies proved very useful. These included John Boyd, *Out of my class* (Belfast, 1985), D.F. Corrigan, *Helen Waddell: a biography* (London, 1986), James Deeny, *To cure and to care: memoirs of a chief medical officer* (Dublin, 1989), Ian Fraser, *Blood, sweat and tears* (London, 1989), R. Finlay Holmes, *Henry Cooke* (Belfast, 1981) and T.M. Johnstone, The vintage of memory (Belfast, 1942). Ambrose Macauley's, *William Crolly, Archbishop of Armagh, 1835-44* (Dublin,

1994) and *Patrick Dorrian: Bishop of Down and Connor, 1865-85* (Dublin, 1987) gave valuable background information on the early days of Queen's. J.R.B. McMinn's collection of letters and documents about J.B. Armour of Ballymoney was helpful: *Against the tide: J. B. Armour,. Irish presbyterian minister and home-ruler* (Belfast, 1985).

Various publications provided useful information on the medical school at Queen's. A special supplement of the Ulster Medical Journal to celebrate the sesquicentenary of the Belfast Medical School contained a number of relevant articles: *The Ulster Medical Journal*, vol. 56 supplement, Aug. 1987. Other valuable material included J.B. Bridges, *Belfast medical students* (Belfast, n.d.), J.B. Bridges and Peter Froggatt, *The Belfast Medical School, 1835-1985* (Belfast, 1985), Ian Fraser, *The Belfast Medical School and its surgeons* (Belfast, 1981), Peter Froggatt "The distinctiveness of Belfast medicine and its medical school" in the *Ulster Medical Journal*, (54), 1985, 89-108, and "The people's choice: the medical schools of Belfast 'Inst' 1835-1949 and the Catholic University (1855-1908) compared" in *Journal of the Irish Colleges of Physicians and Surgeons*, vol.20, no.1, Jan. l991, 49-59, and R.G.Shanks, "The legacies of Sir William Whitla" in *The Ulster Medical Journal*, vol. 63, no.1, (Apr.1994), 52-75.

Various histories of Queen's departments and clubs were useful. These included J.A.Campbell, *The Queen's University of Belfast Department of Geography, Jubilee 1928-78* (Belfast, 1978), T.M. Charlton, *Civil engineering in Queen's, 1849-1963* (Belfast, 1963), Robert Marshall, *The Queen's University Services Club, 1918-68* (Belfast, 1968) and *Queen's Gaelic Football Club, a souvenir history. 1931/2 - 1981/2* (Belfast, 1982).

Some personal reminiscences of life at Queen's were helpful. A typescript lecture of personal reminiscences of Professor H.J.G. Godin, delivered on 23 March 1983 to the Queen's University Association for Women Graduates gave interesting insights into his period at Queen's. The typescript reminiscences of Professor H.A. Cronne covered the years 1922-5. Both these papers have now been placed in the university archive in the Queen's library. Recollections of his time at Queen's are contained in W.H. McCrea's "Clustering of astronomers" in *Am. Rev. Astron. Astrophys.* 1987 (25) 1-22.

Some miscellaneous material is worth special mention. Peter Brooke's 'Religion and secular thought 1850-75' in J.C. Beckett, *Belfast: the making of a city* (Belfast, 1983), 111-28, discussed the cultural and religious background to the British Association visit of 1874. The centenary volume of the *Northman*, 1945, has good articles on Queen's. Valuable insights are contained in Peter Froggatt's "Higher education in Northern Ireland: a Queen's University perspective" in R.D. Osborne, R.J. Cormack and R.L. Miller (eds) *Education and policy in Northern Ireland* (Belfast, 1987), 219-29.

A wide range of other material was consulted, including newspapers, *Who was who,* the *Dictionary of National Biography,* the *Dictionary of Ulster Biography,* (Belfast, 1993) by Kate Newmann and the *Northern Ireland political directory, 1968-93* (Belfast 1994) by W.D. Flackes and Sydney Elliott. *Queen's Calendar, 1922-3* contains an important list of all graduates of Queen's from 1849 up to 1922-3.

Picture Sources

The Editors wish to acknowledge the help of all those who kindly raided their attics for photographs and other illustrations. The staff of the Queen's Audio Visual Services Unit worked beyond the call of duty to produce the best possible images for publication, while Jim McClean and Mark Crean of the Computer Centre produced computer-enhancements of some of the earliest photographs which initially appeared beyond reclaim. Michael Smallman of the University Library showed endless patience in trawling the Archives for material.

In a number of cases it has not been possible to trace the photographers or sources of pictures which have been in the possession of the University for some time. Those illustrations from known sources which appear in the book are listed below.

Pages:

Front and back cover, ii, 178, 186, 189, 193, 208, 210 - Christopher Hill;

vi, 7, 8, 9, 38 (left and bottom right), 42, 47 (top & bottom right), 67 (top), 69 (bottom), 77 (inset), 88, 98, 101, 102 (right), 115, (left), 118, 125, 130, 135, 136 (right & bottom), 137, 139, 141, 158, 161, 167, 173, 174, 176, 180 (top left and bottom right), 182, 183, 188, 207 - Ivan Strahan;

2, 6, 28, 49, 50, 51, 52, 54, 55, 76, 92, 112, 132, 156 - Queen's University Collection;

3, 12, 19 (left), 20, 24, 34, 39, 40, 41 (left), 45, 63, 67 (bottom), 68 (top), 69 (top), 71, 75, 79, 87 (bottom), 104 (bottom), 113, 129 (bottom) - QUB Library Archive;

11, 15 , 18, 21, 38 (top right) - courtesy Brian Walker;

17 (centre) - courtesy SP Tyres Limited;

17 (top & bottom) - courtesy Michael McKeag;

19 (right, top & bottom), 90, 109, 138, 151, 158, 175 (right), 195 (bottom), 196, 198, 201, 202, 205, 211 - QUB Audio-Visual Services;

22, 26 (right, top & bottom), 27 (left, top & bottom) - courtesy Mitchel McCoy;

27 (bottom right) - courtesy Peter Osborough;

29 - courtesy Barrie Hartwell;

31, 44, 47 (left) - courtesy Ulster Museum;

35 (top right) - courtesy Raymond Patterson;

35 (left) - courtesy Mrs D. E. Black;

46 - courtesy Sir Ian Fraser;

64 - courtesy Elizabeth Madill;

65 - courtesy Mr T. A. Thompson;

68 (bottom), 70, 83 - courtesy Bruce Hill;

74 - courtesy Robin Shanks;

77 (bottom right) - courtesy Clare Macmahon;

80 (top and inset) - courtesy Margaret Burch;

80 (bottom) - courtesy Doris Calwell;

81 - Royal Victoria Hospital Archive;

84, 86 - courtesy British Council;

94, 105 (bottom), 107, 128, 146, 165, 195 (top), 203 (top) - courtesy Belfast Telegraph;

99 (left) - courtesy Ove Arup & Partners;

102 (left) - courtesy Henri Godin;

103 (right top, centre and bottom) - courtesy Anna Wilson;

103 (left) - courtesy Leslie Stannage;

104 (top), 108 - courtesy Edith Cunningham;

105 (top) - courtesy University of Hull;

106 - courtesy Moira McKelvey;

117, 123 - Reg Watson;

120 - courtesy Robert Stout;

122 - courtesy Raymond Piper

127 - courtesy Phil Coulter;

129 (top) - courtesy Mike Bull;

136 (top) - courtesy Ian Brick;

143, 144 (top) - courtesy Queen's Festival Office;

148 - Alf McCreary;

160 - courtesy Lesley Bruce;

175 (left)- Maureen Strain;

191 (bottom) - courtesy United International Pictures;

204 (top) - courtesy Irish News;

204 (bottom) - Allan McCullough;

209 - Frank Nugent

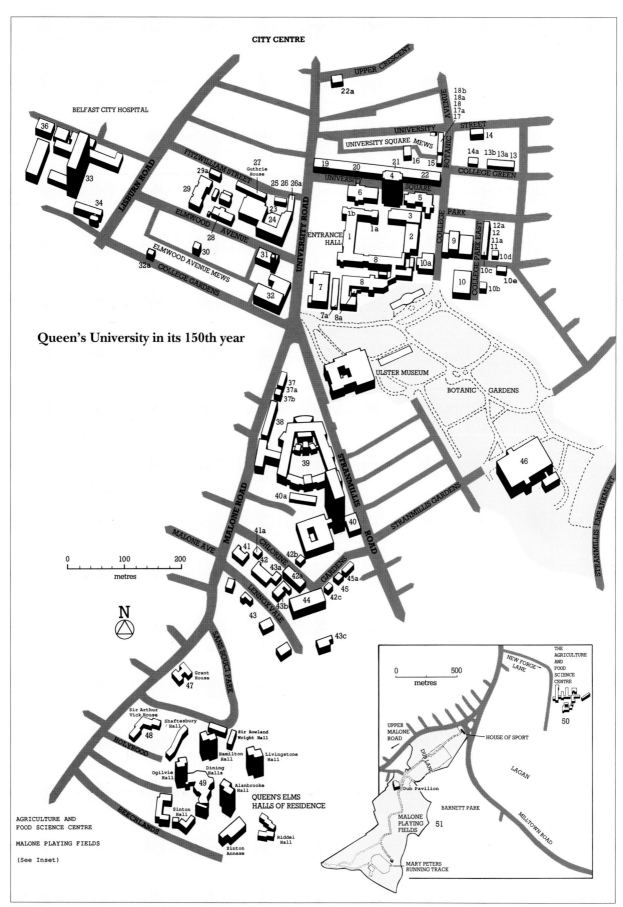

Queen's University in its 150th year

CITY CENTRE

BELFAST CITY HOSPITAL

36
33
34

LISBURN ROAD

FITZWILLIAM STREET
27
Guthrie House
29a
29
25 26 26a
23
24
ELMWOOD AVENUE
28
30
31
32a
ELMWOOD AVENUE MEWS
COLLEGE GARDENS
32

UPPER CRESCENT
22a

UNIVERSITY SQUARE MEWS

18b
18a
18
17a
17

UNIVERSITY
STREET
14

14a 13b 13a 13
COLLEGE GREEN

19   20   21   16 15
UNIVERSITY   4   22
SQUARE
6   5
1b   3
ENTRANCE
HALL   1   1a   2
8   10a
7   8
7a 8a

BOTANIC AVENUE
COLLEGE PARK
9
COLLEGE PARK EAST
12a
12
11a
11
10d
10c
10
10e
10b

UNIVERSITY ROAD

ULSTER MUSEUM

BOTANIC   GARDENS

STRANMILLIS GARDENS

STRANMILLIS EMBANKMENT

37
37a
37b
38
39
40a
40
46

MALONE ROAD
STRANMILLIS ROAD

MALONE AVE

0   100   200
metres

N

41a
CHLORINE
41   42b
42
43a   42a
44   42c
43b   45
43   45a
42c
LENNOXVALE
GARDENS

43c

SANS SOUCI PARK

Grant House
47

Sir Arthur Vick House
Shaftesbury Hall
48   Sir Rowland Wright Hall
Hamilton Hall   Livingstone Hall
Ogilvie Hall   Dining Halls
49   Alanbrooke Hall
Sinton Hall   QUEEN'S ELMS HALLS OF RESIDENCE
HOLYWOOD
BEECHLANDS
Sinton Annexe   Riddel Hall

AGRICULTURE AND
FOOD SCIENCE CENTRE

MALONE PLAYING FIELDS

(See Inset)

NEW FORGE LANE
THE AGRICULTURE AND FOOD SCIENCE CENTRE

0   500
metres

50

UPPER MALONE ROAD
HOUSE OF SPORT
DUB LANE
Dub Pavilion
LAGAN
MALONE PLAYING FIELDS
BARNETT PARK
51
MILLTOWN ROAD
MARY PETERS RUNNING TRACK

Map Key

1 Main University Building (Lanyon)
1a Finance & Information
1b Institute of Continuing Education
2 Administration Building
3 Social Sciences Building
  Economics
  Political Science
  Faculty of Economics
  & Social Sciences
4 Main Library
5 Music
6 Old Library
7 Sir William Whitla Hall
7a South Dining Hall
8 Pure & Applied Physics
8a Conservation Laboratory
9 Pure & Applied Physics,
  Pure Mathematics
10 David Bates Building
  Applied Mathematics
  & Theoretical Physics
  Computer Science
  Computer Centre
10a Old Drill Hall
  Computer Science
10b Computer Science
10c Computer Centre
10d Hope House (Northern Ireland
  Education Support Unit)
10e College Park East Hostel
11 Scholastic Philosophy
11a Philosophy
12 Economic & Social History
12a Modern History
13 Social Studies
13a Audio Resources
13b Politics
14 Education
14a Education
15 Computer Centre
16 Queen's Film Theatre
17 Centre for Social Research

17a Education
18 Computer Science
18a Alliance Française
18b Education
19 English
  Greek, Roman & Semitic Studies
  Arts Central Computing Unit
  Celtic
20 Modern & Medieval Languages
21 Law
22 University Health Service
  Social Anthropology
22a Social Work
  Fendereskey Gallery
  Travel Shop
23 Institute of Irish Studies
24 Students' Union
  Queen's University Travel Centre
  Refectory/Cloisters Restaurant
25 Faculty of Medicine
26 Faculty of Science & Faculty of
  Theology
26a Faculty of Arts, Academic Audit
  Office, International Office
27 Guthrie House
28 Geology (Geosciences)
29 Geography (Geosciences)
  Archaeology
29a Palaeoecology
30 Electron Microscope Unit
31 Elmwood Hall
32 University Bookshop
  University Common Room
32a Festival House
33 Medical Biology Centre
  Biomedical Science
  Biology and Biochemistry
34 Dunluce Health Centre
35 Whitla Medical Building
  Clinical Medicine
36 Pharmacy
37 Computer Centre
37a QUBIS (No. 10 Malone Road)
37b Appointments & Careers

  Advisory Service
38 Biology Building
  Biology
  Psychology (Laboratories)
39 David Keir Building
  Aeronautical Engineering
  Chemical Engineering
  Chemistry
  Civil Engineering
  Psychology
40 Ashby Building
  Electrical & Electronic Engineering
  Mechanical & Manufacturing
Engineering
  Engineering Mathematics
  Faculty of Engineering
  Computer Centre
40a Northern Ireland
  Technology Centre
41a–42c Architecture & Planning
43b Institute of Profession Legal
  Studies
43c Institute of European Studies
44 Science Library
  Queensprint/Textflow
  Audio Visual Aids Unit
45–45a Mechanical & Manufacturing
  Engineering
46 Physical Education Centre
47 Grant House
48 Sir Arthur Vick House
49 Queen's Elms Halls of Residence,
  Shaftesbury Hall, Ogilvie Hall,
  Hamilton Hall, Livingstone Hall,
  Alanbrooke Hall, Dining Halls,
  Sinton Hall, Sinton Annexe
  and Riddel Hall.
50 Agriculture and Food Science,
  Newforge
51 Malone Playing Fields
  Dub Pavilion
  Mary Peters' Track
  House of Sport

Index